10

ADD

THE
UNKNOWN
WAR

THE UNKNOWN WAR

BY

HARRISON E. SALISBURY

PICTURE EDITOR AND DESIGNER: IRWIN GLUSKER

BANTAM BOOKS
TORONTO · NEW YORK · LONDON

For Dmitri Khludov and Viktor Zapolsky, two among the millions
of young men who died for Russia in World War II

THE UNKNOWN WAR
A Bantam Book/October 1978

Published simultaneously in the United States and Canada

*Bantam Books are published by Bantam Books, Inc. Its
trademark, consisting of the words "Bantam Books" and the
portrayal of a bantam, is registered in the United States
Patent Office and in other countries. Marca Registrada,
Bantam Books, Inc., 666 Fifth Ave., New York N.Y. 10019.*

PRINTED IN THE UNITED STATES OF AMERICA

CONTENTS

NOTE

During World War II over 3,500,000 meters of documentary film were shot at the front by Soviet cameramen assigned to produce the official photographic record of World War II. Hundreds of thousands of still photographs were taken by these men and other news cameramen, comprising the largest photographic archive of the war. Of the 243 film photographers assigned to the front, thirty-three, nearly one-fifth of them, died in action. The casualty rate for still cameramen was equally high. No photographers in the war got closer to the action—often they were part of the action themselves, wielding a tommy gun between taking pictures. Much of this unique photographic treasure has reposed untouched in Soviet archives since 1945. Much has never before been seen publicly until it was released specifically for use in the TV series, "The Unknown War," from which many of these photographs have been taken, supplemented by pictures from other sources, including the German archives. One of the bravest of the Soviet World War II cameramen was Roman Karmen, who photographed the siege of Leningrad and who took some of the pictures in this book. Five Soviet photographers died on that assignment. Karmen, codirector of "The Unknown War," died of a heart attack in Moscow in the spring of 1978 while at work on the television series.

A QUIET SUNDAY

he morning of Sunday, June 22, 1941, was unusually fine
in Moscow. This was the summer solstice and the sun rose a little after
3:00 A.M. In Leningrad boys and girls strolled the boulevards for
hours in the romance of the white nights. In all of European Russia
the weather was perfect, the skies clear.

By the time the Moscow subways and streetcars began to run at
6:00 A.M., people were heading for the suburban railroad stations and
a day of rest and bathing in the countryside, of fishing in nearby
sandy lakes and picnicking in the birch-and-pine forests around the
Russian capital.

There wasn't a cloud in the sky and the forecast was for
temperature in the low eighties. Some picnickers stopped to read
Pravda on the bulletin boards at the railroad stations. But there was
no news worth bothering with. The *Pravda* editorial was devoted to
public education. One article marked the hundredth anniversary of
the death of the Russian poet Mikhail Lermontov, and quoted a line
from his poem about the battle Russia fought with Napoleon at
Borodino: "Not in vain does all Russia remember the day of
Borodino!" On the last page of *Pravda*, page four, there was an item
about a cyclotron for smashing atoms which had been built at the
Physics Institute near Leningrad. For those who tuned in on Moscow
radio that morning there was no real news. Just the regular early
morning calisthenics.

It was so fine a day that almost every train was loaded with

At left, a view of Red
Square in Moscow shortly before
the Germans attacked. Above,
German military commanders
assemble at the beginning
of the attack on Russia.

**German Stukas fly toward
Russia on a bombing attack.**

families clutching picnic baskets and string bags in which to bring
back to the city the fish they caught, the mushrooms they picked or
new cucumbers and radishes bought in the country markets.

In the city the big Gorky park filled up. Thousands of strollers
took the air in Red Square and along the embankments of the Moskva
River. Shoppers crowded the Mostorg Department Store and the
shops on Kuznetsky Most and the Neglinaya. There was a holiday air
about it all—the sun, the temperature and the easing of tensions.
Until a few days before many Russians had been worried over rumors
of war. Stories made the rounds that Adolf Hitler, having wound up
his blitzkrieg in western Europe, had decided not to attack England
but to turn instead on Russia despite the pact of nonaggression and
friendship which he had signed with Josef Stalin in August 1939.

Now the fears of war had been quieted. Tass, the official Soviet
news agency, had distributed a statement declaring that the rumors
were false; that Russia was guided by firm friendship with Nazi
Germany; that Germany had submitted no demands to Russia; that
reports of German preparations to attack the Soviet Union were false.
All these rumors, Tass said, had been circulated by parties that
wanted to spoil Nazi-Soviet relations.

While twenty-four years of Soviet rule had not inspired the
Russians with total belief in the truth of their Government's
statements, the Tass declaration was so sweeping that no one could
suppose that the Third Reich and the Kremlin were on anything but
the friendliest terms.

By 11:30 A.M. crowds in the suburban stations had thinned out.
Those who were leaving the city for the day had gone. But the
throngs in the stores and the big municipal food and vegetable markets

had grown larger as Moscow settled into its summer holiday.

Loudspeakers on the principal streets had been playing the usual fare of operetta songs and light marches. But a little before noon they went dead. A moment later an announcer broke in: "*Vnimaniye! Vnimaniye!* Attention! Attention!" He alerted his listeners that there would be an important announcement at noon. As his voice clicked off it was replaced by the ticking of a metronome. Presently he repeated the announcement. Then the metronome resumed.

People halted and began to ask each other what it might mean. This kind of an announcement was not unprecedented but it seldom meant anything good. Traffic slowed down and people gathered in little knots near the loudspeakers. What was happening? They had only a few minutes to wonder. At noon precisely the metronome clicked off and the solemn voice of Yuri Levitan, the official Government announcer, was heard introducing Vyacheslav Molotov, the Soviet Foreign Minister.

"Men and women, citizens of the Soviet Union, the Soviet Government and its head, Comrade Stalin, have instructed me to make the following announcement:

"At 4:00 A.M. without declaration of war and without any claims being made on the Soviet Union, German troops attacked our country, attacked our frontier in many places and bombed from the air Zhitomir, Kiev, Sevastopol, Kaunas and other cities. . . .

"The attack has been made despite the fact that there was a nonaggression pact between the Soviet Union and Germany, a pact the terms of which were scrupulously observed by the Soviet Union.

"Our cause is just. The enemy will be crushed. Victory will be ours."

Molotov spoke less than five minutes, but when he had finished it was as though the sun had been blacked out and the June fragrance vanished from the air. There was a brief pause in the streets. People were too stunned to react. Then in a single universal movement they flooded into the food stores, the meat shops, the jewelry stores, the hardware stores, the state banks. They bought everything they could lay hands on and drew out every kopek of their savings. The banks ran out of currency and had to close by 3:00 P.M. The Russians knew what war meant and they transformed their paper money into flour, sugar, salt, kerosene, sausage and lard. They bought up diamond rings, gold watches, anything of value in the jewelry stores and pawn shops. They even bought shovels and hoes in the hardware stores and chairs and tables in the furniture stores.

If anyone stopped to wonder why Molotov had made the announcement at noon instead of Josef Stalin it is not on record.

How could war have hit Russia like lightning from a clear summer sky? No country on earth had displayed more concern over the danger of attack from abroad. From the moment of the Bolshevik seizure of power November 7, 1917, Lenin and after him Stalin had warned the people again and again that they were surrounded by enemies who might strike without warning, without notice. The Soviet Union had grown up in what it called "capitalist encirclement." The whole population had been trained to bear arms. Every schoolboy and schoolgirl learned to shoot a rifle, handle a machine gun, hurl a hand grenade. The Red Army and the defense industries had first priority in the budget and generations of Russian men and women lived without butter, with little meat, without automobiles and

A section of the crowd in Moscow listening to Foreign Minister Molotov's radio announcement that Germany has attacked Russia.

refrigerators in order to build Russia's military might.

The question of what had happened was inescapable in Russian minds. True, Europe had been at war since September 1, 1939, when Hitler, flush with signing the famous nonaggression pact with Stalin, launched his armies against Poland. Not many Russians were enthusiastic about the newfound friendship with Nazi Germany, which they had been trained to regard as their mortal enemy. But at least they could see the pragmatic results of Stalin's policy. Hitler was now at war with England and France. Western Europe had been ravished but Russia, having divided Poland with Hitler, was at peace.

True, it was an uneasy peace. First there had been Russia's unexpectedly hard miniwar with Finland, finally won in the spring of 1940. But the Finnish campaign and the take-over of the Baltic states of Estonia, Lithuania and Latvia had given Russia a cushion against attack. The frontier was pushed north so that enemy guns no longer could fire pointblank into the Leningrad suburbs. No longer could the Baltic states be used as a jumping-off point for hostile forces, and the newly absorbed Polish territory gave the Red Army defensive depth in the west. And in 1940 Russia managed to get back Bessarabia and part of Bukovina from Romania, which improved defenses in the south.

Many Russians had been alarmed at the speed of the Nazi blitzkrieg in the west. The ease with which the Wehrmacht overran Norway, Denmark, the Low Countries and France worried Soviet citizens. Nor was the blitz against London, Portsmouth, Coventry and other British cities in any way reassuring.

But there had been no change in the comfortable tone of the Soviet press. *Pravda* and *Izvestiya* continued to report in friendly fashion Hitler's successes. There were none of those subtle hints on which the Soviet readers had come to rely as a true guide to Stalin's policy.

Foreign Minister Molotov went off to Berlin in November 1940 and met with Foreign Minister Joachim von Ribbentrop and Hitler. The reports of the meetings were cordial. Even a sudden flurry in April 1941 when the Germans moved into Yugoslavia and Greece

Adolf Hitler posing with his military leaders in August 1940. From left, Keitel, Rundstedt, Bock, Goering, Hitler, Brauchitsch, Leeb, List, Kluge, Witzleben, and Reichenau.

caused only momentary alarm. And when rumors had begun to build up in June that the Germans were turning eastward there came the reassuring statement of the Government news agency, Tass. Certainly if anything dangerous was going on the Government would not have issued a declaration so sweeping and so convincing that all was well between Russia and Germany.

That had been June 14. And now a week later—war!

What had happened?

This was a question which had risen even more sharply in the minds of Josef Stalin's closest associates only a few hours earlier.

These men, members of the Politburo, chiefs of Government departments, diplomats, members of the General Staff, generals of the Red Army, knew a great deal more than their 187,000,000 fellow Russian citizens. But they, too, had been caught in the tragic surprise.

Stalin's associates did not know everything which had happened in the past year. They knew that relations between Moscow and Berlin had not been as smooth and optimistic as they had appeared on the surface, but few had been prepared for the catastrophe of war.

They did not know, of course, because it was one of Hitler's most closely held secrets that as early as July 22, 1940, the Fuehrer held his first detailed High Staff discussion of the "Russian problem" and instructed Field Marshal Walther von Brauchitsch to draw up plans for an offensive against Russia, possibly to be carried out as early as autumn. Nor did they know that in this very month of July 1940 Soviet intelligence agents had learned that the German General Staff had instructed the German Transport Ministry to provide data on capabilities for movement of German troops from west to east. This fact was passed on to Stalin, but he did not reveal it to his military commanders.

A series of reports suggesting German preparations for an attack on Russia came to the Kremlin during the autumn of 1940. Stalin had the world's most effective intelligence network. Spies, underground

The Soviet leaders in January 1941. Left to right, Bulganin, Malenkov, Zhdanov, Shcherbakov, Beria, Andreyev, Dimitrov, Kaganovich, Mikoyan, Shvernik, Voroshilov, Molotov, Stalin, Timoshenko, Kalinin, Badayev, and Popov.

11

German soldiers study map during the move into the unfamiliar territory of the Soviet Union.

agents, Communist Party faithful were active in almost every country in the world. True, Stalin had liquidated much of his intelligence network in Germany at the time of his pact with Hitler (fearing possible embarrassment) but in Tokyo he had a remarkable spy, a German named Richard Sorge. Ostensibly a Nazi newspaper correspondent, Sorge was a close friend of German Ambassador Herman Ott, a closer friend of the German military attaché and privy to every secret received by the Embassy from Berlin, whether by diplomatic pouch or top secret code. There were few confidential matters which Berlin did not share with Germany's Tokyo embassy because it was charged with maintaining closest liaison with Germany's ally, Japan. On November 18, 1940, Sorge dispatched his first warning to Moscow that Germany was making preparations for an attack on the Eastern Front.

There is no evidence that Sorge's warning had any effect in Moscow. It followed a visit November 12–14, 1940, to Berlin by Molotov, a visit which clearly signaled a major change in Soviet-German relations. Stalin wanted a number of things from his Nazi partner. He wanted a free hand in the Balkans, particularly Bulgaria and Romania, and an end to Nazi meddling in Finland. He was hopeful of getting Hitler's support for control of the Dardanelles.

Hitler wanted to size up Russia once and for all before deciding on war. He offered Molotov grandiose words—a place in the world order he was constructing, freedom to expand to the south, into Persia, the Gulf, India.

But Molotov insisted on talking specifics—getting Nazi troops out of Finland, a Soviet pact with Bulgaria, details on how the world was to be carved up. The more Hitler heard Molotov's schoolmaster twang the more his determination to carry war to the east was hardened.

Marshal A. M. Vasilevsky, later to become Stalin's Chief of Staff, came back from Berlin certain that sooner or later Germany would attack the Soviet Union. His view was shared by many of his military colleagues. Did Molotov warn Stalin? No one knows. But on December 18 Hitler placed his signature on the draft of Plan Barbarossa—the detailed outline for the attack on the Soviet Union. The next day, full of smiles, he received the new Soviet Ambassador V. G. Dekanozov, a high official of the Soviet secret police, right-hand man of Lavrenti Beria, the head of the police, and Stalin's closest crony. Hitler had kept Dekanozov waiting a month to present his credentials. Now Hitler was jovial. The two men had a cordial talk. Ten days later Richard Sorge in Tokyo wirelessed in code to Moscow:

"On the German-Soviet frontier eighty divisions are concentrating. Hitler intends to occupy the territory of the U.S.S.R. on the line Kharkov-Moscow-Leningrad."

Sorge reported that a German reserve army of forty divisions was assembling at Leipzig and that twenty German divisions had been

Above, Russians enlist to fight for their country. Below, enlistees prepare to leave for military training.

shifted from France to Poland.

On Christmas Day the Soviet military attaché in Berlin received an anonymous letter. It said that Hitler intended to attack the U.S.S.R. and provided the outline of Plan Barbarossa. The attack was timed, the letter said, for the spring of 1941.

How did Stalin react to this intelligence? No one can now guess his private thoughts, but military men who raised questions about Germany's intentions found themselves quickly and sometimes severely reprimanded. They were told they were suffering from "Germanophobia."

With the new year the intelligence information reaching Stalin grew to a flood. Hardly a day went by without new information on Hitler's intentions. There were almost weekly cables from Sorge in Tokyo. By March 5, 1941, he had sent off a microfilm of a telegram from von Ribbentrop to Ambassador Ott giving the date of the German attack as mid-June. The Soviet military attaché in France, Major General I. A. Susloparov, reported that the Germans planned to strike in late May. Later he corrected the date to late June. As early as January Undersecretary of State Sumner Welles had warned Soviet Ambassador Konstantin Oumansky in Washington that the U.S. had information that the Germans were planning an attack on Russia in the spring. Warnings came in to Stalin from Roosevelt, from Churchill, from friendly diplomats in many capitals and increasingly from his military and intelligence operatives.

The warnings grew more frequent. The Soviet General Staff reported on May 1 that throughout March and April the Germans had concentrated more and more troops on the Soviet frontier. German Air Force reconnaissance became blatant. Between March 28 and April 18 there were 80 Nazi overflights, including one plane which came down near Rovno complete with camera, exposed film and a topographical map. On May 15 Richard Sorge reported that the German blow would come June 20–22 and four days later he advised it would be carried out by nine armies and 150 divisions. A bit later he forwarded the German order of battle. About the same time the Berlin embassy sent in an almost equally comprehensive report on German plans. On June 6 the Soviet intelligence service placed on Stalin's desk an estimate that the Germans now had concentrated 4,000,000 men on Russia's western border. Embassy wives and children began to leave Moscow for their homes in Germany. The Nazi consul in Leningrad canceled an order with a Russian tailor for a new suit. Admiral Nikolai G. Kuznetsov had gathered a mass of naval intelligence pointing to imminent Nazi action. He went to the Kremlin June 13 or 14 and saw Stalin for the last time before the outbreak of war. He reported that almost every German ship had cleared out of Soviet harbors and waters, often leaving without discharging their cargoes. He planned to ask Stalin for orders to put the fleet on the alert but Stalin seemed so uninterested he left without raising the question.

On June 12 Sorge in Tokyo received a message from Moscow expressing strong doubt as to the validity of his reports that the Germans were preparing war. He sent off a new wireless: "I repeat: nine armies of 150 divisions will attack on a wide front at dawn June 22, 1941." He signed the message with his customary code name, "Ramsey."

The message went forward on June 17. Sorge was deeply upset. Something must be wrong at the Moscow center. They doubted his reports. Someone didn't believe him. Could it be Stalin?

German soldiers advancing into the Soviet Union.

STALIN'S BLUNDER

Never had a government information so comprehensive, so accurate, so timely concerning the plans and intentions of its enemy as did Stalin of Hitler. Neither the American breaking of Japan's "Code Purple" nor the British success with Germany's "Ultra" could compare with the data which piled up on Stalin's desk. Stalin's materials were vastly superior to the American and British data. Stalin's information came from scores of sources—high and low. From his own agents. His own military. His own diplomats. From spies. From statesmen of other countries. Even from the Germans themselves. At the last moment the German Ambassador in Moscow, Count Friedrich Werner von der Schulenburg, later to pay with his life for his opposition to Hitler, took the remarkable step of attempting to warn the Russians of the German plans. He called in Vladimir Dekanozov, Soviet Ambassador to Germany who chanced to be in Moscow, and told him how dangerous the situation had become. He urged Moscow to get in touch with Berlin before it was too late. Dekanozov, thinking it was all a German trick, would hardly listen, insisting that the Ambassador must talk to Molotov. Twenty-five years later Vladimir Pavlov, Dekanozov's interpreter, confirmed that the Russians thought von der Schulenburg's courageous warning was only part of a grandiose Hitler blackmail plot.

Blackmail . . . This seems the only comprehensible explanation why Stalin turned a deaf ear to every warning he received. He believed Hitler was capable of blackmailing him but not attacking. He trusted Hitler to live up to the Nazi-Soviet pact and he was prepared (many of his associates believed) to pay a steep price—greater deliveries of oil, of food, of iron ore that Hitler needed for his war machine. Even territorial concessions if need be. This was his ace in the hole. But it turned out to be an ace without value. The one man in the world whom Stalin trusted was not bluffing. This was for real. As of June 21 Hitler had massed on the borders of the Soviet Union 4,200,000 men, comprising 208 divisions, composed of 163 infantry divisions, 21 armored divisions, 14 motorized divisions, one division of cavalry and nine security divisions. He had assembled 3,500 tanks, 50,000 guns, and 3,900 planes. It was the most powerful military force that ever existed.

Whatever Stalin thought about Hitler he had, in fact, taken some elementary precautions. The Red Army had been brought up to a strength of nearly 5,000,000 by June 1, 1941, as against 2.5 million January 1, 1939. He had 2.9 million troops in Russia's western defense districts (true, they were badly positioned). He had begun (much too late) to move important reinforcements west from the Trans-Baikal and Caucasus districts—five armies in all, the Twenty-Second, the Twentieth, the Twenty-First, the Nineteenth and the Sixteenth. But these movements were not due to be completed until late July.

Orders had gone out to speed the preparation of border defenses (a whole new system had to be built because of the extension of Soviet frontiers westward). But Colonel General M. P. Kirponos, the Kiev commander, was reprimanded when he proposed to move his

Stalin in his Kremlin office beneath a portrait of Karl Marx.

troops into the new frontline fortifications. Such action might be taken by the Germans as a provocation.

The possibility of provocations filled Stalin's mind. Soviet anti-aircraft units were forbidden to fire on German planes. This might be taken as a provocation. Army and navy men who talked about possible war with Germany were branded "provocateurs." Some were even arrested. Party political workers lectured the Army men that talk of war was provocational. Russia had no disagreements with Germany. Stalin had assured peace for a long time into the future.

As time wound down only one element of Russia's armed forces —the Navy—was mobilized for war and this by its own initiative. On June 19 at 4:15 P.M. at the urgent insistence of Admiral Vladimir Tributs, Commander of the Baltic Fleet, Navy Commissar Nikolai Kuznetsov put the Baltic fleet on a No. 2 combat alert, just one step shy of a No. 1—total war—red alert. Hours later he ordered the Northern Fleet and the Black Sea Fleet onto No. 2 alert.

The clock ticked on. On Friday evening, June 20, Stalin for the first time must have felt some concern, because in the early morning hours of Saturday June 21 he sent instructions to the Soviet Embassy in Berlin to seek an urgent meeting with Foreign Minister von Ribbentrop to find out what was happening. Von Ribbentrop was to be told that Moscow was ready for any kind of conversations (was this a hint that Stalin himself might come to Berlin?) to ease the situation.

It was a dull Saturday in Berlin. Every hour on the hour First Secretary Berezhkov telephoned the Foreign Office, but Ribbentrop could not be located. Moscow called the Berlin Embassy. Molotov wanted an answer immediately. Berezhkov began calling every thirty minutes. No response from the German side.

Perhaps the lack of response from Berlin played a role in Moscow. Perhaps it was the operational reports from Soviet commanders on the frontier telling of the steady roar of trucks and tanks lumbering up to the border towns. Perhaps it was a last-minute cable from Ambassador Maisky in London reporting the British had just told him they had reliable evidence that the Germans would attack in the morning of the 22nd. Whatever it was, Stalin made one move on that pleasant Saturday afternoon. He telephoned General Tyulenev, who was in charge of Moscow's antiaircraft defenses.

"Comrade Tyulenev," he said, "how are we fixed as far as the antiaircraft defense of Moscow is concerned?"

Tyulenev gave him a brief report.

"Considering the disturbing situation," Stalin instructed, "you should bring the Moscow antiaircraft forces to 75 percent readiness for action."

Tyulenev believed that Stalin must have received some new evidence of the possibility of a German attack. Admiral Kuznetsov later came to the same conclusion.

However, doubt still persisted. Tyulenev checked with GHQ a bit later. They told him the front commanders and intelligence reports continued to emphasize the possibility of a German attack. But when Stalin was informed he replied, "You're just raising a panic."

On the German side of the border there was quiet confidence. The tanks, the troops, the guns, the men were in place. The planes were positioned for takeoff at dawn to attack the concentrations of Soviet aircraft, which had been carefully plotted by reconnaissance flights. There had been one last-minute argument. The original time for the jump-off had been set as 4:00 A.M. But in the north the sun

FOOTNOTE TO HISTORY
In 1939 Stalin and Hitler agreed to sign a pact of nonaggression which, to Stalin's shock, was broken, when Hitler invaded Russia. Here German Foreign Minister von Ribbentrop is shown signing the document. Standing, from left, Russian Ambassador Shkvarzev, Stalin, and Russian Foreign Minister Molotov.

THE GERMAN OFFENSIVE

SWEDEN

NORWAY

Narvik

Petsamo

Murmansk

FINLAND

Archangel

UNION   OF

Helsinki

Stockholm

*LAKE
LADOGA*
Neva R.

Svirstroi

Vologda

SOVIET

BALTIC SEA

Tallinn

ESTONIA

Narva

Kronstadt
Leningrad
Volkhov
Kobona
Tikhrin

Chudovo

Luga R.

Cherepovets

SOCIALIST

Ventspils

Riga

LATVIA

Pskov
Ostrov

Novgorod

*LAKE
ILMEN*

Demyansk

Volga R.

Gorky

Kazan

Libau

Opochka

Dec 1941 Line

Kalinin

REPUBLICS

Velikaya R.

Ulyanovsk

LITHUAN

Taurage

Dvina R.

Smolensk

Moscow
Moskva R.
Kolumna

Kuibyshev

Tilsit
Kaunas

Orsha

Vyazma

Mozhaisk

Yelnya

Ryazan

EAST
PRUSSIA

Alytus

Highway

Dnieper R.

Roslavl

Tula

Neman R.

Minsk

Bryansk

Orel

Vistula

Slutsk

Voronezh

Warsaw

Brest-Litovsk

BYELORUSSIA

Glukhov

Kursk

Nov 1942 Line

POLAND

Rovno

Kiev

Sula R.

Kharkov

Don R.

Stalingrad

Zhitomir

Psel R.

Volga R.

CZECHOSLOVAKIA

Tarnopol

Berdichev

UKRAINE

Dnieper R.

DON
COSSACK

Astrakhan

Vinnitza

Uman

Bug R.

Dnepropetrovsk

Donets R.

Budapest

Ingul R.

Krivog Rog

Zaporozhe

Rostov-
on-Don

HUNGARY

BUKOVINA

BESSARABIA

Nikolaev

*CASPIAN
SEA*

YUGOSLAVIA

ROMANIA

Odessa

CRIMEA

Kerch

Krasnodar

Kuban R.

Voroshilovsk

Belgrade

Bucharest

Sevastopol

Novorossisk

Maikop

Grozny

BLACK SEA

CAUCASUS

0   100   200   300   400 Mi.

would rise at 3:00 A.M. or earlier. Northern group commanders wanted an earlier start. In the south along the 1,800-mile front the sun would not be up until 4:00 A.M. Finally a compromise hour was picked: 3:30 A.M.

The German forces were concentrated in three huge masses—a northern group headed toward the Baltic states and Leningrad, a central Army group directed toward Moscow and a southern group that would attack the Ukraine, seize Kiev and Kharkov and then head for the oilfields of the Caucasus.

All was ready. It was no longer possible to camouflage the mass movement of men nor to still the rumble of equipment and the throb of motors as the troops moved to their starting points. But as far as German intelligence could determine, on the Russian side of the border all was peace and quiet. No troop movements. No unusual alarms. By midnight Nazi diversionary units which had already crossed to the Russian side would cut the lines and snap the cables, severing Soviet military communications between regional headquarters and forward positions.

There was high confidence in the German command. Hitler had told Field Marshal Rudolf Gerd von Rundstedt: "You have only to kick in the door and the whole rotten structure will come crashing down."

Outside the Kremlin in Red Square in the pleasant twilight of the summer solstice boys and girls strolled slowly, arms about each other. Older couples sat in the benches beside Lenin's Masoleum and partook of the fine air. Every quarter hour the clock in the Spassky Tower sounded and on the hour came the reverberating beat of its great chimes. From time to time the meticulously uniformed guards at the Spassky entrance sprang to attention, a shrill alarm bell sounded, the great doors swung back and a long black Zis limousine with gray curtains at the windows to conceal the identity of the passenger whirled up the cobblestones and into the Kremlin compound.

The limousines were bringing to the Kremlin members of the Politburo and the Soviet High Command, summoned at long last by Stalin, to consider the mounting evidence that the Germans were about to go to war against Russia.

General Georgi Zhukov, Chief of Staff, had telephoned Stalin that a German sergeant major had crossed the lines and revealed that the Germans were moving up to takeoff areas for an attack to begin the next morning.

The meeting was held in Stalin's Kremlin office, a plain room paneled in Karelian birch and furnished only with portraits of Marx, Engels and Lenin. Stalin's desk was beside a window looking out over the Kremlin walls. At the other side of the room was a long table covered in crimson baize.

Stalin was not inclined to believe the report of the German deserter.

"Are you sure the Germans didn't send that deserter across the lines themselves?" Stalin asked, looking coldly at Zhukov and Defense Commissar Timoshenko. "You are confident that this is not a provocation?"

The long room was silent a moment. Stalin puffed on his pipe. The members of the Politburo turned their faces to Zhukov and Timoshenko. All knew Stalin was almost pathologically convinced that the Germans, the English, the French and the Americans were

A German soldier questions a Russian who has just escaped from a burning Soviet tank.

trying to trick Russia into war.

Zhukov had brought with him the draft of a directive to the Soviet armed forces warning them of the danger of a German attack at any moment and putting them on a No. 1 "red alert." Stalin paced up and down the room a moment. Then he said: "Let me see your directive." Zhukov handed it over. Stalin reached for a cigarette box, took out two Hertzogovina Flowers, his favorite brand, broke them, smashed the tobacco into his pipe, lighted it, drew on it and said:

"This order is premature. Draw up another saying that on the evening of June 21–22 there may be a provocation on the border. The troops must be ready for it but they must not be incited by any provocations which might lead to complications."

Zhukov and Timoshenko hurried back to Defense Headquarters to issue the directive. The Politburo continued to discuss the situation. Marshal Budyonny suggested that all the Soviet troops east of the Dnieper be ordered to move toward the Soviet-German frontier, the Air Force be put on a No. 1 alert and a deep defense line set up on the Dnieper and the Dvina from Kiev to Riga. Only the last proposal was acted on. Budyonny was named chief of the "Reserve Army" and Georgi Malenkov, Stalin's favorite Party Secretary, was made his deputy. They hurried off to Defense Headquarters. Budyonny's only problem was that he had no troops, arms, planes or guns for the "Reserve Army."

The orders which Timoshenko and Zhukov sent out that night (but not until 12:30 A.M. Sunday, June 22) warned of the possibility of a German attack that might begin with a provocation. The troops were not to be incited by provocations. They were to be placed on a basis of combat readiness, occupying the still-empty firing positions of the border fortifications. Planes were to be dispersed before dawn and placed under camouflage. Preparations must be made for blacking out cities and installations but "no other measures are to be taken without special orders."

The warnings reached the principal Soviet commands between 2:00 and 3:00 A.M. The German attack started before many border units could even be informed. Special representatives of the High Command were sent out to the border military commands but they went by train and none arrived before the outbreak of war.

Molotov, despairing of getting through to von Ribbentrop, finally called in the German Ambassador von der Schulenberg and asked him about the rumors of impending war. Von der Schulenburg, an honest man who knew that war was imminent, was embarrassed. He offered a few painful generalizations and drove back to his embassy. On the way he watched an excursion boat pass by on the Moskva River, lights ablaze, a jazz band playing an American song. About the same time Dekanozov in Berlin had an equally unrewarding meeting with Ernst von Weizsacker, State Secretary of Foreign Affairs.

At about 11:00 P.M. Stalin left the Kremlin by the Borovitzkaya Gate in the usual convoy of three limousines. The procession roared down Kalinin Street, into the Arbat and out Dorogomilovskaya Street and the Minsk chausse. Stalin had a villa a few miles out of town. He never spent the night at the Kremlin. At his villa, alone in the peace and quiet of the summer evening, he worked a couple of hours and went to sleep on his office sofa, which pulled out to make a bed. The time was about 2:30 A.M.

In the Defense Commissariat the night was tense. About midnight

Zhukov got a report from the Kiev military district. Another German deserter had turned up. He had swum the River Bug and told the Soviet border guards that the German attack was to be expected at 4:00 A.M.

Zhukov and Timoshenko nervously telephoned the front commanders—F. I. Kuznetsov in the northwest, D. G. Pavlov in the center, M. P. Kirponos at Kiev. Everywhere there were signs of trouble.

The Naval Commissar, Admiral Nikolai G. Kuznetsov, slept on his office couch that night. He called his principal admirals at

Soviet soldiers being marched
to a prison camp
in the Ukraine, 1941.

intervals. All reported alarming signs of German action. Finally he
dropped off to sleep. At 3:15 A.M. his telephone rang. It was Admiral
F. S. Oktyabrsky, Commander of the Black Sea fleet. The Germans
were bombing the Sevastopol naval base.

Admiral Kuznetsov telephoned Stalin immediately, but the duty
officer said, "He's not here and I don't know where he is." So Kuznetsov
called Timoshenko and relayed the news. A few moments later the
Admiral got an angry call from Georgi Malenkov, Stalin's secretary.

"Do you understand what you have reported?" Malenkov asked.

"Yes," Kuznetsov said. "I understand and I report it on my own responsibility. War has started."

Malenkov immediately telephoned Sevastopol and talked with Oktyabrsky. Bombs exploded as the conversation went on. Oktyabrsky hung up and an aide said knowingly, "In Moscow they don't believe that Sevastopol is being bombed." He was right.

At 3:30 the Western Defense District reported to Zhukov that bombs were falling in Byelorussia. Three minutes later a report came in that the Germans were bombing Ukrainian towns. At 3:40 the bombing of Kaunas and other towns was reported to Zhukov. Shortly before 4:00 A.M. Marshal Voronov, Chief of Antiaircraft Defense, reported to Timoshenko that the Germans were bombing Ventspils and Libau on the Baltic. He was given a big notebook and told to write down his report, word for word. Behind him checking on it all stood L. Z. Mekhlis, Chief of Army Political Police and a crony of Police Chief Beria.

"I left the office with a stone in my heart," Voronov recalled. "I realized that they did not believe that war actually had started."

It must have been at this moment that Zhukov finally telephoned Stalin. Dawn had already come to Moscow. The pale blue sky was streaked with streamers of red. Zhukov got no answer. He kept calling. Finally the officer on duty answered with a sleepy voice.

"Comrade Stalin is asleep," the officer replied.

"Wake him up," Zhukov commanded. "The Germans are bombing our cities."

Zhukov waited. The silence went on for several minutes. Finally he heard the sound of the receiver being picked up and a quiet voice said: "Stalin."

"I'm calling at the orders of the Defense Commissar," Zhukov said. "The Germans are bombing our cities."

There was a long silence.

"Do you understand me?" Zhukov asked.

Again silence. Zhukov only heard the sharp intake of Stalin's breath. Then Stalin spoke.

"Where's the Defense Commissar?"

"Talking to the Kiev Military District," Zhukov replied.

Another silence. What can he be thinking, Zhukov wondered? Stalin spoke again.

"Come to the Kremlin with Timoshenko. Tell Poskrebyshev [Stalin's *chef de cabinet*] to summon the Politburo."

It was 4:30 A.M. by the time Stalin and the Politburo were assembled. Stalin did not greet Zhukov and Timoshenko when they appeared. He simply said: "Report."

Timoshenko reported on the bombing of cities and military attacks along the frontier. When Timoshenko concluded every face turned to Stalin. Stalin stuffed tobacco into his pipe.

"Tell me, don't you think that all this may be a provocation?" he asked. There was a thin note in his voice which sent a signal of fear through the room. For the first time Stalin did not appear confident.

"How can that be, Comrade Stalin?" Zhukov replied. "Our own cities are being attacked by bombs!"

Stalin made an impatient movement of his hand.

"The Germans," he said, "are well-known masters of provocation. They might even begin to bomb their own cities."

No one spoke. Stalin began to pace the room. Suddenly he stopped beside Foreign Minister Molotov. "We must get in touch with Berlin immediately," he said. "Phone the German Embassy."

Molotov picked up a telephone and called the Foreign Office. He

Ukrainian citizens amid the ruins of their bombed home.

talked a moment and hung up. Almost immediately the phone rang back. Molotov listened. "Schulenburg wants to see me urgently. He has an important communication."

Molotov went off to see von der Schulenburg. The generals and the Politburo members sat in their places. Stalin paced the floor. Presently Molotov returned, pale and shaken. "The German Government has declared war on us," he said. Stalin was in the far corner of the room. He turned, took a few uncertain steps, slowly sank into a chair and hunched over the table, his unlit pipe beside him. Finally he straightened up, pointed his finger at Timoshenko and Zhukov and ordered them to issue a directive to the troops to repel the enemy. But not to cross the frontiers. Nor were planes to penetrate more than 150 miles into enemy territory.

The directive was issued at 7:15 A.M. Even at this hour Stalin clung to the hope that it was not a "real" attack but only some aberrant Nazi generals acting on their own. All through the morning the Russians tried by wireless to get in touch with Berlin. They asked the Japanese to convey their message. As Molotov told von der Schulenberg, "Surely we have not deserved this!" Stalin was still willing to negotiate. Sometime during the day he must have realized that it was too late. That the one man whom he had trusted, Hitler, had betrayed him. It was then that Stalin, in the words of Nikita Khrushchev, turned to his associates and said: "All that Lenin created we have lost forever!"

With those words Stalin, the world's greatest dictator, vanished from the scene. He retired to his villa at Kuntsevo and there he sat for days. He did not answer the telephone. He sent no messages to his associates. Nor would he see them. The housekeeper and the guards at the villa glimpsed him occasionally through the half-open door of his study. He sat motionless in his chair, his desk covered with papers, staring into space. They brought him meals but he did not eat. Sometimes he seemed to be asleep but his eyes were open.

The Germans raced across Russia's western approaches. The Soviet losses were frightful. In the West military experts agreed with the Nazi boasts that Russia "will be finished in three weeks." The Soviet general staff, the great military commanders, the Politburo members not used to taking a single step without Stalin's approval, tried to weld Russia into a fighting machine. It wasn't easy. Soviet Ambassador Ivan M. Maisky in London almost lost his mind in frustration. The British Government urgently wanted to consult Stalin on common plans to combat Hitler. Winston Churchill wanted to know how he could help Russia. But Maisky could not even get an answer to his cables and not a line of instructions on how to proceed.

Finally Stalin began to emerge from his seclusion. On July 3 he broadcast to his people, his voice uncertain, breathing heavily into the microphone, punctuating his sentences with long pauses while he audibly gulped water from a glass. It was an address of exceptional modesty. He called the Russian people not "comrades" but used the old Russian expression *bratya i sestri*, brothers and sisters. He invoked the spirit of Great Russian patriotism and the images of the Russian past. He mentioned Marshals Suvarov and Kutuzov who had defeated Napoleon.

Gradually he turned back to the task of directing his country, of leading it in the colossal war into which his fatal blunders had plunged it.

German General Rudolf Gerd von Rundstedt meeting with Hitler during early days of the Russian campaign.

Russian words scrawled on a wall in Brest in July 1941. "I am dying but I do not surrender. Farewell Motherland."

BRAVERY AT BREST

As the Nazi hordes roared over the Soviet border on the mild Sunday morning of June 22, 1941, the Germans intercepted a Soviet wireless exchange in clear (not military code) transmission. The Red Army unit wirelessed: "We are being fired on. What shall we do?" Headquarters replied: "You must be crazy. Why is your signal not in code?"

Admiral Kuznetsov, the Naval Commissar who had by his own authority put the Soviet fleet on war alert (with the result that the Navy took no losses in the surprise attack), waited in his office that morning for some word from the Government. None came. Finally he got into his car and went to the Kremlin. No one was there. He couldn't understand it. On Sunday evening Molotov telephoned to see how the Navy was doing. With Stalin in a state of shock apparently no one had remembered that Russia had a Navy.

Three German divisions smashed across the frontier in the vicinity of Taurage, on the direct Tilsit-Riga highway. The Soviet border post went on the radio: "Osoka calling! Osoka calling! Germans have crossed the frontier. This is Osoka. It's war." But it was twelve hours later, 4:00 P.M., June 22, before the border troops could get a message through to 125th Division GHQ. Within a few hours the 125th Division itself was crushed.

In the Baltic area the Germans had a three-to-one superiority in infantry and two-to-one in artillery. But the figures were deceptive. While the Russians had 170 divisions guarding their western frontier only 58 were in the first echelon when the Germans attacked.

Along the Neman River protecting Kaunas the 128th Soviet Division and the 5th Tank Division were on guard. But within an hour communications were cut. Headquarters radio tried to reach them!

"Neman! Dunai calling. Alytus. Alytus. Alytus. Dunai calling." There was no answer. A courier tried to reach Alytus by car. He did not return. Major Agafonov, a communications officer, set out for Alytus. He met a bus bringing Soviet officers back. They told him there was no point in trying to reach Alytus. It had already been taken by the Nazis. Five hundred Nazi tanks had spearheaded across the Neman River. Kaunas, headquarters of the Northwest Front, was doomed.

The Soviet Air Force on the Western Front was almost wiped out in the first day—900 planes on the ground and 300 in the air. Lieutenant General P. V. Rychagov, Air Commander of the Baltic Military District, was called to Moscow and shot. Lieutenant General Kopets, chief of Bomber Command, committed suicide June 23. He had lost 800 bombers in two days. The Kiev Military District lost 180 planes in the first few hours.

The problem of the Soviet defense was compounded by the belief of many high commanders (reinforced by directives and injunctions from Moscow) that the German attack didn't necessarily mean war. General Ivan I. Fedyuninsky, commander of the 15th Soviet Corps on the River Bug (later to distinguish himself in Leningrad under

Marshal Zhukov), felt that his chief, General M. I. Potapov of the Fifth Army, "was still not quite sure that the Nazis had started a war." When General D. G. Pavlov, Commander of the Western Military District at Minsk, heard of the German attack he said, "It can't be. It's just nonsense." He had told his commanders there might be a raid across the Bug River that night "by fascist bands" and gave orders to seize the "bands" but not to pursue them across the river. Within hours the Nazi panzers had severed Pavlov's communications. He could not find out what was happening, give orders to his troops or ask Moscow for instructions.

There was a special problem in the Kiev Military District, defending Russia's southwest approaches. General Kirponos had been ordered to move his headquarters forward from Kiev to Tarnopol on the Soviet frontier. As the German attack began his whole organization was in motion, the first headquarters echelon arriving in Tarnopol on the evening of June 21, the second not until 6:00 A.M. the morning of the 22nd, having been strafed by Nazi planes enroute. With his headquarters in transit General Kirponos had no way of coordinating defense against the onrushing German panzers. Moscow's orders provided only a foretaste of what was to come.

Everywhere the Nazis plunged forward, smashing the Russian border defenses, penetrating fifty and one hundred miles into Soviet territory before the regional commanders could get a grasp on the problems they faced. Everywhere huge pockets of Soviet troops were left behind, sometimes valiantly fighting their way back to their own lines, sometimes throwing up a circular defense and fighting it out with the bewilderingly mobile Nazis, sometimes surrendering in masses so great even the efficient Germans were hard put to cope with them.

Sometimes valiantly fighting . . . In a hundred, two hundred, possibly three hundred different areas Red Army units fought on behind the Nazi lines, out of touch with their commands (which often had been destroyed), resisting as well as they could against this enemy which had struck with such surprise.

The key to the center of Russia's western border was the frontier city and fortress of Brest-Litovsk on the River Bug. From Brest a good highway ran northwest of the vast Pripet marshes, 250 miles to Minsk, capital of Byelorussia, and on through Orsha, Smolensk, Vyazma and Mozhaisk to Moscow itself. This was the main route to the Soviet capital, the one Napoleon had followed, and here under Field Marshal von Bock, Hitler had concentrated his strongest striking force. The force marshalled against Brest-Litovsk was headed by Field Marshal von Kluge's Fourth Army, comprising 29 infantry divisions and the brilliant General Heinz Guderian's Second Panzer Group which included five armored and three motorized infantry divisions. Army Group Center was supported by Field Marshal Albert Kesselring's Second Air Fleet of 1,000 planes, the strongest of Hitler's air groups.

Von Kluge swept across the Bug, through Brest-Litovsk, and within four days Slutsk, 60 miles south of Minsk, had fallen. On June 27 Minsk was encircled and the city fell. The Germans took 300,000 prisoners. The Soviet Third, Tenth and Thirteenth armies were destroyed and the Fourth and Eleventh armies desperately damaged. General Pavlov, Soviet Front Commander, his Chief of Staff General Klimovsky and many other officers were recalled to Moscow and shot.

But far behind the lines on the River Bug the ancient fortress of Brest went on fighting. Although the fortress dated to the eighteenth century and had been massively reconstructed in the middle of the nineteenth century, it was not suited to contemporary warfare. Brest itself was an historical anamoly. It had been the western guardian of Russia for centuries but fell to the Germans in World War I. Here the representatives of the fledgling revolutionary Government of Lenin were compelled to sign the humiliating peace with Germany in which the Bolsheviks gave away two thirds of European Russia. Brest was retained by Poland after World War I and came back to Russia only in the 1939 partition.

In the slightly less than two years after Brest fell into Soviet hands a modern fortified zone had been built around the old Brest fortress, but it was not complete and in no condition to serve as a bastion against modern weapons. Moreover, on the morning of June 22 most of the Brest troops were at their summer camps on training maneuvers and Moscow's post-midnight warning of possible Nazi attack came far too late to summon them back. In fact, to the elements of the Sixth Orlov Red Banner Division and the 42nd Rifle Division that chanced to remain in the fortified area, the Nazi attack came as a complete surprise. They totaled about two regiments with few guns and almost no tanks.

Soviet border guards at Brest, detachments of NKVD troops

A German antitank gun crew cheers destruction of Soviet tank.

under the command of Lavrenti P. Beria, the Soviet Chief of Secret Police, had reported the Nazi preparations for war but got nothing for their pains but a warning to beware of provocations.

When the Germans moved forward on the morning of June 22 about 3,000 Soviet troops managed to assemble in the Brest fortified area. They were assaulted by the 45th German Division numbering close to 20,000 men. The fortified area had been surrounded by noon, and the Germans poured artillery fire into the old redoubts and newly constructed but not completed concrete bunkers. Eight assaults were carried out that day and the Nazis succeeded in occupying part of the Kobrinsk fort, the central part of the Terespol fort and a part of the Volinsk hospital.

All day the Brest wireless operator tried to contact headquarters —any headquarters—division, Army, even Moscow. Finally he began broadcasting in the clear : "This is the Brest fortress. We are fighting. Losses are insignificant. Munitions okay. We are preparing our guns and tanks for action. We await orders! We await orders!"

Over and over the message was transmitted. No orders ever came. No one—as far as Soviet historians have been able to discover —ever heard the message.

The battle went on. Day after day. The Germans drove harder and harder and slowly began to pinch the Russian defenders into a smaller and smaller area. Supplies ran out. There were more dead and wounded than men able to man the guns. On June 29–30 the Germans mounted a final offensive and overran all the principal installations. The battle was over, or so the German military logs and regimental reports have it. The Russians say that until the middle of July small bands of Red Army men in outlying bunkers and isolated cellars fought on until the last were killed, starved to death or flushed out.

All of the leaders of the defense were killed—Captain Zubachev, Commissar E. M. Fomin, Major P. M. Gavrilov, Political Worker S. S. Skripnik. Or so it was long assumed. Years later it was discovered that Major Gavrilov, badly wounded, had fallen prisoner to the Nazis. At the end of the war he was released only to be sent to Stalin's prison camps. After Stalin's death in 1953, this hero of the Brest defense was liberated.

Not a word of the bravery of the Brest defenders appeared in the Soviet press, although some members of the garrison escaped, fought with the Byelorussian partisans and gradually made their way back to the Red Army lines.

Little by little the legend of the defenders of Brest spread by word of mouth. The year 1941 was a year when the Red Army needed such legends for the troops who reeled back under Nazi blows. Two or three small stories about Brest finally were published but it was not until 1954, after the death of Stalin, that the heroism of the fort's defenders began to be publicly acknowledged. Book after book appeared about them. Many were written by the writer S. S. Smirnov, who swore to dedicate his life to the memory of this small band of Soviet men and women who gave their lives in the early days of the war to halt the onrush of the Hitler juggernaut. No one knows why the heroism of Brest was hardly mentioned during the war and during Stalin's lifetime. Perhaps it was simply because the episode was not known in Moscow because of the total destruction of the Soviet line of command. Perhaps Stalin thought the legend of Brest would remind people of the terrible disasters of the war's first days. It is hard to tell, but one thing is known. When the Brest defenders who had been Nazi prisoners of war were returned to the Soviet Union in 1945,

A German soldier combs the Russian forest for snipers.

most of them were sent straight from Hitler's concentration camps to those of Stalin in Siberia.

The panzers drove forward. By July 16 Guderian had seized Smolensk, the last important town before Moscow—120 miles to the east. Another huge concentration of Soviet troops was surrounded, principally the Soviet Sixteenth and Twentieth armies. By the time the Smolensk pocket was liquidated three weeks later another 300,000 Red Army men had been taken prisoner.

The story was not much different on the other fronts. To the north the Germans raced through Lithuania and Latvia, most of whose inhabitants greeted them as liberators. Lithuania and Latvia had been forcibly incorporated into the Soviet Union only a year earlier; few inhabitants had any love for the Soviet Union. Within two weeks the Germans had turned the Pskov-Ostrov-Opochka line, seizing Ostrov on July 5 and Pskov on July 9. The Russians had hoped to set up a new defense line on the Velikaya River, 125 to 150 miles southwest of Leningrad, but the Nazis were too swift. In less than three weeks of fighting the Germans had cleared most of the natural barriers to their drive upon Leningrad.

Why had the fighting gone so badly for the Red Army? Basically because of the German tactical surprise. In three weeks, of the 31 front-line divisions of the Soviet Northwest Front 22 had lost half or more of their strength. On the whole Soviet front 28 divisions had been obliterated and more than 70 divisions had lost 50 percent or more of their strength. Six days after the war started the 2nd Corps of the Thirteenth Army on the Western Front reported it had no ammunition, no fuel, no food, no transport, no means of communication and no instructions as to where to evacuate wounded if means of evacuation could be contrived. This was a typical corps. By June 29 the Western Front had lost 60 important supply depots (Stalin under Police Chief Beria's influence had insisted on putting the big depots close to the frontier instead of in rear areas). The Front had lost 2,000 freight cars of ammunition (30 percent of its total), 50,000 tons of gasoline (50 percent of its reserve), 40,000 tons of forage (the Red Army still used a lot of horses) and almost all its hospital and engineering supplies.

Russian soldiers throwing grenades during early days of the war.

In Moscow, the only description for the atmosphere was unreal. Stalin once again was meeting his political aides and his generals in the Kremlin.

The Kremlin had been dressed in camouflage—that is, the gilt domes of the churchs and towers had been smeared a dirty green and freizes of canvas disguised the dense cluster of old buildings. The vast pavements of Red Square were crisscrossed with geometric designs, intended to disorient the Nazi bombers. Enormous concentrations of antiaircraft guns had been mounted inside the Kremlin and on the roofs and in courtyards of buildings around the triangle-shaped half-mile square. No real German air attacks occurred until July 22 and work went on much as usual. The confusion of the first days of war, when it was discovered that no one had bothered to provide bombproof quarters for Stalin and the General Staff, had somewhat dissipated. General Tyulenov, Chief of Moscow Air Defense, provided the political and military leadership with his own underground headquarters. At the Byelorussian station of the Moscow metro a

wallboard partition separated the General Staff from a public shelter crowded with women and crying babies. Better arrangements were soon made in the Kirov Street station.

The first discussions of collaboration between Russia and the West were held in late June between Foreign Minister Molotov (Stalin was still in a state of shock but, of course, no one but the Politburo knew this) and Sir Stafford Cripps, the British Ambassador, who had flown in from London. The talks seemed somewhat at crosspurposes. Molotov kept asking why Rudolf Hess had flown to England in late May, just before the Nazi attack. Molotov's questions suggested that he thought Hess had been trying to get the British to gang up with Hitler in attacking Russia.

More serious talks were held by the now somewhat recovered Stalin and Harry Hopkins, who flew to Moscow as President Roosevelt's representative, on July 28. Hopkins talked for hours with Stalin in the Kremlin and met with all Stalin's top aides. He found Stalin (he thought) in the best of spirits, confident of victory, in possession of himself, his mind quick and seeming to grasp every detail of the war. They talked facts and figures about what Russia needed and what the United States could provide.

Before Hopkins left Moscow August 3 Stalin assured him that the Red Army would hold the line on which it now stood or within fifty or sixty miles of it through the winter and in the spring would launch a great counteroffensive. He had no doubt that Soviet forces would hold Kiev, Leningrad and Moscow.

Hopkins cabled Roosevelt from Scapa Flow on his return via Scotland: "I feel ever so confident about this front. . . . There is unbounded determination."

At the moment Stalin gave Hopkins his pledge about Kiev, Leningrad and Moscow, the Germans were opening wide the jaws of a vast pincers which was to close around Kiev in what would prove to be the worst single Soviet defeat of the war. In fact, two days earlier on July 29 Marshal Zhukov had candidly warned Stalin that he was courting disaster unless he immediately abandoned Kiev and ordered the troops of the Southwest Front withdrawn eastward beyond the Dnieper.

Stalin exploded. Within forty minutes Zhukov had been removed as Chief of Staff and sent out to command the Reserve Front.

To the north the drive of Field Marshal von Leeb on Leningrad had taken him to the hastily thrown up Luga line, only sixty miles from Leningrad. He was about to assault and crush a force of largely untrained volunteers which manned the line and head straight for Leningrad. He already was closing in on Baltic Fleet headquarters at Tallinn.

On the main Moscow Front the Germans were busily cleaning up their vast encirclement of the Smolensk region, preparatory to moving forward again on the Moscow highway.

Optimistic and self-confident as Stalin may have appeared to Harry Hopkins, he was losing and losing catastrophically in the great battle of the Soviet system against the Nazi system.

One of Hitler's panzer units passes through a Russian village. Front right, a Mark III tank; behind it, a half-track cargo and personnel carrier. Left, trucks followed by motorcycle troops.

After the capture of Kiev, two Germans overlook the Dnieper River and the city.

THE TRAGEDY OF KIEV

Kiev is the ancient capital of Russia, a lovely city whose origins go back to the misty days of the founding of Rus, the first Russian state, a city of trade and commerce, culture and religion, set on the high eastern banks of the Dnieper River. In the time of the Goths and the Varangians Kiev was a transshipping point for the trade in honey and furs and mead and amber and beautiful white slaves from the north, for the rubies and emeralds and spices and gold of Persia and the East.

In Kiev the Orthodox Church became Russia's official faith when Vladimir at the end of the tenth century invited the advocates of the Christian, Jewish and Moslem doctrines to argue the relative merits of their religions. He picked Christianity and, so the legend goes, toppled the ancient heathen idols into the River Dnieper and subjected his people to mass baptism in the river. Whether the legend is true or not, to this day the great Cathedral of Saint Sophia and the magnificent Pecherskaya Lavra remain the jewels of the Russian Orthodox church.

In June of 1941 Kiev was a city of 1,000,000. It was famous for its Podol, the old Jewish district and trading area on the low land beside the river, and for the Kreshchakh, a slowly curving boulevard in the center of town where generations of Kievlyans strolled in idle pleasure under great chestnut trees whose limbs crossed above the street, turning the promenade into a green esplanade.

Kiev was not just another city. It was the capital of the Ukraine, a symbol of Russian tradition unlike any other city in the Soviet Union.

Perhaps it was this tradition—a feeling that the loss of Kiev meant more than the loss of such a town as Minsk, the capital of Byelorussia, Riga, the capital of Latvia, Kaunas, the capital of Lithuania, or the bustling industrial cities of central Russia—that affected Stalin's judgment in his military decisions with respect to Kiev and the Southwest Military Front which defended it.

The commander of the Kiev defenses was Colonel General Mikhail P. Kirponos, who had succeeded General Zhukov in this post in January, 1941, a few months before the start of the war. Kirponos was a Red Army general who had started his service in the Czar's army and had joined the Bolsheviks shortly after the Revolution of 1917. He had been Chief of the Leningrad Military District before coming to Kiev and, while Nikita Khrushchev did not hold him in high esteem, he was regarded by his fellow Red Army generals as a careful, able and experienced leader.

No regional Red Army commander had been more alert to the likelihood of German attack than Kirponos. A week or more before June 22 he became convinced that war was imminent. He sent Stalin a personal letter asking permission to evacuate 300,000 civilians from the frontier region along the River Bug and to prepare his defense works. In fact, Kirponos ordered some of his troops to occupy the uncompleted sections of frontier fortifications. The move had hardly started before it was reported by the secret police to Moscow. Kirponos received a sharp reprimand from Chief of Staff General Zhukov and orders to bring his troops back immediately. This action was probably instigated by Stalin's Police Chief, Beria.

The Germans did not catch Kirponos by surprise. He had been expecting the attack. But he might as well have been totally offguard since he had been prevented from taking necessary measures to meet the Nazi thrust. As quickly as possible he shifted his headquarters back to Kiev. Tarnopol, where he had been ordered to set up shop on June 21, was quickly overrun by the Germans.

Kirponos was a first-class man. He had good field commanders and in the early days of the war his troops managed to fall back in better order than those on the Western Front to his north. But the disarray of the Western Front exposed his command on its northern perimeter. He was compelled to waste strength in a futile counter-offensive ordered by Moscow on the evening of June 23. His staff tried to persuade him against carrying out this move but the Political Commissars insisted and politics carried the day. The weakened, disorganized Soviet troops without air support or intelligence as to the location of the Nazis fought hard but to little purpose.

Danger to Kiev began to take shape about July 1 when the front to the north had fallen into bits and General (later Marshal) Konev's powerful Nineteenth Army was switched from the Kiev approaches to the Western Front to try to stem the German breakthrough. That was when Nikita Khrushchev arrived in Kiev to take over the job of mobilizing manpower and resources to put the Kiev fortified region into battle readiness. On July 7 the Nazi 11th Armored Division broke through the Berdichev fortified zone on the Soviet frontier, about eighty miles from Kiev. Kirponos appealed in vain for reserves from Zhukov who warned sternly, "I cannot understand how you could permit the enemy to penetrate the fortified zone." By the 9th the Germans had appeared at Zhitomir, seventy miles west of Kiev on the direct route. On the 12th Kirponos moved his headquarters to Brovari, a suburb of Kiev on the eastern bank of the Dnieper, and on the same day Kleist's Nazi armor penetrated into the Kiev fortified zone to within twelve miles of Kiev.

The war had been on for only three weeks and the Germans were almost within shouting distance of the capital of the Ukraine. In another few days two of Kirponos' armies, the badly weakened Sixth and Twelfth armies, covering his southern flank, had to be pulled back to the southeast, giving up Vinnitsa. For the first time a clear threat arose that Kiev itself might fall into encirclement.

As so often happened, the orders to the Sixth and Twelfth armies to withdraw came too late—Soviet commanders always delayed proposals for retreat until the last moment because they knew Moscow might take reprisals against them. The delay compelled the reassignment of the two armies to the South Front, taking them out of Kiev's command. Both commanders of the armies, Lieutenant General I. N. Muzychenko and General G. P. Ponedelin, were wounded and captured by the Germans. Both generals were sent to prison camps by Stalin when they were released from German captivity at the end of the war. Stalin considered them traitors and ordered their families confined as well. The same treatment was meted out to Tank General M. I. Potapov, Commander of the Fifth Army, also captured by the Germans in the Kiev battle. After Stalin's death all three were freed and returned to Army commands.

Nikita Khrushchev, second from right, conferring with comrades in Kiev.

As July neared its end the Germans had begun the deep encirclement of Kiev. Their lines touched the Kiev suburbs north and northwest of the city, curved around and made a deep penetration to the southeast, beginning to push past Kiev toward the great bend of the Dnieper.

Khrushchev, Kirponos' political officer, tried to get weapons from Moscow to arm the workers of Kiev. He talked to Stalin's protégé, Party Secretary Malenkov, who said there were no rifles to spare. Malenkov suggested that the Kievlyans fight with pikes and swords and homemade weapons. Even spears. As for ammunition, he said Kiev could make fire bombs out of bottles of gasoline.

General Zhukov, as Chief of Staff, spent some time on the Kiev Front and on his return to Moscow became more and more concerned about the developing situation. Finally on July 29 he met with Stalin and warned him that Germans were in a position to strike at the weak northern flank of the forces protecting Kiev and might easily encircle them from the rear. He suggested that the Southwest Front be strengthened with the assignment of a new army but that as rapidly as possible all Soviet forces, including those defending Kiev, be withdrawn to the east bank of the Dnieper.

"What about Kiev?" Stalin asked him.

"Kiev will have to be surrendered," Zhukov said.

Stalin exploded. He would not even think of giving up Kiev.

But Zhukov's fears were well founded. On August 2 von Kleist hurled his Sixth Army and part of the 1st Tank Group at the hinge of the Soviet Sixth and Twelfth armies, slicing through the Uman area and leaving the two Soviet armies and part of the Eighteenth Army encircled. South of Kiev the Germans raced for Dnepropetrovsk and Zaporozhe on the Dnieper. By the time the Germans cleaned up the Uman pocket they had taken another 103,000 Russians prisoner, more than 300 tanks and 800 guns. For practical purposes the Germans had undermined the Soviet position in the Ukraine west of the Dnieper.

By the first days of August the Germans had concentrated more than twenty divisions on the Kiev front.

In his original directive to his armies Hitler had specified that the initital objective of the three great thrusts of his troops would be Leningrad. Once Leningrad had been taken the northern arm of his forces would swing around to the south and envelop Moscow from the rear. Meantime the southern arm would have smashed across the Ukraine. Then, with a final direct thrust by the Central Front, Moscow would be taken from all sides and Soviet resistance would be crushed.

All of this, he estimated, would take not more than six weeks for the German panzer divisions, fine-tuned by their exploits in western Europe. By the last week in July Hitler was somewhat behind his timetable but not enough to seriously affect his confidence nor that of his military leaders. There was, however, constant bickering among the commands about priorities and allocation of forces. Most of Hitler's advisers by this time believed he should concentrate on the central thrust against Moscow. Hitler, however, had other ideas. He was possessed by determination to capture and destroy Leningrad which he perceived as the embodiment of the Bolshevik doctrine that he so hated. And he was determined as swiftly as possible to get into his hands the rich grain and food reserves of the Ukraine together with its coal and iron deposits and heavy industries.

In a series of conferences from July 23 to 26 Hitler decided to switch Hoth's important panzer group from the Central Front to the Leningrad direction and he assigned Guderian's Second Panzer Group to assist von Kleist's 1st Panzer Group in the Ukraine. This meant that progress on the center would be slowed while the Nazis concentrated on the targets of Leningrad and Kiev.

While military authorities, especially in Germany, still argue about the wisdom of Hitler's decisions, the immediate effect on the defense of Kiev was catastrophic. The bulk of the Soviet force defending Kiev was concentrated north and northwest of the city. It was against this force that Guderian was now to be unleashed.

Almost every evening Stalin conferred with the Kiev commanders. The conversations were conducted over the special military Baudet telegraph wire. The Baudet machine was set up next to the office of Stalin's *chef de cabinet* Poskrebyshev, just beside Stalin's personal reference library attached to his Kremlin office.

On the night of August 4 Stalin had one in this series of conversations with his Kiev commanders. He ordered some changes in the composition of the Southwest Front commands and once more took occasion to emphasize that the Germans should not be permitted to cross the Dnieper. He ordered new fortified zones to be set up to protect the area south of Kiev from German attack. Kirponos and Khrushchev once again promised to hold the line but asked for more men and supplies. Stalin said they'd have to get by for the most part on their own resources as Leningrad was now doing. For example, Leningrad was now turning out its own SRS rockets and why hadn't Kiev started to do this?

Kirponos and Khrushchev said they'd be glad to turn out SRS weapons but they didn't know how to do it—would Stalin just send them a sample and the plans for its construction?

Stalin said this was their own fault. Their assistants had the details, they just hadn't paid attention. However, he relented and said he'd send them a battery of SRS weapons and plans for making them. The SRS was the famous Russian *katyusha*—the multibarreled rocket which up to that time was Russia's most closely held secret weapon.

The next day Stalin rejected a proposal by Marshal Budenny that the troops south of Kiev be permitted to withdraw to the line of the River Ingul.

Words do not win battles. For all Stalin's exhortations, the danger to Kiev steadily grew. By August 8 the Germans had pushed into the Kiev suburbs of Mysheloka and Sovka and from the heights could look down on the southern portion of Kiev. Stalin called Kirponos on the direct wire: "We've gotten evidence that the Front has lightheartedly decided to surrender Kiev to the enemy because it hasn't got enough strength to defend it. Is that true?"

Squaring his shoulders (to confirm Stalin's "report" would have been the equivalent of a death sentence) Kirponos said with all the vigor at his command: "They've told you lies. We will hold the city. However, a German attack by three divisions in the southern sector has pierced our lines to a depth of two and a half miles. Yesterday the enemy lost 4,000 dead and wounded and we 1,200. And I must report that I have no more reserves in this sector."

Stalin said Kirponos would have to hold out for a couple of more weeks, after which he hoped to send him some help. Meantime, he added, his tone becoming less menacing, "Take all possible and all impossible measures to defend Kiev."

So it went. Threats from Stalin, brave promises by Kirponos, deadly attacks by the Germans. The battle for Kiev was reaching its climax.

German troops move through a burning Ukrainian village.

Stalin thought he had the answer. He would form a new Army Group northeast of Kiev and to the east of the crumbling Western Front. This powerful group, plentifully supplied with tanks from the GHQ reserve, would serve two purposes. It would protect the distant southwestern approaches to Moscow and it would engage Guderian's panzers and save Kiev. Stalin had little respect for any man. But he had great respect for Guderian. He had followed the exploits of the famous Nazi panzer commander in western Europe. He knew Guderian was a danger which must be met and coped with if the Red Army was to stabilize the front against Hitler.

On August 8 Stalin called into the Kremlin a scrappy, self-confident commander, General A. I. Yeremenko. Most of his experience had been with cavalry and armored forces, and he had done well in the tough battles around Smolensk. Stalin had decided to give Yeremenko command of what was to be called the Bryansk Front with headquarters about 200 miles southwest of Moscow and 220 miles northeast of Kiev.

Yeremenko got to the Kremlin as an air raid was fading away. After some sparring about, Stalin appointed him to the Bryansk Front.

"Leave tomorrow," Stalin said, "and waste no time. Guderian's panzer group is operating in the area and hard battles are in the offing. You'll have to deal with the mechanized troops of your 'old friend' Guderian whose habits you ought to know from previous encounters on the Western Front."

Yeremenko's task, said Stalin, was to destroy Guderian.

In his cocky way Yeremenko promised that "in the very nearest days I will unconditionally destroy Guderian."

Stalin was impressed. "There is the kind of man we need in these complicated conditions," he told his companions.

Perhaps Yeremenko was too cocky. Perhaps the situation was beyond him. But things did not change. The Nazis raced across the Ukraine. They captured Krivog Rog on the southern Dnieper August 15, the Black Sea port and shipbuilding center of Nikolaev August 17. Yeremenko engaged Guderian on the 16th near Konotop and Chernigov, northeast of Kiev. But Yeremenko's promises were vain. His forces did not smash Guderian. To the contrary.

The deadly threat to Kiev grew. On August 16 Chief of Staff Marshall Shaposhnikov and his deputy Marshal Alexander M. Vasilevsky proposed to Stalin that the Soviet forces north of Kiev be moved to the east bank of the Dnieper. Stalin refused. He was still confident Yeremenko could handle Guderian. On August 19 General Zhukov (then on the Western Front) again warned Stalin of the danger of encirclement of Kiev from the rear, followed by a Nazi thrust on Moscow. He was told that Yeremenko and the new Bryansk Front was designed to meet precisely this threat. The next day Stalin approved moving the Fifth Army on Kiev's northern flank to the east bank of the Dnieper but gave strictest orders that Kiev must be held at all costs.

Zhukov made one more attempt. He called Stalin directly and warned him of the peril to the Kiev troops unless they were immediately pulled back. Stalin insisted that Kirponos and Khrushchev were still confident of holding the Ukrainian capital and that Yeremenko could deal with Guderian.

Stalin was immovable and the danger grew. Yeremenko got into more and more trouble. A massive air strike was ordered against Guderian. Some 450 planes participated. Guderian kept going.

GHQ was at its wit's end. "At the very mention of the cruel

Ukrainian citizens welcome a German soldier by presenting him with food.

necessity of giving up Kiev, Stalin would fly into a rage," Vasilevsky recalled. Everyone knew Kiev should be evacuated and the troops saved. No one could bell the cat. No one was willing to stick his neck out with Stalin. And as always happens in war when one thing goes wrong another follows. The Fifth Army was unable to carry out its withdrawal over the Dnieper successfully and suffered heavy losses. A new Thirty-seventh Army had been formed by Kirponos to protect the western face of Kiev. It was formed from units of smashed-up divisions, and General A. A. Vlasov was put in charge of it by Khrushchev. Vlasov proved an able commander and in the most difficult days held the western gates of the city against German attack. Later Vlasov was to become famous as the most important military defector from the Red Army. Under German auspices he put together several divisions from Red Army prisoners. He was captured at the end of the war and executed by the Russians.

Stalin's son, Yakob, center, in a prison camp. The Germans captured him in July 1941.

Day after day and night after night the circle around Kiev narrowed. Marshal Zhukov, before being sent off by Stalin to take over the collapsing Leningrad front, warned Stalin again that he must yield Kiev. This produced an angry order by Stalin to Kirponos on September 11 that "Kiev is not to be surrendered and bridges are not to be demolished without permission from General Headquarters." Stalin added: "Kiev was, is and will be Soviet. I do not permit you to retreat."

Marshal Budenny, an old cohort of Stalin, tried as General Commander of the Southwest Front to get Stalin to yield. The only result of this was that Budenny was removed from command and Marshal Timoshenko was named to his place.

Kirponos, despite the urgings of his fellow officers, refused to make a direct request to Stalin for permission to withdraw—and in fact it was already too late. The great Nazi loop had been closed. Finally, on September 14 at 3:25 P.M., General V. I. Tupikov, Kirponos' Chief of Staff, on his own initiative advised the General Staff in Moscow that time had run out. "The beginning of a catastrophe which you can well conceive is only a couple of days away."

Tupikov was right. But still there was no change. He was branded a panicmonger. On September 16 General Ivan Bagramyan flew out of the Kiev encirclement to the headquarters of Timoshenko and Khrushchev. They ordered him to return instantly to Kiev, command Kirponos to abandon Kiev, get across the Dnieper as fast as he could with as many troops as possible and draw back to the Psel River. Bagramyan flew into Kiev and gave the order which had been transmitted orally to him.

Kirponos refused to act without written instructions.

Kirponos said: "We were forbidden to withdraw personally by Comrade Stalin. He ordered us not to halt our defense of Kiev. We can violate this order only if we have a written order from the Command of the Southwest Front or a new order from Comrade Stalin."

At twenty minutes to midnight September 17 Shaposhikov authorized withdrawal from Kiev but said nothing about withdrawing to the Psel River line.

Late that night Kirponos ordered his forces to begin their retreat. It turned into a rout. Kirponos and his staff fell back in a column of about 1,000 men, 800 of them staff officers. They were quickly surrounded by the Germans and most of them killed not far from the Sula River. Among the dead were Kirponos, his Military Commissar M. S. Burmistenko and Chief of Staff General Tupikov. There have long been rumors that Kirponos and perhaps the others committed suicide. The Germans claimed they took 665,000 prisoners in the cleanup. The Russians contended the figure was far less. The numbers were not so important as the results. The defeat at Kiev cleared the path for the Germans all the way into the north Caucasus and set the stage for the Nazi drive on Moscow.

Long afterward Marshal Bagramyan, who fought his way out of the encirclement, tried to puzzle out why Stalin had committed such a terrible error. It was, he thought, because of his confident words to Hopkins. Stalin had promised that Kiev, Leningrad and Moscow would be held. He was afraid of the propaganda consequences of Kiev's surrender. For this he gambled—and lost possibly a million fighting men, the whole of the Ukraine and brought Moscow itself to the brink of catastrophe.

THE RUSSIAN DUNKIRK

Bombardment of the Tallinn harbor.

owhere along the smoke-clouded 1,800-mile Eastern Front was there a sign of a turn in the tide. Everywhere the Nazi panzers, the gray-clad Nazi infantry, the swastika-marked planes of the Luftwaffe struck and struck again. There were no secure points on the whole Soviet front, only areas where for the moment the pressure eased a bit, usually because Nazi motorized units had outrun supplies, fuel or ammunition, or where they were compelled to halt and deal with the huge "cauldrons" of Soviet troops thrown into encirclement.

The Soviet Navy, the only armed force which had been fully alert to Hitler's attack, had been able to play little part in stemming the Nazi tide. Actually the Navy had been thrown off stride by the changes in Soviet frontiers carried out in 1939–40.

The Baltic fleet, the principal naval force, had been based since its founding by Peter the Great at Kronstadt, the naval fortress at Leningrad. But with the take-over of the Baltic states in 1940, headquarters had been shifted to Tallinn on the Estonian coast. Forward bases had been established at Libau, near the East Prussian border, and Riga, the capital of Latvia.

Admiral Vladimir Tributs had been nervous about these forward positions from the start. Stalin wanted to station a battleship at Libau but Tributs managed to block that. As portents of war gathered he grew nervous about the submarine brigade and light naval craft stationed at Libau. With some difficulty he got permission to move the ships back to Riga in May. At Stalin's insistence two old battleships, the *Marat* and the *October Revolution*, had been stationed at Tallinn. There were neither booms nor torpedo nets to protect the ships, and in the days before June 22 Tributs got increasingly nervous. Permission to pull the battleships back to Kronstadt came on the eve of the war. On the evening of June 21 the *Marat* safely made its way back to Kronstadt. *October Revolution* did not move until early July.

Tributs's concerns were valid. Libau was swept up in the first hours of the Nazi attack. There had been no real coordination between land and naval forces concerning the protection of the Baltic naval bases. Nor were there plans for evacuating civilian population, stocks of matériel or army and naval facilities. The reason for this was that for the past decade Soviet military doctrine had proclaimed that if war came it would not be fought on Soviet soil. It was to be carried immediately to enemy territory and would, the propaganda proclaimed, be fought "with little blood." In other words, the Soviet had prepared itself to fight the kind of offensive war Hitler had unleashed against Russia. But it had not prepared itself for defense against such a lightning attack.

Nowhere was this more evident than in the Baltic region where the population, with unconcealed impatience, awaited the arrival of the Germans. There were large German minorities in all the Baltic states. Since the time of the Hanseatic League and the Baltic barons German influence had been strong.

Now in Tallinn when Soviet sailors walked the boulevards in their navy whites they passed sidewalk cafés where men lounged in summer linens under gaily colored awnings and ladies in low-cut gowns languidly sipped their ices. This was Soviet territory, but the influence of bourgeois Estonia had hardly ceased.

It was a peaceful scene, yet the Nazi panzers were thundering down the Baltic highways only miles away. And the peace was deceptive. Hardly a night passed without a murderous attack on Soviet officials, soldiers and naval men. This had been going on long before June 22. It did not halt with the outbreak of war. Wives of naval officers were not encouraged to join their husbands.

The situation at Riga was even more precarious. The Germans bombed Riga in the first hours of war, and when they dropped parachutists there were few Soviet forces to cope with them. Vice Admiral V. P. Drozd entered Riga on the night of June 24 aboard his flagship, the 7,000-ton *Kirov*, pride of the Baltic. He found the city crisscrossed with random shooting. Fires burned. No Soviet police appeared. Admiral Tributs concluded that Riga would fall almost as quickly as Libau and he gave orders that the port be evacuated.

This was easier said than done. The only mine-free route lay through the narrow and shallow Muh-Vain Strait. The passage had not been used by heavy ships since World War I. Drozd set draggers and trawlers to deepening the shallow passages. First the freighter *Vtoraya Pyatiletka* was sent through. Then the *Kirov* and the large icebreaker *K. Voldemars* set out with the destroyers *Stoiky, Smetlivy* and *Grosyashchy* ahead. The cruiser moved slowly but grounded on blockships sunk in the channel in World War I. Drozd inched the *Kirov* over. At midnight he ran aground but was pulled off by tugs, but at daylight he went bow on into a shoal. After three hours he managed to get off and made it into Tallinn. Two days later the Germans broke into Riga and on July 1 paraded down the main street.

All through early July the tensions rose in Tallinn. Languid men and women lolled on the white sands of the Pirita beaches ostentatiously turning their heads away as detachments of Baltic sailors roared by in trucks and detachments of people's militia went out of the city to try to hold off the Germans. No plans had been made by the Army to protect the Baltic Fleet's headquarters from attack by the Germans. Some 25,000 men and women with picks and shovels hurriedly threw up improvised trenches and dug tank ditches. This stopped the Germans for the moment.

Nikolai Mikhailovsky, a Soviet Naval correspondent, and an elderly Dostoevsky scholar named Orest V. Tsekhnovitser shared a room at the Golden Swan Hotel. Sometimes they strolled through the medieval streets of the Old City and into the formal grounds of Kadriorg Park. They visited the little house where Peter the Great lived while his workmen constructed the port of Revel, the port now called Tallinn. Sometimes they sat in the old cathedral, Tom Kirka, six centuries old. It was hard to believe when you sat within the six-foot walls of the cathedral that out in the sunny July afternoon Nazi tanks were driving along the coastal roads, firing pointblank into the hastily constructed volunteer-manned defenses only seven or eight miles outside the city.

As July idled by the dangers grew. The Soviet Eighth Army, which had been retreating steadily and fighting all the way from the East Prussian frontier, was supposed to protect Tallinn. But now it was falling back again on Narva, well to the east of Tallinn. By August 8 Tallinn's land communications both east and west had been severed by the German panzers. No longer was it possible to com-

Russian sailors in the Baltic fleet on land duty near Tallinn.

municate with Leningrad by telephone. It was time—some said it was past time—for the Soviet Naval Command to consider means of getting out of Tallinn.

The lines pressed close to the city and German shells began to rain down. The six-inch guns of the *Kirov* and the 4.5-inch guns of the destroyer leader *Leningrad* returned the fire. By August 23 a full-scale duel was going forward between German long-range guns and the fleet artillery. On that day alone 600 German shells fell in the harbor area and German planes bombed the fleet.

Life in Tallinn withered. The streets fell empty. Streetcar service ended. The radio loudspeakers went silent. Newspapers failed to appear. Mikhailovsky took a turn in Kadriorg Park. The red squirrels chattered at him. No one had fed them lately. The park was empty of people.

Admiral Tributs took over defense of the city on August 17. His principal manpower was what was called the 10th Corps, actually about 4,000 worn-out and dispirited troops, as many sailors as could be spared from the fleet and some workers from the factories, about 20,000 men in all. It was strictly a pickup force and it could not have withstood the Nazis had it not been for the heavy firing of the guns of the *Kirov*, the *Leningrad* and the *Minsk*.

Tributs began to evacuate the wounded and those not needed for defense of Tallinn. He sent off 3,500 wounded in the transport *Baltika* which managed to reach Kronstadt in spite of being hit by a mine. But the *Siberia* with 3,000 wounded was sunk in an air attack. Many of the wounded were saved.

The final Nazi assault opened August 19. Tributs was moving people and ships out of the harbor as rapidly as he could. Vsevolod Vishnevsky, a naval correspondent, and many others were ordered to sleep aboard the *Virona*. Orders for evacuation might come at any time.

Vishnevsky made hurried jottings in his notebook:

"Black smoke . . . Two fighters overhead . . . The *Tsiklon* moves away . . . Two torpedo boats come into the harbor . . . Sailors from the *Kirov* and a minelayer off to the front singing . . . The *Virona* prepares to depart . . . Many fires . . ."

On the 25th smoke screens were laid over the harbor and tugboats repeatedly shifted the position of the *Kirov*, the *Minsk* and *Leningrad* to keep them out of range of Nazi gunners. A convoy of nine transports made it back to Kronstadt but the transport *Daugava* was sunk. Minesweepers were ordered to clear a path for the fleet to leave the harbor.

Orders from Moscow for the evacuation of Tallinn came through on the morning of August 26. Vishnevsky had a last look around the city. The main streets were barricaded and machine-gun fire echoed around the Rusalka monument. The Russians were slowly falling back toward the harbor. Vishnevsky went back aboard the *Virona*. He took out a copy of Tarle's *Napoleon* and read it as dense black clouds of smoke rose over the city. The oil tanks had been set afire.

In the morning the smoke was so dense Vishnevsky could hardly breathe. The power station, grain elevators and arsenal were being destroyed. Vishnevsky made one last foray into town to the almost deserted newspaper office. There he picked up bundles of the last edition of the newspaper *Sovetskaya Estonia* and brought them back to the harbor. Then he took a cutter and went aboard the *Leningrad*. Mikhailovsky, Professor Tsekhnovitser and many other journalists boarded the *Virona*. Johannes Lauristan, Chairman of Soviet Estonia, was supposed to board the icebreaker *Surtyl*. It had already left with a theatrical company. He went aboard the minelayer *Volodarsky*.

More than 190 ships prepared to move out of Tallinn harbor, including more than 70 transports of more than 6,000 tons. There were 10 minesweepers and 17 trawlers to sweep a path through the mines which the sailors said were thick as soup with dumplings.

As night fell the ships moved out. The weather was bad. The wind came up. Rain gusted down. Now the harbor was dark and empty. Only two cutters remained and the *Pikker* which was to bring the military council out to the *Kirov*. The minelayer *Amur* stood at the channel entrance. When all were out it was to be sunk to block access to the harbor.

Nearly 23,000 persons had been loaded onto the evacuation ships, and 66,000 tons of military matériel. At 4:00 A.M. the Military Council left for the *Kirov*. At 7:00 A.M. Admiral Panteleyev went aboard a cutter and joined the *Minsk*.

The array of ships rendezvoused off Tallinn and at noon August 28 the passage to Kronstadt began. There was no air cover, nor could any be expected until the ships arrived in the vicinity of Kronstadt.

Admiral Panteleyev watched the progress from the *Minsk*. First, Convoy No. 1—nine transports including the *Virona* and an escort of three submarines, five trawlers, five minesweepers and five cutters. Next, Convoy No. 2 including the big transport *Kazakhstan*. There were four convoys in all. No. 3 was the largest, including the transports *Luga*, *Tobol*, *Luçerne*, *Balkhash* and the *Vtoraya Pyatiletka*.

The *Minsk*, heading a detachment of twenty-one naval vessels, pulled away at 5:15 P.M. and the rear guard of thirteen ships at 9:15 P.M. The line of ships stretched out fifteen miles.

There was plenty of light in the sky and German bombers were not long in moving in. The first ship to go down was the transport *Ella*.

It was between 9:00 and 10:00 P.M. when the *Virona* went down. She had been attacked fiercely by Nazi aircraft. Professor Tsekhnovitser cried out repeatedly: "Be calm. Panic is the most dangerous thing." Suddenly Mikhailovsky felt the deck rise up beneath his feet

Soviet convoy at Tallinn.

and the next thing he knew he was in the water, blood flowing from his head, blinding his left eye. He turned on his back and watched the Nazi planes dive down, then he swam a while. He swam past a floating body, the skull crushed. He recognized a schoolgirl he had been talking with on the *Virona* a few moments before. He had begun to lose strength when a cutter almost ran him down. Strong hands reached and pulled him aboard.

Admiral Panteleyev witnessed the tragedy of the *Virona*. He saw it list and heavy smoke appear. The rescue ship *Saturn* hurried forward but hit a mine and sank. Then the *Virona* went down as did the transport *Alev* and two more transports. The gunboat *Sneg* picked up dozens of survivors. A commissar on the *Sneg* said bitterly: "Did you ever think we would drown like blind cats in a puddle? Where were our planes?" He did not know there were no planes left with a range to cover the Tallinn exodus.

The poet Yuri Inge watched the *Virona* sink. He was aboard the icebreaker *Voldemars*. He had his notebook in hand and was taking down his impressions for a poem which had already taken shape in his mind. A friend heard him exclaim: "The bastards!" Then the *Voldemars* was sunk and Inge died with it.

It was a night of horror. At 9:00 P.M. the submarine *S-5*, escorting the *Kirov*, hit a mine and sank. Then a paravane of the *Kirov* caught a mine and began to draw it aboard. Sailors managed to cut it loose at the last moment. The minelayer *Gordy* blew up at 9:36 P.M. Then the transport *Yakov Sverdlov* went down, having taken a torpedo aimed at the *Kirov*. Shore batteries opened up and a German torpedo boat made a try for the *Kirov* but was beaten off by the cruiser's main guns.

A paravane on the destroyer leader *Minsk* drew a mine aboard at 9:40 P.M. It exploded, and Vice Admiral Panteleyev estimated the vessel shipped 650 tons of water. The minelayer *Skory* and a tugboat took the *Minsk* in tow but were sunk by mines. The *Minsk* was dead in the water and did not resume movement until after daylight the next day. The rear guard was virtually obliterated. The *Sneg* and the *Tsiklon* were sunk at 10:00 P.M. Then the squadron leader *Kalinin* was lost, followed by the minelayers *Artem* and *Volodarsky*. The transports *Luga*, *Everitis* and *Yarvamaa* were sunk.

The passage to Kronstadt was like a passage in Dante's hell. Of 29 large transports, 25 were lost, three were beached and only one reached Leningrad. In all, 38 noncombatant ships were lost and more than 10,000 lives. In addition 10 warships, mostly gunboats, minesweepers and small craft went down. The biggest losses were the *Ivan Papanin* with 3,000 aboard; the *Vtoraya Pyatiletka* with 3,000, the *Luga* with 300 wounded, the *Balkhash* and the *Tobol*, each carrying several hundred. Of 67 non-Navy ships 34 were lost; of more than 100 naval craft 87.5 percent were saved along with 18,000 personnel.

The Russian Dunkirk was more deadly than its British counterpart. The British operation was much larger, involving the safe evacuation of 338,226 men with a loss of between 9,000 and 10,000. The British employed 1,084 ships in the evacuation, most of them very small, and lost 108. The distance was 40 to 50 miles compared with more than 200 for the Tallinn-Kronstadt passage. And the British had command of sea and air.

The casualties did not end with the arrival of the ships at Kronstadt. There remained the case of Captain Vyacheslav Kalitayev, Commander of the transport *Kazakhstan*. This ship carried out 3,600 troops. Kalitayev was one of the most experienced Baltic skippers.

The *Kazakhstan* quickly attracted the attention of Nazi bombers. Wave after wave of JU-88s struck at the ship. Kalitayev was on the bridge when a bomb hit there, destroying the bridge and killing the commander of the antiaircraft battery and all those on the upper bridge. The *Kazakhstan* was left without command. It lost speed and dropped out of the convoy. Fires raged in the hold. Finally a crewman managed to steer the *Kazakhstan* aground on a spit of land called Vaindlo, about sixteen miles off the coast. There the passengers were removed and the seven surviving members of the crew managed to get the *Kazakhstan* into Kronstadt, September 12.

Everyone assumed that Captain Kalitayev was dead. But he was not. He had been thrown unconscious into the water and by good luck was picked up by the submarine *S-322* and brought back to Kronstadt, arriving ahead of the *Kazakhstan*.

An investigation was ordered immediately as to why Kalitayev had "left" his ship. Surviving crew members told how he had been blown off the bridge. But suspicious investigators of the secret police were not satisfied. They rounded up some passengers to swear that Kalitayev had leaped into the water to save his own life. He was put before a firing squad and executed seventeen days after the seven other surviving crew members were awarded medals for bravery.

Not until January 27, 1962, was the reputation of Kalitayev rehabilitated by the Leningrad District Military Court, partly as a result of tenacious investigation by the naval correspondent and playwright Aleksander Zonin who had been a passenger on the *Kazakhstan*. In his own lifetime Zonin could not get his account of the disaster published and he himself was expelled from the Communist Party and arrested in 1949. He died shortly after being released after Stalin's

Smoke screen over a ship at Tallinn while convoy was under dispersal order.

death in 1953. Two other correspondents, Vladimir Rudny and Georgi Bregman, then took up the case. Kalitayev's widow, the actress Vera Tutcheva, was finally officially informed the charges had no foundation more than twenty years after her husband had been shot.

The losses of the Tallinn evacuation surrounded the Baltic fleet with an atmosphere of suspicion and hostility. There was a search for scapegoats. Admiral Pantaleyev told of being confronted by a high officer, possibly Police Chief Beria, who demanded to know: "Why didn't our fleet fight? Why have the fascists been able to fight and we have not?"

Panteleyev tried to explain the complex situation at Tallinn.

The "high officer" did not agree. "The staff is not supposed to concern itself with that kind of business," he said. "It must work out active operations and fight and attack."

Panteleyev concluded that the staff of the fleet had come close to being found guilty by the high officer for the tragedy which had occurred.

The Tallinn disaster has been endlessly analyzed by Soviet naval specialists. The distinguished Soviet naval historian, Captain V. Achkasov, concluded twenty-five years later that the real cause was to be found in the reluctance of anyone in the Baltic fleet, the Leningrad command or Moscow itself to order the fleet to prepare to evacuate.

The reason, he said, was the knowledge on the part of the commanders that they would subject themselves to the gravest charges of cowardice, panic and possibly treason. The consequences could be fatal. Rather than risk a firing squad they subjected their commands and their country to the greater risk of total disaster.

LENINGRAD IN DANGER

Leningraders killed by a German shell on the Nevsky Prospekt.

Nowhere in Russia had it been more difficult to believe in the tragedy of war than in Leningrad, the magnificent capital which Peter the Great built on the Gulf of Finland in the eighteenth century to provide his country with what came to be called its "window on the West."

The city had been christened St. Petersburg in honor of its great founder. Always it had been different from the rest of Russia, more cosmopolitan, more European, a mixture of non-Slav peoples, Germans, Swedes, Dutch, English, French and Italian. Foreigners were drawn to the new Russian capital for service with the Czar and for trade and commerce. "Piter," as the city was affectionately called, was Russia's artistic and cultural center, the city of Pushkin, Russia's greatest poet, of the brilliant and gloomy Dostoevsky, of ballet, of music, of revolutionaries and aristocrats, of Nicholas II and finally of Vladimir Ulyanov, better known as Lenin.

No longer was Leningrad the capital of Russia in 1941. The city's name had been changed to Petrograd at the start of World War I because Nicholas thought "Petersburg" had a German sound. Then Lenin moved the capital back to Moscow in 1918, fearing German occupation, and it never moved back. When Lenin died in 1924 his name was given to the northern capital on the Neva with its miles of boulevards, great brooding palaces, magnificent vistas, the Fortress of Peter and Paul, St. Isaac's Cathedral, the Kazan Cathedral, the Winter Palace and the great Hermitage buildings.

Announcement of war on June 22 had caught Leningrad at the height of its summer fete. In those June days the sun never sets in Leningrad. It is the time of white nights when the city stays up all night, when young men and women stroll the streets long after mid-night, singing and holding hands and poets compose sonnets along the canals where Pushkin walked. The thought of war seemed unbelievable.

But it was only too real. Leningrad, like the rest of Russia, was ill-prepared for the Nazi attack. Andrei Zhdanov, the powerful Communist Party boss, was not even in the city. He was on the Black Sea on vacation. The Leningrad commander in chief, Lieutenant General M. M. Popov, wasn't in town either. He was on an inspection trip around his defense district that had taken him to Arctic Murmansk and would not bring him back to Leningrad until the day after war started.

Clearly, the German attack was no more expected in Leningrad than it was in the Kremlin. Nor when it came was there realistic understanding of its meaning. The initial response of Party Secretary Zhdanov (when he got back to Leningrad), of General Popov, the Leningrad commander, of General Kiril Meretskov who arrived in Leningrad as the representative of the High Command, was that Leningrad was in splendid shape. Its frontier against the Finns to the north had been comfortably pushed back to give Leningrad a cushion of about one hundred miles and the Soviet had occupied the Hango peninsula as a protection to the naval base of Kronstadt. To the west the absorption of the Baltic states had pushed the frontier four hundred miles to the west. What was there to worry about?

To be sure, the approaches to Leningrad from the southwest were not too secure and orders were given to speed up work on the

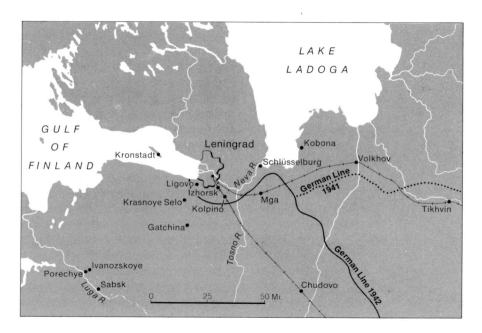

THE BATTLE OF LENINGRAD

Pskov-Ostrov fortified area, to start a new secondary defense line along the Luga river, 120 miles southwest of the city, and to build defenses around Volkhov, southeast of the city.

Naturally, volunteers swarmed to the colors. There were 100,000 the first day and more than 200,000 before the week's end—more than could comfortably be absorbed by the Red Army. But the great concern in the first days was not about the land fighting. Everyone was confident that the Red Army could hold the Germans hundreds of miles away from Leningrad. What everyone feared was air raids. The bombings of western Europe, of Madrid, of Rotterdam, of London, of Coventry had cast a long shadow of terror. Leningrad was afraid of German bombs and the first concern was for the children. Authorities decided to move 400,000 children out of the city. In one week 212,209 children were sent away, mostly into the nearby countryside, many of them, as it turned out, directly into the path of the advancing Germans. But of that danger in early July no one was really thinking.

One danger which leaped immediately into the mind of Moscow was Leningrad's huge defense industry. Leningrad's population was over 3,000,000. It had a work force of 780,000 and 520 factories. Much of the Soviet's advanced machine and technological industries were here, including many defense plants like the great Kirov steel works which made the 60-ton KV tank, larger and superior to any possessed by the Germans and of whose existence the German generals did not dream. The Kirov factory director flew to the Urals on the second day of the war to investigate the possibility of shifting KV production to Chelyabinsk. He reported that it could be done but recommended delaying the move. Moscow accepted his recommendation but ordered the KV put on serial line production. By July KV production had been doubled. But the delay in moving the plant to the Urals was to cost the Soviet Union dearly.

There was a quick shift of Leningrad factories over to military production and by early July five new factories were turning out artillery, eleven were producing mortars including the famous *katyusha* multibarreled rocket and twelve were making tanks and armored cars. Leningrad distilleries cut down production of vodka and started turning out Molotov cocktails, bottles filled with alcohol or gasoline, for throwing at Nazi tanks.

Almost immediately Leningrad discovered that it was expected to meet most of its military needs on its own. Colonel B. V. Bychevsky of the engineering service found a shortage of mines and explosives. He asked Moscow for new stocks. Moscow said: "There are more important fronts than yours. Use your local resources." The job was turned over to Mikhail Basov of the industrial department of the Leningrad City Party Committee. He got 40,000 mines from the Aurora factory and 60,000 from the Woodworking trust and found plenty of explosives in the city's construction organizations. Civilian construction was halted, including work on a subway system, and the crews set to building fortifications.

There was one bonus from the decision not to move the KV assembly lines to Chelyabinsk. The 31-car train protected with machine guns and armored cars provided for the tanks was turned over to the Hermitage museum and more than 500,000 objects of art were loaded aboard—Rembrandt's "Holy Family" and "Return of the Prodigal," Titians, Giorgiones, Rubenses, Murillos, Van Dycks, Da Vinci's "Madonna Litta" and "Madonna Benois," Raphael's "Madonna Alta," collections of Grecian marbles and Scythian gold. It was taken to the Urals and safely stored there for the war's duration. Later a second trainload was sent off. A third never made it.

For the most part it was the big industrial plants which were shipped out of Leningrad—the Nevsky machine-building plant by August 1, a portion of the Kirov and Izhorsk works about the same time. By August 27 nearly 60,000 freight cars of machinery had been sent away and by September 1, 92 large plants had been evacuated, many of them only in part.

This was part of an extraordinary effort which gained momentum as the summer of 1941 wore on—a drive to move vital factories and institutions out of the Nazi path. If the task had been tackled late and with some irresolution it gained speed under the force and drive of Aleksei Kosygin who in July was named to coordinate the movement.

Great factories like Serp and Molot, Elektrostal and the First State ballbearing plant were moved out of Moscow to Magnitogorsk and Nizhny-Tagil in the Urals. The Moscow State auto plant went to Ulyanovsk on the Volga and to two Urals cities. The evacuation of Byelorussia got underway too late and most of the industry of Minsk had to be left behind. Some installations like the great Dnepropetrovsk hydroelectric plant could not be moved. The dam was blown up to deny the Nazis its use. In all, no less than 2,593 individual plants, some large, some small, were moved east during 1941 and, difficult though the task proved to be, production from these transplanted steel, machinery and weapons factories at their new locations deep in the distant Urals and Siberian industrial cities kept the Red Army going.

Not all the early decisions proved wise. The Kharkov tractor factory was evacuated to Stalingrad where a year later it and the Stalingrad tractor factory were trapped in the greatest battle of the war.

When the Nazis poured into the Baltic states and drove westward, trainloads of food supplies and fuel were in the Soviet railroad system headed for delivery points already or soon to be in German hands.

Anastas Mikoyan, in charge of food and fuel, tried to divert the

Citizens dig antitank trenches outside Leningrad in July 1941.

trains to Leningrad, the only convenient metropolis where surplus storage facilities could be provided. But Andrei Zhdanov, Leningrad Party boss, angrily protested to Stalin. Leningrad had enough on its hands without being saddled with improvising storage for surplus food it didn't need. The trainloads were diverted elsewhere and Zhdanov came bitterly to regret his hasty decision.

Another problem in Leningrad came back to haunt the city. There was a program to evacuate adults who weren't essential to the war effort. But Leningraders didn't want to go. They saw no necessity for it and they wanted to stay and fight for their city. By August 11

some 467,000 persons had been sent out of the city and it was decided to evacuate another 400,000. The number was increased to 700,000 a few days later. But as fast as people were sent out of the city in July and August new throngs entered, refugees from the Baltic states being swept up in the German drive.

Summer was well advanced before anyone even began to think of food supplies. Leningrad, like the rest of Russia, had enjoyed plentiful food in the last two or three years. The outbreak of war brought a rush on the food stores, but after a few days things came more or less back to normal. There was no rationing during the first month of war. Then on July 18 the whole country was put on a ration of 800 grams, almost two pounds, of bread a day. The meat ration was 2,200 grams—about six pounds a month for workers and a pound and a half for children and dependents. The ration of cereals, fats and sugar was ample for ordinary needs. The Russian diet is based on bread and the July 18 quantities were within normal consumption limits. Nothing to worry about. Leningrad got the same ration as the rest of the country. As Leningrad evacuated its children ample food, especially meat, butter, cheese and eggs, was sent with them so they would not suffer. In the so-called commercial stores for high prices you could buy anything you wanted without ration cards. Restaurants served meals without coupons. There was nothing in July in Leningrad to compare with the severe rationing and deprivation which England had endured since the spring of 1940. Nothing gave the Leningraders a feeling of alarm at the closeness of the invader to their city.

In fact, the Germans were drawing nearer and nearer. Field Marshal von Leeb had a powerful force, 21 to 23 divisions spearheaded by von Hoth's Fourth Armored, possibly 340,000 men in all. He had 326 tanks and 6,000 guns which gave him a superiority over the Soviet defense forces as of July 10 of 2.4 in infantry, 4 in artillery and 1.2 in armor. He had about 1,000 planes. The Russian defenders about 100.

The Nazi steel fist pulverized every defense the Red Army put up. Now von Leeb was approaching the makeshift Luga line, only half finished and hardly more than half manned. Marshal Voroshilov, one of the Soviet's most senior military men, a veteran of the Civil War, an old associate of Stalin's, had been placed in general charge of the Northwest Front protecting Leningrad. His problem was the same which had confronted the Soviet commanders since June 22—how to slow down the Nazi drive. Great hopes had been placed on the Luga line. Colonel Bychevsky, the engineering specialist, worked twenty-four hours a day to strengthen the improvised fortifications. He placed giant landmines under buildings at Strugi Krasnye, Gorodishche, and Nikolayevo, which he expected the Germans to occupy. On July 13 he touched them off electronically from Gatchina, causing heavy Nazi casualties. That evening after a frantic conference at Smolny, one-time institute for training young noblewomen and now the headquarters of the Communist Party, four guerrilla battalions were ordered to penetrate the German lines to sabotage their advance. There was an air of desperation about the conference. A few hours later Bychevsky got a frantic call—the Nazi 41st Panzers had smashed across the Luga at Porechye and seized a foothold at Ivanovskoye within the Soviet defense system. A similar attempt was barely beaten off at Sabsk.

The Germans at Ivanovskoye were being held up by People's

Volunteers from Leningrad who poured out of boxcars directly into the fire fight. If German tanks broke through here they had a clear well-paved highway straight to Leningrad without a single organized unit or defense position to halt them before they reached the Winter Palace.

Bychevsky rounded up a company of field engineers and 1,000 mines and set off by a roundabout route to avoid Nazi dive-bombers. At Ivanovskoye he found Marshal Voroshilov and General Popov standing on an open hillside watching the Volunteers struggle back from an unsuccessful counterattack. Soviet artillery was laying shells into the heart of the village, setting peasant *izbas* afire, and Nazi tanks could be seen maneuvering on the edge of the village. Shells were exploding. Splinters filled the air. Voroshilov stood like a stone image. As Bychevsky watched, General Popov leaped into a tank and headed for the village. "What the hell!" Voroshilov exclaimed, trying to halt the general. Soon the tank was hit by a shell and Popov, unhurt, clambered out and rejoined Voroshilov.

Voroshilov and Popov ordered the Germans driven back beyond the Luga—an order which the Volunteers could not fulfill—and dashed off. At Sredneye, a few miles away, Voroshilov found Red Army men falling back in confusion. He jumped from his car, re-formed them and, pistol in hand, led them in a charge across the field, halting the Germans in their tracks.

But personal bravery was no answer to the German tanks. The Nazi forces could not be driven back across the Luga. That night Moscow agreed to release three to five tanks for each division defending Leningrad, and Zhdanov and Voroshilov issued a solemn proclamation:

"Over the city of Lenin, cradle of the Proletarian Revolution, there looms the immediate danger of the invading enemy."

A Soviet counterattack drove a Nazi spearhead moving northeast in the Novgorod area back about thirty miles. For the moment the imminent threat to Leningrad eased. Von Mansteen noted in his diary: "It's impossible to say that the position of the corps at this moment is very enviable. The last few days have been critical and the enemy with all his strength is attempting to close the ring of encirclement."

The Soviet respite was brief. By early August von Leeb was on the move again. He had twenty-nine divisions at 80 to 90 percent of full strength. Opposing him, the Russians had fifteen weak divisions. Chief of Staff Halder wrote in his diary August 3: "Army Group Nord obviously should not meet with irresistible difficulties."

Von Leeb pushed forward August 7–8. The remnants of the Luga line cracked immediately. Vsevolod Kochetov, a Soviet war correspondent, arrived at the front near Opolye that night. He camped in a churchyard among the tombstones. It was a fine warm night but he was awakened by what he thought was the eruption of a volcano. The earth shook. A blinding light filled the sky. It was, he realized, German railroad artillery. He started out for headquarters and found the roads jammed—peasants driving cows and pigs, carts of household belongings, mongrel dogs barking, Red Army trucks filled with soldiers, bleary and mud covered, soldiers on foot without guns, bandages over their heads and eyes, some supported by comrades, slogging hopelessly with heads down and eyes averted. Kochetov had never seen so terrifying a sight.

Von Leeb broadcast to his troops:

"Soldiers! You see before you not only the remains of the Bolshevik Army but the last inhabitants of Leningrad. The city is empty.

German infantry troops combing a forest south of Lake Ladoga in the autumn of 1941.

One last push and the Army Group Nord will celebrate victory!"

There was some truth to von Leeb's call. There were no Soviet reserves left. The units at the front were worn and debilitated, many only a fraction of their stated strength. As Chief of Staff Nikishev reported August 13 to Moscow: "Even the smallest breakthrough can be halted only by hurried improvisations of one unit or another."

The Leningrad leadership had thrown in manpower lavishly. In the third week of July Zhdanov sent 100,000 persons to work on the Luga Lines and another 87,000 to strengthen the Gatchina fortified zone in Leningrad's suburbs. More than 500,000 persons, including women and children of 14 and 15, were mobilized to dig trenches and ditches. The curators of the Hermitage Museum did pick and shovel work. So did the actors of the Leningrad theaters. Seven divisions of Peoples Volunteers were formed, each with a stated enrollment of about 15,000. Some 90,000 Communist Youth and Communist Party members went to the fighting front from Leningrad in the summer of 1941. There weren't enough arms to go around. Some used guns that had last been fired in 1914 against the armies of Austria-Hungary and Germany. Many had no guns.

In mid-August a massive shift of forces was ordered, thousands of Soviet troops were withdrawn from the relatively inactive Finnish front north of Leningrad and switched to the endangered approaches

Soldiers in front of the great
Kirov steel plant in Leningrad.

west and southwest of the city. It was a badly planned movement,
ordered too late. For a week almost every unit defending Leningrad
was on wheels.

There were few in Leningrad now who did not grasp the peril.
The danger had first been presented to the city at a rally for the
Leningrad Party *aktiv* on Sunday, July 24. At Zhdanov's call all Party
members swore an oath "to die before yielding the city of Lenin."
Then they sang the *Internationale*.

Despite Zhdanov's determination, despite the mass oath, despite
the desperate work of hundreds of thousands of civilians and the
bravery of the Volunteers, the Nazis pushed ahead and on August 16
Zhdanov summoned his top Party workers again to Smolny for frank
talk.

A. K. Kozlovsky, a Party worker, put his impressions into his
diary:

"Today I was at the narrow *aktiv*. Report by Marshal Voroshilov.
Then Comrade Zhdanov spoke. In the most active and direct
manner he laid out the situation of the Leningrad front. . . .

"The Red Army will not permit the enemy to break into the city.
Today we are beginning to form new workers units on the factory
principle. The city will be surrounded by a belt of forts."

Hitler had switched more armor to von Leeb. He was certain the fall of Leningrad was at hand. The German radio broadcast that the naval base of Kronstadt was burning. German passes for cars entering the city had been printed. So had invitations for a victory banquet at the Winter Palace. Leaflets warned the Leningraders: "You will perish in the wreckage of Leningrad. . . . We will level Leningrad to the earth and destroy Kronstadt to the water line."

The Berlin radio broadcast: "Only hours remain before the fall of Leningrad."

Four days later after a full Party *aktiv* meeting at Smolny Zhdanov proclaimed: "The enemy is at the gates. It is a question of life or death."

Leningrad, Zhdanov prophesied, would become the grave of the Nazis.

The city took on the appearance of a fortress. Leningrad men and women threw up 450 miles of antitank ditches, 18,000 miles of trenches, 15,000 reinforced concrete bunkers, 22 miles of barricades. Leningrad was preparing to fight the Germans street by street, block by block, building by building in the fashion of Madrid in the Spanish Civil War. A curfew was imposed. Security was tightened. Air raids began.

Behind the scenes there were quarrels, confusion and possibly even conspiracy. Some time in August, or even before, Stalin had become suspicious of the leadership of the Leningrad Command. He became querulous and bitter in telephone conversations with Marshal Voroshilov and Party Chief Zhdanov. He followed the details of defense arrangements with intense care, often changing and vetoing proposals by the Leningrad leadership. He flew into a violent rage August 21—the day the "Enemy is at the gates" posters appeared on the Leningrad streets. He objected to a new city defense command set up by Zhdanov and Voroshilov without consulting him. Possibly he thought the two were trying to avoid responsibility if Leningrad fell. Possibly he feared a plot to surrender the city. Possibly others among Stalin's associates had been critical of Zhdanov and Voroshilov because of the advance of the Germans. In any event he accused the Leningrad leadership of panic. He called Zhdanov and Voroshilov "specialists in retreat." He revised and rejected their troop dispositions and administered a formal reprimand.

But Stalin did not halt there. His mind was filled with suspicion and concern. He dispatched to Leningrad a powerful commission of inquiry. It included Foreign Minister Molotov, Stalin's favorite Party Secretary Georgi Malenkov (a sworn foe of Zhdanov), Naval Commissar Admiral Kuznetsov, Air Marshal P. F. Zhigarev, Artillery Marshal Voronov and Aleksei Kosygin, chief of evacuation planning.

The group flew to Cherepovets (because the main Leningrad line had been cut by the Germans) and then by train north through Tikhvin and Volkhov to the little station of Mga, twenty-five miles southeast of Leningrad. The date was August 28. It was night. An air attack was in progress. The party got off the train and walked down the tracks where they boarded an interurban streetcar and a bit later were met by limousines sent to meet them by Zhdanov.

Mga. It was not a name which any of them had heard before. But it was one long to live in their memories and those of the people of Leningrad. Two days later, August 30, a Nazi unit would capture Mga, cutting the last rail link between Leningrad and mainland Russia. From that day forward for nearly 900 days Leningrad would be in blockade.

Factory worker putting out an incendiary bomb that has just dropped through the roof.

THE CIRCLE CLOSED

The battle for Mga was one of those accidental happenings of war whose consequences could not be foreseen. No one, German or Russian, intended to fight a battle at Mga. It was an obscure railroad station, a small freight transfer point southeast of Leningrad. It was not on the main Moscow-Leningrad line, but on the roundabout northern railroad, a branch line which made a connection to Moscow at Vologda, 360 miles to the east of the northern capital. It suddenly became important after the 20th Nazi Panzer Division, having broken across the Luga line, captured Chudovo, cutting the main Moscow-Leningrad line, called the October Line in memory of the 1917 revolution, and headed northeast along the Tosna River toward Lake Ladoga.

The 20th Panzers actually wanted to push north for Leningrad, but a detachment of workers at Izhorsk, south of the city, diverted them and so, following the line of least resistance, the 20th approached

Leningraders who have just survived Nazi bombardment of the city center.

Mga. Ahead of the panzers a broken Soviet unit, the Forty-eighth
Army, now at less than division size, stumbled eastward. It no
longer had any capacity to fight. The Nazis pushed through Mga with
virtually no opposition on August 30 and reached the banks of the
Neva River. The first word Leningrad command had of the breakthrough came from a young girl who saw the Nazi tanks. The Naval
Commissar, Admiral N.G. Kuznetsov, happened to be sitting alone in
Admiral Isakov's office at Smolny Party Headquarters. The telephone
rang and he answered it. A girl told him excitedly that the Germans
had reached the banks of the Neva. Kuznetsov reported this to the
Leningrad commander, General Popov. He hadn't heard about it,
thought the girl was panic-stricken, and brushed it all off.

For a few days the Leningrad command tried to conceal the loss
of Mga while they desperately sought to recapture it. But the

counterattacks failed and the Germans were to stay on the Neva until 1943. Failure to report the loss of Mga strengthened Stalin's distrust of the Leningrad command. His high-powered commission, headed by Molotov and Malenkov, went over plans for the defense of the city, approved arrangements for evacuation of 1,000,000 Leningraders, arranged (or so they thought) for the evacuation of scientific institutions and defense plants, checked the placement of street fortifications and inner city defense rings, shifted commands and responsibilities. Reluctantly Stalin released for the city's use four days of Leningrad tank production, both 60-ton KVs and workhorse T-34s, and ordered ten rifle battalions—perhaps 10,000 men—in to reinforce the battered defense forces.

One other move was made. A new Fifty-fourth Army had been created and put under command of Marshal G. I. Kulik. It was based in Volkhov, east and slightly south of Leningrad. Kulik's mission was to protect the Leningrad-Vologda railroad (including Mga), to relieve German pressure on Leningrad and prevent the city's encirclement.

It is hard to imagine a worse choice for the role of Leningrad's savior. Kulik was a police general. His roots were in the secret police apparatus and he was employed by Stalin for shady and sinister missions. His appearance on any front was like the black spot for honest Red Army commanders. Invariably he found treason and promptly reported it to the Kremlin. Commander after commander was removed and/or shot at his orders. As a military leader he proved worthless. His name thirty years later causes Red Army men to curse.

This was the man to whom Stalin gave authority to try to save the endangered city. The results were only to be expected. Many Soviet military writers credit Kulik directly for the loss of Mga, specifically for the failure of the Red Army to retake the railroad and, thus, for permitting Leningrad to fall into encirclement and the horrors that followed. Anastas Mikoyan, writing as late as 1977, blamed Kulik totally for the disaster. Kulik had been directed to put a division or two at the disposal of the Leningrad front to protect the railroad. He did not do so. This was only one of the major disasters attributed to Kulik. Eventually, according to Nikita Khrushchev, even Stalin had too much. Kulik was removed from command and shot.

But whatever his future might be, Kulik played a fateful role in the Leningrad tragedy. The entire nature of the events surrounding Leningrad's fall into encirclement are still, more than thirty-five years later, enshrouded in sinister puzzles.

To this day the real purpose of Stalin's high-level mission to Leningrad in the closing days of August and early September is not clear. Was Stalin hoping to save Leningrad? Or was he preparing to make the best of its loss and intending to blame those who were in command of the city's defense? Georgi Malenkov, the party secretary, was a vicious political opponent of Andrei Zhdanov, the Leningrad Party boss. Was Malenkov trying to save the city or was he arranging his rival's downfall and trying to get out of Leningrad what could be gotten before the deadly last act?

Evidence is hard to come by. For years after World War II the sending of the mission headed by Molotov and Malenkov to Leningrad was given a prominent place in all Soviet histories and in the biographies of both men, especially that of Malenkov. By the time many of these enconiums had been published Zhdanov was dead of a

Five Soviet leaders: from left, Molotov, Stalin, Voroshilov, Malenkov, and Beria.

heart attack in 1948 and most of his associates had been arrested and shot in what was called the "Leningrad Affair." They are not alive today to tell their side of the story and few if any of their archives have ever been published. Today's Soviet accounts do not even mention Molotov and Malenkov.

There are some clues as to what really was going on. The main preoccupation of the mission seems to have been with getting matériel out of Leningrad rather than sending in reinforcements. The fact that encirclement was completed before the mission left Leningrad was a fact which no one had counted on. Men like Kosygin were specialists in evacuation. Marshal Voronov, the artillery specialist, made arrangements for shipping heavy guns and ammunition *out* of Leningrad to assist other hardpressed fronts, particularly Moscow.

There is one hard bit of evidence concerning Stalin's intentions. Admiral Kuznetsov stayed on in Leningrad after his colleagues had returned to Moscow. After a risky flight at low altitude over Lake Ladoga to avoid Nazi fighter planes, Kuznetsov met Stalin in the Kremlin at noon September 13, an unusual hour. Ordinarily appointments with Stalin were at night. He found Stalin restless, nervous and full of questions which centered on the extraordinarily serious situation in Leningrad. "It is possible that it may be abandoned," Stalin said. He ordered Kuznetsov to prepare the Baltic fleet for scuttling. Not one warship was to fall into Nazi hands or the guilty parties would be "strictly judged," that is, put before the firing squad. He instructed Kuznetsov to send instant orders to the fleet and shore installations to prepare everything for destruction. To Stalin's amazement Kuznetsov refused. Such an order, Kuznetsov said, could be signed only by Stalin himself. Stalin told Kuznetsov to cosign the

order with Marshal Boris Shaposhnikov, Chief of Staff. Kuznetsov and Shaposhnikov agreed they would not sign such a telegram. Instead they prepared the order and sent it to Stalin for signature. Stalin delayed a bit but finally sent it off. A year later Kuznetsov had reason to congratulate himself on his caution. Police Chief Beria sent a report to Stalin charging Admiral Tributs with "panic" in preparing to scuttle the fleet. Kuznetsov reminded Stalin that it was Stalin's orders on which Tributs acted.

Kuznetsov was convinced by this and other circumstances that Stalin was prepared to abandon Leningrad. Not because the Soviet leader wanted to yield the northern capital, but because he felt the decision was inevitable.

In case Leningrad had to fall Stalin was preparing the appropriate scapegoats—Voroshilov and Zhdanov. And possibly Kuznetsov, Tributs, and Shaposhnikov as well.

It was, of course, a time of unbearable tension. The Kiev tragedy was playing out to an inevitable and terrible conclusion. If Stalin was not aware of this in the first days of September he would be within the week. The Germans were on the verge of capturing two of Russia's ancient capitals, the capital of ancient *Rus*, Kiev, and Peter

the Great's capital, Leningrad. At any moment the threat to Moscow itself was bound to be renewed. All of this in less than ten weeks of war.

Perhaps the best measure of Stalin's real feeling was conveyed by a message which he dispatched to Winston Churchill, his old enemy, on September 4. Russia, he said, faces a "mortal menace."

He asked Churchill to open a second front in France or the Balkans capable of drawing off 30 to 40 German divisions, and he asked for 30,000 tons of aluminum, 400 planes and 500 tanks by October 1.

"Without these two forms of help," he said, "the Soviet Union will either suffer defeat or be weakened to such an extent that it will lose for a long period any capacity to render assistance to its allies.

"I realize that this message will cause dismay to Your Excellency. But what is one to do? Experience has taught me to look facts in the face, however unpleasant they are, and not to fear to express the truth however unwelcome it may be."

The message was presented to Churchill by Ambassador Ivan Maisky. Churchill felt there were clear hints in Stalin's words, and the melodramatic manner in which Maisky delivered the message, that Stalin was considering the possibility of a separate peace.

Eleven days later Stalin frantically asked Churchill to land twenty-five to thirty divisions at Archangel or through Iran. Whether Stalin or Churchill appreciated the irony or not, Archangel was the very port to which, at Churchill's urging, David Lloyd George sent British forces ashore in 1918 to try to strangle the infant Bolshevik regime of Vladimir Lenin.

Churchill responded to Stalin tactfully, trying to explain the impossibility of an instant second front, promising all possible aid in war matériel and suggesting that if Stalin was compelled to abandon Leningrad and the Baltic Fleet the British, at least in part, would make good the Russian loss of naval strength. Stalin tartly responded that he would submit his bill to the Germans if he lost the fleet.

Leningrad's agony grew. On September 6—with members of Stalin's High Commission still in the city—the reality of encirclement burst on the brains of the men charged with its leadership. Mayor Peter S. Popkov realized that Leningrad was on the verge of exhausting her food supplies. The State Defense Committee had found on August 27 that Leningrad had seventeen days of flour supplies, twenty-nine days of cereals, sixteen days of fish, twenty-five days of meat and twenty-eight days of butter. It was decided (at the very moment the last railroad line was being cut!) to ship in enough food to assure Leningrad a 45-day supply. Eight food trains a day were directed to the city—August 31, the day after rail communication had ended. Somehow by barge, riverboat or raft the supplies were supposed to get into the city via Lake Ladoga.

Reality was finally coming. And on September 2 the Leningrad ration was cut in half—to a pound of bread a day for workers and half a pound for children and dependents. All food, including meals in restaurants and canteens, was put on ration.

Then came Popkov's discovery of September 6. Even with the ration cuts the city stood on the brink of starvation. There was only 14 days' supply of flour left, 23 days of cereal, 19 days of meat, 20.8 days of fats and sugar and confectionary for nearly 48 days. By the end of the month Leningraders—if they ate anything at all—would be eating candy and cake.

A Soviet antiaircraft battery defending Leningrad.

Fire brigade at work at a Leningrad power plant after artillery attack.

Leningrad had been remarkably free of Nazi air attack. But now the planes began to appear and on September 4 the first German shells from long-range guns hit the city. The day of September 8 was a fine one, clear skies, warm autumn weather, and the evening promised to be fine as well. The poet Vera Inber went to the Musical Comedy Theater to see *The Bat*. There was an air raid alarm but the play went on. The audience could hear the antiaircraft guns barking. When Vera Inber and her friends emerged they saw a strange reddish light in the sky. It was the reflection of a fire which was devouring the Badayev food warehouses in the southwest quarter of the city. A pillar of smoke and flame rose thousands of feet into the air and when it was over Leningrad's principal stocks of food had been destroyed. The acrid smell of burned sugar, the rich fumes of burning oil and flour, the smell of carbonized meat pervaded the city.

No one after Badayev could be in doubt that Leningrad was in peril—if not from the Nazis, surely from starvation.

Two days later an unknown official from Anastas Mikoyan's Food Ministry arrived in Leningrad to see what might be done to stave off immediate starvation. His name was Dmitri V. Pavlov and his tough, realistic, almost brutal decisions were to govern the life—and death— of Leningraders for months to come.

It was at this moment that Stalin moved. Von Leeb was driving for the kill. His commanders could see in their binoculars the spires of Leningrad's Admiralty, the dome of St. Isaacs, the needle of the Fortress of Peter and Paul. Von Leeb had twenty-nine divisions at his command. He was plowing through to Leningrad from the southwest, smashing into the suburbs of Krasnoye Selo and Ligovo toward the Kirov factory. He was driving up the Moscow-Leningrad highway beyond Izhorsk and Kolpino.

To fend off the Nazis Voroshilov had little but broken units. The last reserves had been thrown in. He himself had been reprimanded by Stalin as never before. He had tried to conceal the loss of Mga and been found out. The same thing happened when the fortress of Schlisselburg at the point where the Neva River flows out of Lake Ladoga fell. Voroshilov tried to keep it secret, hoping to recapture the position. He didn't take it back and Stalin again found out.

Finally the old cavalryman went to the front near Krasnoye Selo himself. He had a detachment of marines, clad in their traditional long black cloaks, hidden in the underbrush. Above the field a dogfight was in progress between Soviet and Nazi planes. Colonel Bychevsky arrived in time to see Voroshilov plant himself ahead of the young sailors and call on them to fight for the Motherland, for the Party, for their sailor's honor. The marines stood behind Voroshilov, some in steel helmets, some with their blond hair tousled by the wind. Finally Voroshilov said simply: "Let's go." The young detachment moved straight toward the German positions, shouting: "Hurrah!" Voroshilov stalked firmly ahead. They crossed a highway and drove the Nazis out of the small village of Koltselevo. The Nazis counterattacked. The marines fought back. They returned again and again. But the Nazis were too strong. Soon the Soviet force had to fall back and Krasnoye Selo was lost.

Word of Voroshilov's action spread across the front. Was it an act of pure heroism? Or did the old fighter expect—and perhaps hope—to go down under Nazi fire rather than face disgrace and possible execution which was so often the fate of commanders whose performance displeased Stalin?

Exactly when Stalin decided to make his last move on Leningrad is obscured by a controversy among Soviet authorities, the kind that so often clouds critical points in Soviet history. On September 8 or 9 (depending on which of his versions is correct) Marshal Zhukov was called into the Kremlin from Yelnya about 230 miles east of Moscow and just south of Smolensk. He had just conducted the most successful counteroffensive the Russians had thus far mounted against the Germans.

Zhukov entered Stalin's office sometime during the evening and found him having supper with members of the Politburo, Molotov, Malenkov and Alexander Shcherbakov, the Party boss of Moscow, among them. Stalin greeted Zhukov warmly (the last time they had met Stalin had fired Zhukov for warning him that Kiev should be abandoned).

He wanted, Stalin told Zhukov, to send him to another front. He wanted him to leave immediately for Leningrad.

"It is an almost hopeless situation," Zhukov recalled Stalin saying. "By taking Leningrad and joining up with the Finns the Germans may strike at Moscow from the northeast and then the situation will become even more critical."

Stalin handed Zhukov a slip of paper. "Give this to Voroshilov," he said. "The order naming you commander will be issued when you arrive in Leningrad."

The slip of paper said: "Hand over command of the front to Zhukov and fly back to Moscow immediately."

Stalin added that things were in bad shape around Kiev and a new commander, Timoshenko, was replacing Budenny in charge of the Southwest Front. Zhukov recommended that Marshal Konev be named to take Timoshenko's position as commander of the Western Front and again warned Stalin that he had better get the troops out of Kiev while there was still time. Kiev would have to be surrendered. There was no alternative. Stalin said he would talk over the Kiev situation with Timoshenko, and Zhukov went off to gather a small staff. He picked Lieutenant General M. S. Khozin and Major General I. I. Fedyuninsky to be his chief aides and flew to Leningrad the next day. Flying low to avoid harassment from Nazi aircraft, Zhukov landed at Leningrad and went straight to Smolny Institute, Party headquarters. Guards stopped him and he waited outside for fifteen minutes before he and his party could be identified. Then Zhukov went in and found Voroshilov, Zhdanov and Party Secretary A. A. Kuznetsov in the midst of a discussion about blowing up industrial plants and other objectives in the event Leningrad had to be abandoned.

Zhukov handed Stalin's note to Voroshilov. The old cavalryman paled. Zhukov asked for the operational charts and Voroshilov handed them over. Zhukov signed a receipt and went to the direct Moscow telephone. He called GHQ. Marshal Vasilevsky answered. "I have taken over command," Zhukov said curtly. "Report to the High Command that I propose to proceed more actively than my predecessor."

That was it. Voroshilov did not speak with Moscow. He left the room without a word. "They've called me to headquarters," Voroshilov brokenly told his colleagues. "Well, I'm old and it has to be!"

Within an hour Voroshilov and his staff were on the way to Moscow and possible execution and in Zhukov's hands was placed the fate of the citadel of the Bolshevik Revolution.

THE CRISIS DEEPENS

In September the days in Russia begin to shorten rapidly. Autumn, with winter just ahead, comes in swiftly. But September of 1941 was an exception. Never had the weather been more beautiful. Sunny days. Blue skies. Cool nights. The scent of sunflowers and rye along the dusty roads, pungent fires of peat and birch on the hearthplaces of the thatched huts of the peasants, evening clusters of women gossiping around the village wells, not many men now among them.

In Moscow the streets were filled with mustard-colored trucks and soldiers in mustard-gray uniforms, the smell of cheap gasoline mingling with that of crushed leaves from the lime trees on the boulevards that covered the pavements like a blanket. Only a few *babushki* with their baby carriages sat on the park benches. Everywhere people strode purposefully, an ear out for the air raid alarms that had sounded more and more often.

It was such a September as Russia had seldom known, and to the men in the Kremlin it was a September which seemed to have no end. Every day arose a thousand alarms. Every day fewer ways to meet them. The deadly net around Kiev and the southern Soviet armies had been pulled tight. Kiev, the Ukraine and a thousand thousand fighting men were lost. When had any country suffered such a loss? How could the Germans be halted from overrunning the whole Ukraine, the Don country, the Kuban, even the Caucasus, the riches of its oil fields just ahead, with visions of Persia and India not much further distant?

To the north Leningrad was in agony, the most deadly battle the war had yet seen. Zhukov became a man of terror, demanding that no one retreat, yanking out commanders if they gave up a foot of soil, on the go twenty-four hours a day, a figure who seemed not human, his harsh voice flogging the men and the officers into the lines. Let them die. But halt the Germans. No one believed the Germans could be halted except, perhaps, Zhukov and Zhdanov by his side. The men and women of Leningrad fought and fought and fought. They took the streetcar to the war. Now the lines began just beyond the Kirov steel works. Everyone was in the first line, even the composer Shostakovich, writing his Seventh Symphony ("Leningrad"). The Russians and Germans battled over the heights where the Pulkovo observatory was located. They fought for the building where Pavlov conducted his famous experiments on dogs. They fought all night and into the next day and the day after that. A suburban railroad station changed hands five times in two days and still the battle raged.

But there seemed little on which hope might be founded. When

the tired, bloody agonized Leningrad defenders dropped of their wounds or were killed, who would take their places and where was the ammunition to come from, let alone the food that melted away almost as Dmitri Pavlov, the food commissioner, doled it out?

Perhaps there was one tiny ray of hope. The pace of the Nazi advance had slowed with the arrival of Zhukov and his terrible anger, his terrifying demands, his total unwillingness to permit anyone to do anything but fight no matter how hard, how tired, how dangerous. How many commanders were broken in rank, how many were sent to the execution wall, will never be known. But it was more than a few. A frightful tactic. But what else was he to do?

Yet, Stalin could not be certain Leningrad would hold. Every preparation had been made to blow up the city. The great buildings were mined, the warships prepared for destruction. Now all he could do was wait and see. As he waited the sands ran out for Kiev. Finally the order had to be given—weeks too late—for the armies to pull out. All Stalin could do was to try to conceal the extent of the debacle from the outside world with bold words and intense security. Even many of his closest associates did not know the full price paid for his Kiev disaster.

Stalin had one genuine ace in the hole but he could not be certain of playing it. Despite the catastrophes of the first three months of war he had engaged his reserves with parsimony. Not even marshals like Zhukov, Timoshenko and Vasilevsky were fully informed on the number of divisions held in the GHQ reserve, nor the number of tanks and big guns. In addition, Stalin had the strength of the Red Banner Far Eastern Army, forty divisions of excellently trained and equipped troops. Only one or two groups had been withdrawn to the west because Stalin felt he must maintain a balance against possible Japanese entry into the war. But now he had received through his spy in Tokyo, Richard Sorge, unassailable evidence that the Japanese, despite every German entreaty, were not going to enter the European war. Instead they had their eyes fixed on Southeast Asia and the Pacific. If worst came to worst—and it looked as though worst would come to worst—Stalin could draw on the fine troops of the Far Eastern Army in a final effort to turn the tide.

Now there began to be ominous signs that the Moscow front was once again becoming active. Hitler's finest armored commander, Guderian, continued to play cat-and-mouse with General Yeremenko and his Bryansk front. Many of Stalin's military advisers, including Zhukov, had warned Stalin to keep close watch lest the Germans attempt a sudden breakthrough in the Bryansk direction.

Unknown to Stalin and his staff, Hitler on September 6 had issued Directive 35, putting into motion Operation *Typhoon*, the plan designed to seize Moscow, crush the Soviets and, hopefully, end the war.

Hitler told his troops:

"After three and a half months of fighting, you have created the necessary conditions to strike the last vigorous blows which should break the enemy on the threshold of winter. All preparations within the capability of human strength have been completed. . . . Today begins the last decisive battle of the year."

Hitler had mustered a remarkable force under Marshal von Bock. He had 77 divisions, more than a million men, 1,700 tanks, 4,000 guns and 950 planes. The Nazi forces were deployed in three groups, each with a fist of panzers at the head. A northern group led by Hoth's Panzer Group would drive from north of Smolensk, about 340 miles from Moscow, in a pincers movement on Vyazma, 120 miles east of Moscow. The southern wing of von Kluge's Fourth Army and Hoepner's 4th Panzer Group would move from a start line around Roslavl, south of Smolensk, and curve around to Vyazma. Hopefully the pincers would clamp shut on the main Moscow defense group. Guderian and von Weich's Second Army would jab northeast from Glukhov in the direction of Orel and Tula, attempting to split Yeremenko's Bryansk group and open the way to Moscow from the southwest.

It was a fairly simple plan and the Germans had every reason to believe that it would succeed. Against them they calculated the Russians could not muster more than 70 to 100 poorly equipped and badly understrength divisions. The actual Soviet force, according to Marshal Vasilevsky, was about 800,000 men, 6,800 guns, 782 tanks and 545 planes.

One German marshal was despondent about the Hitler plan. This was Marshal von Leeb. He still had not taken Leningrad. He was certain that just a bit more pressure would enable him to crack open the city. The high command had begun to discuss the fall of the city in its communiqués. Goebbels called a special press conference in Berlin and announced that all the Leningrad defense forces had been drawn into a noose. They could starve or they would be exterminated. It made no difference to the Germans. "The fate of Leningrad has been sealed," the German radio proclaimed. But already von Leeb had been ordered to transfer his armor to the central front for the attack on Moscow. He pleaded with Chief of Staff Halder who let him

A Soviet artillery unit in action.

keep it on a day-to-day basis. The Germans were so close to Leningrad, right on the city limits, that the guns of the cruisers *Gorky* and *Petropavlovsk* in the Neva could fire into the German lines. The *Marat* and the *Maxim Gorky* stationed in the commercial port and Kronstadt joined in the bombardment. The Germans rained down leaflets: "Save your lives. Beat the Political Commissars—throw a brick in their snouts." Halder began to think that Leningrad would fall. He reported "very good progress" on September 12 and let von Leeb keep his armor for another few days. But time was running out. The armor had to be moved to Moscow. On September 17 the order came through. The armor had to go. The Hoepner group must wheel out of line and join in the Moscow attack.

That day Halder wrote in his journal:

"There will be continuing drain on our forces before Leningrad where the enemy has concentrated large forces and great quantities of matériel and the situation will remain tight until such a time when Hunger takes effect on our ally."

Secretly Hitler approved a policy declaration that:

"As a beginning we will blockade Leningrad (hermetically) and destroy the city, if possible, by artillery and air power. . . .

"When terror and hunger have done their work in the city, we can open a single gate and permit unarmed people to exit.

"In the spring we will enter the city (not objecting if the Finns do this before us) sending all who remain alive to the depths of Russia, or take them as prisoners, raze Leningrad to the ground and turn the region north of the Neva over to Finland."

It was a few days before the Leningrad defenders noticed. Then they spotted German troops digging in. Word came from agents behind the German lines. The tanks were moving south. Leningrad had been saved from German capture. But another ordeal was just beginning.

On the 27th of September the British cruiser *London* dropped anchor at the mouth of the Dvina River, twenty miles north of Archangel. It brought an Anglo-American mission to Russia to talk with Stalin. Heading the Americans was W. Averell Harriman, personal representative of President Roosevelt. Heading the British group was Lord Beaverbrook. There had been some sparring between Harriman and Beaverbrook over how much and how fast aid should flow to Russia, but essentially both men and their principals, Roosevelt and Churchill, wanted to help all they could. They wanted to keep Russia in the war and while they did not know how bad things were they knew they were bad enough.

Foreign Minister Molotov met the group at Archangel and, after a big banquet with many vodka toasts to victory, the party flew into Moscow, arriving on September 28. They flew the last miles at elevations of 500 to 800 feet. Soviet antiaircraft guns opened up on them as they approached the Central Airport. Harriman who was stationed in London immediately felt he had entered a war zone. The flash of Soviet guns twinkled on the horizon, there was a full blackout and the Kremlin was heavily camouflaged.

Harriman found that most Americans in the Embassy thought Moscow would soon fall. Neither the British nor the American ambassadors were optimistic about Russian chances.

But at the Kremlin the atmosphere was different. Stalin was formal but frank. He was going to hold Moscow at all costs. He might

Food rations cards used during the Leningrad blockade.

have to retreat to the Urals but he would keep on fighting. Hitler, he said, had made a fatal mistake by dividing his forces into three groups. Had he concentrated on Moscow he would have overridden the city on the crest of the first wave. Stalin brushed aside his miscalculation over Hitler's intentions, merely saying that if Hitler had given him another year it would have been different. He said the Germans had twice as many planes as he did and three or four times as many tanks. Then he listed his needs. They were colossal—1,100 tanks a month, 4,000 tons of barbed wire a month, 5,000 jeeps, 8,000 to 10,000 trucks a month, as many thousand tons of armor plate as the United States could spare, planes by the hundred, and on and on. He was willing to take troops from the British immediately wherever they could be landed.

Stalin justified his signing the pact with Hitler in August 1941, saying that Prime Minister Neville Chamberlain was really more interested in turning Hitler against Russia than in setting up a genuine collective security system. When the chance came to make a deal with Hitler he took it because he thought it was in Russia's best interests.

As for the military situation, Stalin thought the Russians could hold Leningrad (this was October 1 when the evidence that the Nazis had shifted strength away from Leningrad to the main Moscow front was incontestable). He expected Soviet forces to hold the Crimea with the help of forces from Odessa. He did not, however, reveal that the movement of 80,000 troops and possibly 350,000 civilians out of Odessa had already begun and that Odessa would be surrendered to the Germans October 16.

He made an interesting remark about the Ukraine. He said the situation there was difficult (Kiev had been lost September 20) and that Russian forces were fighting in territory which was not altogether friendly to the Soviets. This was an allusion to the fact that many Ukrainians had since the 1920s been hostile to Soviet rule and had welcomed the Germans, sometimes villagers offering the traditional platter of *kleb i sol*, bread and salt.

On the morning of October 3, 1941, Harriman and Beaverbrook flew out of Moscow, back to Archangel and reboarded the cruiser *London*. They had been given gala banquets at the Kremlin, had been toasted with vodka, had dined on endless courses, including mountains of caviar, fish, suckling pig, chicken, pheasant, ice cream and fresh fruit flown in from the Crimea. The atmosphere in the Kremlin was overflowing with confidence and determination. And seldom had Harriman seen such luxury as at the Kremlin dinner. Only on one night had Stalin appeared nervous, querulous, argumentative, smoking one cigarette after the other. For the rest he seemed open, jovial, patient, smoking his pipe, talking in statesmanlike tones, quick with figures, bargaining closely, but a realist who seemed to have not only his country but the difficult fortunes of war totally under command.

Harriman caught a bad cold on the *London* and went to bed for five days with sinusitis. When he finally managed to get about a bit, on October 7 or 8, he asked General Ismay who headed the British military delegation what he thought about the Russian Front. Ismay predicted the Russians would hold on for three more weeks. Harriman noted in his diary that the British were consistent in one thing: for the last three and a half months they had been saying the Russians would hold out for three more weeks.

Up to this point German war losses totaled 550,000 men. Soviet losses, killed or taken prisoner, were 3,000,000.

THE BATTLE OF MOSCOW

little after 6:00 A.M. on the foggy morning of October 5, 1941, two airmen, Major G. P. Karpenko and Major D. M. Gorshkov, took off in a P-2 fighter from Luberts airfield just outside Moscow on their morning "milk run." Their job each day was to fly west along the Moscow-Warsaw highway and advise on what they saw. They flew

Margaret Bourke-White's famous photograph shows field tracers over the Kremlin during a German air raid early in the war.

the route every couple of hours and reported to Lieutenant General P. A. Artemov, Chief of the Moscow Military District.

Artemov had ordered the patrol as a precaution in late September as the Germans approached closer to Moscow. The airmen flew out two hundred to three hundred miles and scanned the ground at low altitude for signs of action.

The weather improved as the airmen flew west, and when the sun rose the mist burned off. In the first hundred miles, as far as Medyn, everything seemed normal. Thirty miles further west at Yukhnov where the highway crossed the Ugra River, the pilots saw a few military units and some peasants with carts, probably refugees. When the airmen arrived over Spas-Demensk, 185 miles west of Moscow, they spotted two columns of tanks, trucks, guns and armored vehicles strung out over twenty miles of highway, moving east. The airmen clearly saw Nazi swastikas on the vehicles.

Quickly the fliers returned to Moscow. To the airmen the situation seemed frighteningly clear. Yesterday the Nazis had been at Roslavl, 235 miles southwest of Moscow. They obviously had broken through and now were on the move 65 miles east of their last reported position.

At 10:00 A.M. the airmen's information reached Colonel N. A. Sbytov of the Moscow Air Command. He could not believe it. If the report was correct the Germans were only 175 miles from Moscow on an almost open highway.

The German assault on Moscow had opened on September 30—at the height of Stalin's meeting with the British and Americans. It was undoubtedly this fact, carefully concealed by Stalin from his visitors, which gave him an occasional air of nervousness and preoccupation, particularly since the German drive had burst with enormous force. Guderian's Second Panzers jumped off from positions east of the Desna River and just south of Yeremenko's redoubtable Bryansk group. Moving rapidly in fine weather, Guderian advanced fifty miles on the first day. He advanced almost as far the next day and was now approaching Orel, a key center about two hundred miles southwest of Moscow. Once again the Bryansk command had proved no match for the fast-moving Nazi armored specialist.

Late in the evening of October 1 (after he had given a lavish banquet at the Kremlin for Harriman and Beaverbrook) Stalin summoned one of his finest armored commanders to the Kremlin, General Dmitri Lelyushenko. Stalin told him that Guderian had broken the Bryansk Front and was threatening Orel. Lelyushenko was instructed to take charge of an armored force just being thrown together and try to halt him. The command was to be ready for action in three or four days. Lelyushenko's orders were not to let Guderian seize Orel.

Hardly had Lelyushenko started to put his staff together than another call came from the Kremlin. It was now very late at night. He found Stalin with Voroshilov, Mikoyan and Marshal Shaposhnikov. Shaposhnikov spoke: "The situation has changed. Guderian is already close to Orel. You and General Zhigarev [Commander of the Air Force] must go immediately to Orel and work things out on the spot."

Stalin spoke up: "You must not let them come further than Mtsensk." Stalin took a red pencil and drew a line across the map at the River Zusha where it passed through Mtsensk. By dawn Lelyushenko and a motorcycle regiment were roaring down the

German soldier in foreground has just thrown a hand grenade, baseball style, as he leads a charge. Smoke in rear rises from a burning Soviet town.

southwest highway toward Orel.

At midmorning October 2 Lelyushenko arrived at Tula, a famous old Russian arms center about one hundred miles south of Moscow and a hundred miles from Orel. He picked up new forces as he went along and twenty-four hours later arrived at Mtsensk. Guderian had already taken Orel and his vanguard was arriving at Mtsensk.

Guderian's breakthrough was extraordinarily critical. The attention of the High Command and Stalin was almost entirely focused on it. It had to be stopped or the Germans would arrive in the suburbs of Moscow within three or four days. Marshal Shaposhnikov fed armored forces and mixed brigades to Lelyushenko as rapidly as he could collect them. On October 4 he telephoned and promised that by the next day he would send Lelyushenko two divisions of katyusha rocket launchers. The weapons were still so secret Lelyushenko didn't know how to use them.

"Be careful you don't lose them," Shaposhnikov said. "If you do, your head will answer for it. That's what the High Command [Stalin] says."

Shaposhnikov promised he would send specialists to instruct Lelyushenko in employing the new weapons. Lelyushenko was now engaging Guderian's advance forces. By October 5 a major battle could be expected.

The fixation of Stalin and the High Command on Guderian and the Bryansk breakthrough probably produced inattention and skepticism at word of the appearance of an armored column on the Spas-Demensk highway. Sbytov, the first general to hear the news, decided to consult his chief, Major General K. F. Telegin.

Telegin was in a delicate position. His command was a rear element unit. He had only peripheral access to the High Command. He was supposed to get intelligence briefings from the High Command, not the other way around. But the fact was that he had laid on his own reconnaissance flights because information from the Bryansk Front was shaky. Actually, although Telegin didn't know it, Yeremenko had lost communication with Moscow and had for practical purposes fallen into encirclement. However, neither he nor the High Command were quite aware of this. High Command communications with the principal Western Front and Reserve Front commands were also almost peripheral.

Telegin had heard from a colleague that morning that the Germans were claiming a big breakthrough in a gigantic operation against the Russian Front. He also had reports that some units of the Soviet Forty-third Army had been halted by military policemen at Maloyaroslavets, seventy miles west of Moscow and far east of the zone they were supposed to be defending. How to put this all together puzzled Telegin. He hadn't a word in the High Command's intelligence briefing that suggested a major breakthrough. Telegin and Sbytov decided to send out another plane and see if they could verify the earlier report. About noon the second plane returned with news that the column was now approaching Yukhnov, nearly fifty miles east of Spas-Demensk.

Telegin was still reluctant to alarm the High Command. These were the days when Stalin was sending "panicmongers" to penalty battalions or putting them against the wall. Telegin called the duty officer at GHQ who reported no special news from the front. He called Marshal Shaposhnikov who said, "All is quiet if you can call war quiet."

Puzzled and cautious, Telegin ordered a third patrol sent out.

Meantime he started making a list of units he could throw together if it proved to be true that the Nazis were racing toward Moscow on the main Warsaw highway.

At 2:00 P.M. Sbytov reported three fighter planes had come back. They had undergone heavy antiaircraft fire. The head of the Nazi armored column was seven to ten miles west of Yukhnov.

Telegin called Shaposhnikov again and got a sharp reply. He sent out a fourth reconnaissance. At 3:00 P.M. the plane was back. The Nazis were at Yukhnov.

Telegin took his courage in his hands and telephoned Shaposhnikov. The Marshall could hardly believe the news. It contradicted all his information. A few minutes later Poskrebyshev, Stalin's *chef de cabinet*, was on the phone. Then Stalin himself. He listened quietly to Telegin and told him to put together a scratch force capable of holding the so-called Mozhaisk defense line, fifty to sixty miles west of Moscow, for five to seven days.

Before Telegin could get to work Lavrenti P. Beria, the police chief, was on the wire. He denounced Telegin's information as coming from provocateurs and asked where Telegin had got his report. Telegin named Sbytov. A little later Telegin found that Beria's deputy had browbeaten Sbytov and forced him to resign his command. Somehow, Telegin managed to get Sbytov out of police clutches and set about putting together some units to try to halt the Germans.

Above, German tanks advance after leaving a village in flames. At right, Muscovites dig antitank ditches in the suburbs.

That evening General Zhukov at his headquarters in Leningrad had a call on the Baudot telegraph line from Stalin. He asked about the situation in Leningrad. Zhukov reported that the Nazis had ceased attacking and apparently were moving their armored forces toward Moscow.

Stalin listened and then said he wanted Zhukov to come to Moscow immediately. A critical situation had arisen on the Moscow Front, particularly in the Western Front sector and around Yukhnov.

Zhukov agreed to leave in the morning. As it turned out he was delayed by a day because of a crisis concerning the Fifty-fourth Army, and before Zhukov got to Moscow the situation had gotten much worse. Not only was Yeremenko now fully encircled and no longer in touch with Moscow, but also the bulk of the main western force around Vyazma had fallen into the Nazi loop, as had been planned by Hitler's command in laying out Operation Typhoon. It may have been the evening of October 6 that Air Marshal A. Ye. Golovanov was called to the Kremlin and found Stalin alone in his office. He was seated at a table with an uneaten meal before him. Golovanov entered but Stalin did not rise or give any sign of having seen him. Golovanov realized something serious must have happened but did not dare break the silence. Finally Stalin spoke. "We are in great trouble," he said slowly. "The Germans have broken through our defenses near Vyazma. Sixteen of our divisions are encircled."

Golovanov stood silent. Then Stalin spoke again, as much to himself as to the Air Marshal. "What shall we do? What shall we do?"

At dusk on October 7 Zhukov landed at Moscow Central Airport. He was taken immediately by Stalin's personal bodyguard to Stalin who was at his villa outside Moscow, ill with the grippe. When Zhukov entered Stalin got up and went to a map.

"We're in serious trouble on the Western Front," he said. "A very grave situation has developed and I can't get a detailed report on the true state of affairs. Go at once to the Western Front. I'll be waiting

An airplane spotter in Moscow's Red Square in 1941.

for your call."

Zhukov went to Marshall Shaposhnikov, who was preparing situation charts for him. Shaposhnikov told him that Western Headquarters was located at Krasnovidov, close to the old Napoleonic battlefield of Borodino, about fifty-five miles west of Moscow. This was where Zhukov had his headquarters during the Yelnya conteroffensive a few weeks earlier. Zhukov and Shaposhnikov had a glass or two of strong tea. Each was exhausted. Then Zhukov set out in the pitch-black night to find the beleaguered headquarters. He studied the situation maps by flashlight and periodically halted his car and jogged for two or three hundred yards to keep from falling asleep.

It was early in the morning of October 8 when Zhukov arrived at Western Front Headquarters. He found there General Konev, the Front commander, Marshal Bulganin, then Konev's political officer, General Malandin, Konev's Chief of Staff, and Marshal Sokolovsky, representative of GHQ in Moscow. The small room was lighted by miners' candles. Everyone looked worn and tired.

Bulganin said he had just spoken with Stalin but could give him no specific information because they did not know what was happening to the tens of thousands of troops encircled around Vyazma.

It is difficult to reconstruct the complex pattern of events which Operation Typhoon set in train. The task is made more difficult by quarrels among the Soviet commanders over responsibility for the Vyazma disaster, probably the second largest of the war.

Marshal Konev, who was in command of the Western Front, made every effort to demonstrate that it was not his fault. He said he had warned Stalin about the imminent Nazi attack (just as Stalin, in turn, warned him). He pointed out that in spite of the threatening situation he had been compelled to give up two full-strength divisions to the GHQ reserve on Stalin's orders just before the attack began.

After the Nazi encirclement was threatened on October 4 Konev said he telephoned Stalin, warning him of the likelihood of a German breakthrough in the rear of his Nineteenth, Sixteenth and Twentieth armies, and that Stalin took no action. He conceded that the telephone connection was broken during this conversation but contended that later he had reached Marshal Shaposhnikov at GHQ and proposed that his forces be drawn back to the Gzhatsk line on the River Vop. Shaposhnikov, in Konev's version, agreed to report Konev's recommendation to Stalin but Konev got no word until the next day when it was too late.

The fact is, as Konev conceded in his memoirs, that he could find no record in the GHQ archives of either of these conversations, neither that with Stalin nor that with Shaposhnikov—a curious circumstance since the GHQ archives seem to be remarkably complete.

Violent disagreement over Vyazma erupted after World War II between Konev and Marshal Rokossovsky, another of Russia's great wartime leaders. At the time of the encirclement Rokossovsky, in command of the Sixteenth Army, was serving under Konev. Unexpectedly and for reasons which to this day are not clear, Konev on October 5 ordered Rokossovsky to turn over command of his units to General Yereshakov, commander of the neighboring Twentieth Army, and go with his staff to Vyazma. There he was to take command of a group of (encircled) divisions, halt the German drive on Vyazma (which the Germans already held) and prevent the Nazi offensive toward Yukhnov (already well underway).

The order was so strange that Rokossovsky and his staff could not believe their eyes. They insisted that it be repeated in writing and Konev sent a signed copy, countersigned by his political officer, Marshal Bulganin, by plane.

Only after receiving the signed copy did Rokossovsky gather his staff and set about the impossible task. It resulted in nothing except further to disorient the troops of the Sixteenth Army, now floundering with virtually no direction. Rokossovsky found no troops when he got to Vyazma and had a ticklish time slipping out of encirclement.

According to one account—which Konev denied—Konev promptly accused Rokossovsky of saving his own skin by slipping through the lines with his staff but leaving the Sixteenth Army behind.

Rokossovsky saved himself by presenting the written copy of the order signed by Konev and Bulganin to Marshal Voroshilov who muttered: "Strange . . ." The charge against Rokossovsky could have been most serious, as he had been among the Red Army officers sent to concentration camps four years earlier and released only in time to return to duty with the advent of World War II.

Konev, in his memoirs, blamed the Vyazma disaster on the lack of timely orders to retreat. He said he had given orders to his forces to fall back on October 5, even without authorization, but because they had not been trained in "fighting retreats" the action was not well carried out. He called October 4 "the most responsible day" of his

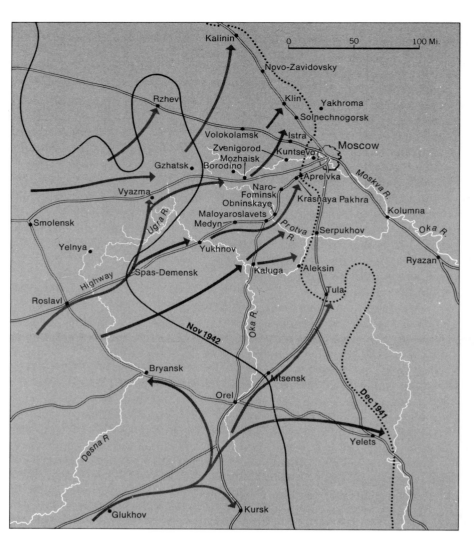

THE BATTLE OF MOSCOW

whole four years of service in World War II, presumably meaning it was the most fateful.

The question of responsibility for the Vyazma disaster is still unresolved. Zhukov, while showing a good deal of restraint in various versions of his memoirs, was inclined to put considerable blame on Konev. In fact, of course, the German attack was so strong and so meticulously carried out, it would have been difficult for any maneuver by the weaker Soviet forces to have been successful.

At 2:30 A.M. October 5 Zhukov telephoned Stalin from Konev's headquarters and warned him that the point of greatest danger appeared to be the main highway from Mozhaisk to Moscow. He said all available forces should be concentrated there to prevent a Nazi breakthrough.

Stalin asked him about the Sixteenth, Nineteenth and Twentieth armies and the shock group of General Boldin of the Western Front and the Twenty-fourth and Thirty-second armies of the so-called Reserve Front, commanded by Marshal Budenny. Zhukov told him they had all been encircled west and northwest of Vyazma.

"What do you plan to do?" Stalin asked.

"I was about to visit Marshal Budenny."

"Do you know where his headquarters is?"

"No. But I'll look around near Maloyaroslavets."

"Good. Call me when you get there."

Zhukov drove off in the foggy night and at about dawn at the railroad station at Obninskoye, seventy miles from Moscow, saw two signalmen laying a cable across the Protva River. The signalmen, after Zhukov had identified himself, directed him back to a hill located in a forest to the left of the bridge. There Zhukov found Budenny's political commissar, L. Z. Mekhlis, who was on the telephone dressing someone down. Mekhlis was another of the police generals whose paranoia, vindictiveness and inefficiency marked their every assignment.

Mekhlis had no idea what had become of Marshal Budenny. He had gone to the Forty-third Army the day before and hadn't been seen since. Search parties had not been able to locate him. Neither Mekhlis nor Major General A. F. Anisov, Budenny's Chief of Staff, could give Zhukov any information on the whereabouts of the Reserve Army's forces.

"You can see what a situation we're in," Mekhlis said.

Zhukov decided he would drive through Maloyaroslavets and Medyn toward Yukhnov in hope of locating Budenny and his troops. The countryside was familiar to Zhukov. He had grown up in the nearby village of Strelkovka and his mother and sister and her four children still lived there. He could not but worry that the Nazis might seize them. (Three days later he managed to evacuate them to Moscow.)

Zhukov found Maloyaroslavets deserted but he spotted two light tracked vehicles in front of the City Hall, and when he went inside he found Budenny. Budenny said he had been out of touch with Konev for two days and that his own headquarters had moved and he did not know where it was. Zhukov told him he would find it beside the railroad bridge at the Protva River, seventy miles from Moscow, and filled him in on the encirclement at Vyazma.

"Things are no better here," Budenny said. "The Twenty-fourth and Thirty-second armies have been cut off and we have no defense front anymore. Yesterday I nearly fell into enemy hands."

"Who is holding Yukhnov?"

The German Army advances into the Caucasus region, 1942.

Moscow scenes. Above, left to right, actors from the Moscow Art Theater form a People's Defense League. Sandbagged buildings on a main street. A blimp to prevent dive bombing flies above Pushkin Square. A barrage balloon about to be raised over the Bolshoi Theater. Below, a ruined apartment building after German bombing. Women and children take shelter during an air raid in the Mayakovsky station of the subway.

"I don't know. We have a small detachment on the Ugra River two infantry regiments but no artillery. I think the enemy has Yukhnov."

"Then who is covering the road from Yukhnov to Maloyaroslavets?"

"When I came through there I saw only three policemen at Medyn."

At Medyn Zhukov found no one but an old woman rummaging in the wreckage of her house. Zhukov tried to talk to her, but she went on digging. Another woman appeared and said the old woman had occupied the house with her grandson and granddaughter. A bomb had hit it the day before and the children had been buried. The woman was out of her mind with grief.

Zhukov drove on toward Yukhnov but soon encountered a Soviet tank brigade. The Germans had captured Yukhnov and crossed the Ugra River. There was heavy fighting near Kaluga but Kaluga itself was still in Russian hands.

Zhukov went on to Kaluga, where on the next day a staff officer finally caught up and gave him a message from Shaposhnikov advising him that Stalin wanted him back at Western Front Headquarters.

A High Commission had been sent to Konev's headquarters. It was headed by Foreign Minister Molotov and included Georgi Malenkov, the Politburo Secretary, Marshal Voroshilov (who had not, after all, been shot by Stalin for his conduct of Leningrad's defense) and Marshal Vasilevsky. Already Molotov had instructed Konev on Stalin's order to transfer five or six divisions to the Mozhaisk defense line. Konev found the order totally unrealistic. It was not possible to

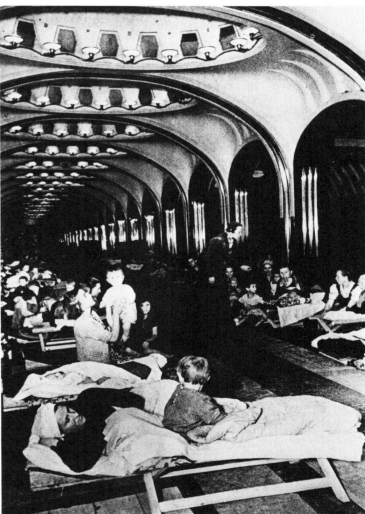

disengage a single unit from the fierce fighting then in progress.

By the time Zhukov got to Western Front HQ on October 10 Stalin had decided to put him in charge. Zhukov got the order from Stalin personally by telephone. Konev was to be his deputy. According to Konev, Stalin took the move on the recommendation of the High Commission with his full concurrence. In reality Stalin had probably already decided on the move when he called Zhukov back from Leningrad. The order was effective at 6:00 P.M. October 11.

Zhukov, in his usual way, took over with total vigor and concentration. Konev was dispatched immediately to set up a new defense force at Kalinin, about a hundred miles north and slightly west of Moscow. Then Zhukov turned to the task of setting up a stable defense line that would run south from Kalinin through Volokolamsk, Mozhaisk, Naro-Fominsk, Serpukhov and Tula.

Although Zhukov expressed total confidence in his ability to save the capital there was at this moment no reasonable grounds on which success might be guaranteed. Every previous defense line had been smashed or encircled by the hard-hitting Nazi panzers.

Stalin agreed to consolidate the Reserve Front with Zhukov's command. Zhukov said he must have large reinforcements very soon. The Germans could be expected to strengthen their drive rather than relax. Zhukov put experienced commanders in charge of each critical area—Rokossovsky at Volokolamsk, Lelyushenko at Mozhaisk and, after he was wounded, General Govorov, General Golubev in the Maloyaroslavets sector and General Zakharin in the Serpukhov area.

Zhukov's principal task was feeding in new forces and organizing them in depth. The Mozhaisk line was strong because of natural conditions, protected by the Lama, Moskva, Kolocha, Luzha and Sukhodrev rivers; small rivers but rivers with steep banks. Zhukov set up headquarters at Albino, near Mozhaisk. The weather had begun to hint of winter. First snow fell October 9 and by October 13 heavy rains and sleet turned the battlefields into mud. The pavement of the Warsaw and Mozhaisk highways began to break up under the impact of the heavy German fighting machines.

But there was no relaxation of danger. The Germans continued to push forward. On October 13 Kaluga, 85 miles south of Moscow, fell. On October 14 Kalinin, 75 miles to the northwest, was abandoned. If the Nazi spearheads could be pushed further east, Moscow easily could fall into extended encirclement, just as had Kiev. Hitler believed that Moscow was his. Goebbels proclaimed that the annihilation of the Soviet armies at Vyazma had "definitely brought the war to a close." German light-armored cars broke through the perimeters and plunged into the suburbs of Moscow. One light tank penetrated to the highway beside the Khimki Station on the Moscow River within the city limits. Its burned carcass lay beside the road until after the war, evidence of the peril to Moscow.

The Party had organized the city for defense. Hundreds of thousands of Moscow residents labored on antitank ditches. Jagged railroad iron hedgehogs protected all approaches to the city. Moscow boiled with rumors: that the Nazis were about to enter the city; that the capital would be abandoned; that the "Jews are leaving the city." Suddenly railroad stations were jammed with people trying to get out of town. On October 13 the city Party organization was assembled by City Party Secretary A. S. Shcherbakov and warned that Moscow was in the gravest danger. The next evening, after receiving news of the fall of Kalinin, Stalin decided to evacuate the Government. Word went out before dawn on the 15th. All important Government and

With the heavy rains of November 1941, Nazi forces ran into trouble as the Russian roads turned to mud, soon covered by snow.

U.S. Ambassador Lawrence Steinhardt, right, greets Harry Hopkins, President Roosevelt's special emissary to Russia, at the Moscow airport, July 1941.

Party bodies, all ministries, most of the Moscow organization was to be moved out. But part of the Politburo, the State Defense Council, the High Command and General Staff would remain.

The foreign diplomatic corps would be moved to Kuibyshev on the Volga. At the American embassy there was something like panic. The U. S. military attachés thought the Russians were done for. Major Ivan Yeaton gave them only a few days. Colonel Philip Faymonville thought it might be over in a few hours. There were no militia on the streets. All had been commandeered for the front. Suddenly a message arrived. Ambassador Lawrence Steinhardt was called to the Kremlin. There he found Sir Stafford Cripps, the British Ambassador. Foreign Minister Molotov told them they were being evacuated immediately to Kuibyshev. He and Stalin would join them in a day or two. The battle for Moscow would go on.

Marshal I. T. Peresypkin was called to the Kremlin October 15 to meet with Stalin. He ran into a group of Party secretaries who had been called in for a Party Central Committee meeting in early October. The meeting was never held because of the military crisis.

Peresypkin was ordered by Stalin to set up communications with the new site of the High Command, a site which had not yet been picked. Peresypkin proposed Kuibyshev because of the excellence of communications. Stalin turned that down. There would be too many foreigners in Kuibyshev, he said. Peresypkin proposed Kazan, also on the Volga. Stalin turned that down too and suggested a third city, the name of which is still not released by Soviet censors. It was a small provincial town, not even on a main rail line. Peresypkin was dismayed. Communications were not good to this point. Nonetheless, the General Staff headed by Marshal Shaposhnikov set out on the 17th, leaving a small group headed by Marshal Vasilevsky in Moscow. Peresypkin set up a communications center on two railroad communications trains and named it Victoria, for the victory he hoped would come.

Confusion reigned. The railroads were besieged. Nazi leaflets showered down. Rumors spread about that Jews were fleeing the city with their gold and other possessions. Some said that Party members spread these rumors. Some said the Nazis were responsible. Whatever the case, the Party organization eventually broadcast a formal denial. Smoke belched from the chimneys of the Lubyanka headquarters of the secret police as thousands of files were burned. Some people found their own dossiers, half burned, floating through the air. Roads to the east developed massive traffic jams. Police and military detachments cleared ways through the jams, simply overturning cars in ditches or running them off the roads, so that convoys could get through, sometimes shooting drivers whose trucks or cars had broken down.

On the morning of October 16 no subways were running in Moscow. The streetcars had halted. The bakeries and food stores had closed. Workers appeared at their factories and in many places found the gates locked and offices closed. Many had no money because the cashiers' offices had shut down—there was no more paper money left in the banks and Finance Minister Zverev had flown off to Kuibyshev. The situation was reported to Stalin at an emergency meeting in the Kremlin. "Well, so what," he said. "I think it will be worse." However, he gave orders that food stores and commissaries be reopened and that transport facilities resume functioning. He also ordered hospitals

Russian airplanes guarding Moscow.

and clinics to stay open and told the Party secretaries to get on the radio and try to quell the panic.

No one knows whether Stalin stayed in Moscow. He sent his son and daughter, Vasily and Svetlana, to Kuibyshev. Visitors to Stalin's Kremlin office recall it being stripped of furnishings, even the pictures from the walls. He was in Moscow on the evening of October 15–16 because that night he visited the wounded General Yeremenko in the hospital on Serebryansky Pereulok in the heart of Moscow, but another official described the Kremlin on October 19 as "dark and empty."

Stalin did not stay long absent from Moscow. There was an ill-tempered meeting of the State Defense Council October 19 at which it was voted to continue to defend the capital. A decree placing the city in a state of siege was issued and plastered up October 20. On the 19th Stalin gave Zhukov permission to withdraw to a new inner defense line which at some points was only a few miles from Moscow. This ran from Novo-Zavidovsky through Klin, the Istra reservoir, the town of Istra, Zharvoronky, Krasnaya Pakhra, a favorite Moscow picnic place, Serpukhov to Aleksin.

There were no end of alarms. The line creaked and sagged and here and there gave way a little. But it held. By now the Soviet forces were concentrated. They were fighting with their backs to the capitol. Supplies and communications were no trouble. Command was simplified. Tula, the ancient gunmakers' city, had become the southern anchor post and while the Germans gained a bit more to the north and the pressure did not diminish, the forward momentum slowed to a crawl.

On November 1 Stalin called Zhukov to the Kremlin. Did they dare hold the traditional November 7 parade through Red Square. Zhukov thought a bit and said yes. The Germans were in no position immediately to renew their offensive. But there must be effective air cover.

The November 7 parade was held. Snow fell lightly. Marshal Budenny took the salute from Lenin's mausoleum. Tanks moved out of Red Square straight on to the front. Stalin delivered the traditional anniversary address at a mass meeting the evening before in the Mayakovsky station of the Moscow subway.

Russian troops parade in Red Square on the anniversary of the Bolshevik Revolution, November 7, 1941.

Moscow had held out—but for how much longer? Zhukov knew the Germans were gathering new strength for one last try. He managed to pry out of Stalin another 100,000 men, 300 tanks and 2,000 guns, including some which were flown out of besieged Leningrad.

Hitler had determined on November 7 to continue the attack on Moscow. Whether he took the capital or not he hoped to break through to the rear and sever Moscow's communications with Siberia. General Halder convened a meeting at Orsha November 15 and outlined the objectives of the attack. They were to try to advance as far as Gorky, two hundred miles east on the Volga. The Nazi commanders did not receive this news with enthusiasm but none seems to have complained. Field Marshal Guderian later said that he was beginning to get nervous. He had heard that the Russians were massing new divisions from Siberia on his southeastern flank near Ryazan and Kolumna.

The Nazis broke through at Klin compelling Rokossovsky to retreat with his Sixteenth Army toward the Istra reservoir and River. There was a violent row over Rokossovsky's action. He had been ordered by Zhukov to stand firm but he went over Zhukov's head and got approval to withdraw from Marshal Shasposhnikov at GHQ. This produced a fiery blast from Zhukov: "I command the troops of this front! Not a step back are you to retreat."

On November 19—the day after the second Nazi drive on Moscow had opened—Stalin telephoned Zhukov.

"Are you sure we are going to be able to hold Moscow?" he asked. "I am asking with an aching heart. Tell me honestly, as a member of the Party."

"There is no question that we will be able to hold Moscow," Zhukov responded. "But we will need at least two more armies and two hundred tanks."

"I'm glad you are so sure," Stalin said. "Call Shasposhnikov and tell him where you want the two reserve armies concentrated. They will be ready by the end of November, but we have no tanks for the time being."

Zhukov called Shasposhnikov and arranged to send the First Shock Army, then being formed, to the area of Yakhroma, and the Tenth Army to the area of Ryazan.

At times it was touch and go with the new Nazi offensive. But for all the fire and thunder, dangerous as was the German movement, it began to peter out.

The Germans attacked once more in the Tula area and were repulsed. On November 29 a German unit smashed across the Moscow-Volga canal northwest of Moscow and seized a bridge near Yakhroma. On December 1 the Nazis launched a sharp attack along the Minsk-Moscow highway and advanced to Akulovo and Golitsyno where they were halted, having lost 50 tanks and 10,000 dead. On December 2 the Germans advanced to a point five miles northeast of Zvenigorod, a northwestern Moscow suburb, and a small advance was made in the Naro-Fominsk sector December 1 in a breakthrough to Aprelevka.

In the twenty days of the second Moscow offensive the Germans had lost 155,000 dead and wounded, 800 tanks, 300 guns and 1,500 planes.

On December 5 Field Marshal Guderian entered this note in his journal: "The offensive on Moscow has ended. All the sacrifices and efforts of our brilliant troops have failed. We have suffered a serious defeat."

LENINGRAD IN BLOCKADE

One day in mid-October Vsevolod Kochetov, a newspaper reporter, and his wife, Vera, were walking in Leningrad's Nevsky Prospekt near the offices of the *Leningradskaya Pravda* where Kochetov worked. Near the door of a pharmacy they noticed an old man lying on the sidewalk, his hat fallen off and long matted hair flowing over his shoulders. They tried to get him to his feet but the man protested feebly. Kochetov went into the drugstore and asked for help. The clerk was indignant.

"What do you think, young man," he said, "that this is a first aid station? Hunger is a terrible condition. Your old man has collapsed from hunger."

Kochetov realized for the first time that he was in the presence of a victim of starvation. He tried to get a policeman to help but by that time the old man was dead.

The impact of hunger on Leningrad came swiftly. D. V. Pavlov, Leningrad's food dictator, had cut rations drastically. For October nonworkers and children got a ration of one-third of a pound of poor-quality bread a day. They got one pound of meat a month, plus a pound and a half of cereals, three-quarters a pound of sunflower-seed oil and three pounds of cookies or candy. Nothing more. And much of the time even these rations were not available or substitutes were issued—fish for meat, cheap candy for fats and oil. Into the bread went larger and larger quantities of substitutes, cellulose, straw, god-knows-what. New ration cards were issued, bringing the total down to 2,421,000. All special rations were halted. Violaters were shot.

Pavlov collected food wherever he could. He ransacked the suburbs and gathered in ten thousand tons of potatoes and vegetables before the fields froze hard. He salvaged eight thousand tons of malt from the breweries and five thousand tons of oats from military warehouses. Horses were slaughtered. Twigs were collected and stewed. Peat shavings, cottonseed cake, bonemeal was pressed into use. Pine sawdust was processed and added to the bread. Moldy grain was dredged from sunken barges and scraped out of the holds of ships. Soon Leningrad bread was containing 10 percent cottonseed cake that had been processed to remove poisons. Five hundred tons of flour was gathered by sweeping out old warehouses.

It grew colder. Snow fell in mid-October. There was a two-gallon ration of kerosene in September, none in October or the months that followed. People grew thinner. More thin and more yellow. Some began to look like beasts. And they fought over a crust of bread. Or over nothing. Bombs and shells rained down. In October 7,500 shells, 991 explosive bombs, 31,398 incendiaries. In November, 11,230 shells, 7,500 bombs. In December, 6,000 shells, 2,000 bombs. Buildings burned down. People were trapped in the wreckage. More and more often no one was able to get them out.

But the spirit of the city did not vanish. The Leningrad Philharmonic gave a concert October 25. Listeners sat in their overcoats. There was no heat. The Leningrad bookstores, some of them one hundred years old or more, stayed open. Book publishing halted but

A starving man with his food ration of one day.

a new edition of Dickens's *Great Expectations* had come off the presses just before the siege began and there were stacks of the new book in the stores. Professor Orbeli, director of the great Hermitage Museum, sponsored a celebration of the eight hundredth anniversary of the birthday of Nizami, national poet of Azerbaijan. The famous Pulkhovo Observatory was in the front lines, under artillery fire by the Germans. Professors A. N. Deich and N. N. Pavlov organized night expeditions to the broken building. They crawled out under Nazi fire and removed priceless scientific records.

November was the month hunger really took hold. People tore wallpaper from the walls and scraped off the dry paste which they thought was made of potato flour. They chewed the paper and some even ate the plaster. At least, they said, it filled their stomachs. Guinea pigs, white mice and rabbits vanished from the laboratories. So did cats and dogs from the streets.

"Today it is so simple to die," Yelena Skryabina wrote in her diary. "You just begin to lose interest, then you lie on the bed and you never get up again."

The ration was cut and cut again and the position of the city did not improve. All efforts to lift the siege failed. Instead, the Germans in a sudden forward thrust captured the rail junction of Tikhvin, 130 miles southeast of Leningrad, on November 8. Tikhvin was a key station on the northern rail branch to Vologda. Its capture ruptured hopes of moving quantities of food into Leningrad over Lake Ladoga. Supplies had come in very slowly and now unless Tikhvin was recaptured a wilderness road 220 miles long would have to be built to the easternmost extremity of Ladoga. Hitler's plan of starving Leningrad to submission seemed about to be fulfilled. Starvation deaths began to mount. In November 11,000 had been recorded, compared with 12,500 killed and wounded in shelling and bombing during September, October and November.

A black market in food flourished—a diamond ring for a few pounds of coarse black bread. Thieves knocked down old women and stole their ration cards. The Leningrad streets grew dangerous at night. Or even in broad daylight for the weak, the old, the hungry. The sex drive disappeared in the starving people and the birthrate fell to the vanishing point.

Time was running out for Leningrad. Little food came in over the rapidly freezing Lake Ladoga. Planes brought only tiny cargoes of the most precious drugs. Efforts were made to ship people out of Leningrad but German dive-bombers sank the ships. The gunboat *Konstruktor* went down on the lake with a loss of 204, mostly women and children. Ice closed the lake November 16, only about 25,000 tons of food having been brought in since September—a 20 days supply for the city transported in in 65 days.

The city started November with a little more than two weeks supply of food on hand.

Hitler broadcast: "Leningrad's hands are upraised. It falls sooner or later. No one can free it. No one can break the ring. Leningrad is doomed to famine."

It was hard to challenge Hitler. How could the city hold out? On the day Tikhvin fell Leningrad had 7 days supply of flour, 8 days of cereals, 14 days of fats, 22 days of sugar. No meat. The closest point to which trains could now come was the tiny station of Zaborye, 110 miles from Volkhov. The distance from Zaborye to Ladoga was 220

A column of Germans taken prisoner by Russians at Leningrad.

miles and no road.

Rations were cut again, even though this doomed people to faster starvation. Workers got 300 grams—about two-thirds of a pound—of bread daily. Everyone else got half that much. Troops were cut to 600 grams of bread and 125 grams of meat.

The only hope was that the ice would freeze on Lake Ladoga and food could be brought in over the frozen lake. But the ice formed slowly. On November 20 the ration was cut again to 250 grams of bread for factory workers and 125 (two slices) for everyone else. Frontline troops got 500 grams.

This cut consumption of flour in Leningrad to 510 tons a day for a population of about 2,500,000. By one estimate this doomed one-half of Leningrad's population to death by starvation. But there was no alternative. The product which Leningraders called bread henceforth contained 25 percent of "edible cellulose." Teams were sent into the nearby countryside to collect pine and fir bark. Each district of the city was given a quota for producing edible sawdust.

The official history of Leningrad concluded that:

"November was the most alarming month of the whole blockade not only because of the difficulties but also because of the uncertainties. War is war. And it was difficult to predict how events would develop around Leningrad. The Fascist command might again mount an offensive toward Svirstroi or toward Vologda. Such a possibility could not be excluded."

On December 1 the poet Vera Inber was walking down Wolf Street and saw a sight she had never before seen, a woman pulling a child's sled on which lay a corpse, tightly wrapped in a sheet like an Egyptian mummy. This would soon become so common no one would give it a second glance. On this day Leningrad entered the ninety-second day of the blockade.

There had been several feeble and unsuccessful efforts to break the Leningrad blockade in late September and October. None succeeded and in November the Fourth Army, which was supposed to protect the single railroad line to Ladoga, slowly fell back and finally yielded Tikhvin on November 8.

Radical action had to be taken. The situation was placed in the hands of General K. A. Meretskov, the able and tough-minded commander of the Seventh Special Army, defending the Svir River just north and east of Tikhvin.

Meretskov flew into Bolshoi Dvor where the Fourth Army Headquarters were located and whipped the bedraggled command into shape. With General Fedyuninsky of the Fifty-fourth Army an offensive was mounted to drive the Germans back. It finally got going December 5, but not without a fierce row between Meretskov and G. I. Kulik, the notorious police general whom Stalin sent in to speed up preparations for the attack. Fedyuninsky attacked from the north, employing 60-ton KV tanks which had somehow been sent over the ice of Lake Ladoga.

There was furious fighting in bitter cold and on December 8 the city was captured. Without it Leningrad could not have survived. Only the next day, December 9, the Leningrad streetcar system halted. There was no coal to run the power stations. The city was almost without electricity. No light for the city. No power in the factories.

Pavel Luknitsky, a war correspondent, wrote in his diary

December 11: "A dark night . . . Tikhvin has been liberated in the nick of time. . . . Snow drifts in the streets. People with exhausted faces walk slowly—dark shadows in the streets. And more and more coffins . . . hunger and cold and darkness . . ."

Colonel General Franz Halder entered the notation in his log December 13:

"The Commander of the Army Group is inclined to the view—after the failure of all attempts by the enemy to liquidate our foothold on the Neva—that we may expect the complete starvation of Leningrad."

The one hope for Leningrad was Lake Ladoga. No one was certain that an ice road could be constructed, but it was the largest lake in Europe and when it froze the thickness of the ice usually was three to five feet. Generally ice formed in late November. The ice road idea was not a new one in Russia. The Russians had conducted operations on the frozen Finnish Gulf during the Civil War and an ice railroad had been built over Lake Baikal during the 1904 war with the Japanese.

Orders to construct a road were issued November 3 and the first reconnaissance party went out on the ice November 17. Over most of the route there was four to eight inches of ice and the great open water *polynia* was rapidly shrinking. On November 19 General N. F. Lagunov, in charge of the ice road, drove across the lake and back. That was one day before the Leningrad ration was cut to two slices of sleazy bread a day per person.

The next day the first convoy moved out across the ice, 350 horse-drawn sledges. The column stretched over five miles. It reached Kobona on the opposite shore at midevening, loaded up and started back. In the early hours of November 21 the first tons of food via the ice road arrived on the Leningrad side. Sixty trucks delivered 33 tons of flour to Leningrad November 23. On the 25th the delivery was 70 tons; November 26 154 tons. By November 30 the ice road had delivered 800 tons of flour, two days supply at starvation rations.

Gradually the road improved, especially after the recapture of Tikhvin. But scores of trucks fell through open patches in the ice. The Germans strafed the route but the supplies kept on. Deliveries crept up to 700 tons on December 22 and 800 tons by the next day. That day Party Chief Zhdanov ordered an increase of the Leningrad ration of 100 grams (about a slice of bread) for workers and 75 grams for all others. One reason he was able to do this was because of the shrinkage of population. The best guess on the number of Leningrad deaths in December was 53,000 persons, but statistics no longer were accurate. Frozen bodies had begun to pile up around the entrance to the city morgue, hospitals and cemeteries.

Zhdanov's Christmas ration boost was a gamble. The radio no longer worked for lack of power, and Party workers hardly had the strength to spread the good news to the people. On December 26 there was a meeting at the Writers Union. The novelist Vera Ketlinskaya spoke. Soon, she was sure, Soviet troops would recapture Mga. The siege ring would be broken. Thousands of tons of food waited for Leningrad just beyond the ring of encirclement. Perhaps by New Year's the worst would be over.

But it was not to be. A weak offensive was launched by the starving Red Army troops but they could not wrest Mga from the Germans. By New Year's deliveries over Lake Ladoga, the "road of life" as Leningraders called it, were dropping again. As of January 1, 1942, Leningrad had only two days of flour in reserve. One day a Ladoga driver, Filip Sapozhnikov, came back late to his barracks after delivering his load of flour. He found a note: "Driver Sapozhnikov. Yesterday, thanks to you, 5,000 Leningrad women and children got no bread ration." The margin was that thin.

Temperatures on the ice road ranged between twenty and forty below zero. The north wind was relentless. Party Chief Zhdanov took iron measures to increase deliveries but, as the Leningrad official history noted, "Never had Leningrad lived through such tragic days. . . . In the evening the city sank into impenetrable darkness. Only the occasional flicker of fires and the red flash of exploding artillery shells lighted the gloom. . . . The great organism of the city was almost without life, and hunger more and more strongly made itself known."

In the subterranean cellars of the Hermitage Museum people lived, worked, studied, died. It was lighted by tiny candle stubs. Scholars warmed their ink with their breaths to keep it from freezing. There were two thousand people living in the cellars. In those arctic days Leningrad artists kept themselves alive by painting. Alexander Nikolsky, chief architect of Leningrad, held an exhibition in the Hermitage cellars. He sketched plans for the future city, an Arch of Triumph, a Park of Victory. "To yield our city is impossible. Better die than give up," he wrote in his diary. Captain A. V. Tripolsky, a Soviet submarine commander, visited Director Orbeli in his cold dark Hermitage office. Orbeli lighted a candle in Tripolsky's honor. When he left Orbeli, Tripolsky went down the steps of the Neva embankment and out onto the Neva ice where the *Polar Star*, once the Czar's yacht, was frozen in the ice. He arranged with the chief electrician to

Trucks moving across the melting ice road on Lake Ladoga, trying to supply food to the blockaded city.

Leningraders filling water buckets from broken water main on the Nevsky Prospekt. Below, corpse of a starvation victim is pulled across a bridge on a sled.

throw a line ashore. Soon Orbeli had a light in his room and an electric heater.

More and more often Orbeli got requests for coffins. The Hermitage had a stock of packing cases and was almost the only source in the city for coffins. Finally Orbeli had to refuse the requests. The Hermitage carpenter had died of starvation.

The heaps of bodies grew so large that engineering teams were brought in to dynamite long trenches in the frozen earth. One of these great trenches eventually became the Piskarev Cemetery. Steam shovels were put into action. Vsevolod Kochetov saw them working one night. He thought new fortifications were being built.

His chauffeur corrected him: "They are digging graves—don't you see the corpses? There are thousands. I go past here every day and every day they dig a new trench."

"Never in the history of the world," comments Leningrad's official history, "has there been an example of tragedy to equal that of starving Leningrad."

Often people just laid down in their beds. They stopped eating. Toward the end they began to cry in a high-pitched note that never halted, their skeletal faces contorted. "Hunger psychosis," the doctors called it.

Nikolai Markevich, a correspondent for *Komsomolskaya Pravda*, wrote in his diary January 24, 1942: "The city is dead. There is no electricity. Warm rooms are most rare. No streetcars. No water. Almost the only kind of transport is sleds . . . carrying corpses in plain coffins, covered with rags or half clothed. Daily six to eight thousand die."

It was then that the worst horror appeared—murderers, criminals of all kinds, even cannibals ranged the city. Gangs preyed on the young, on lonely pedestrians, women on the street at night. They entered unguarded apartments. Some haunted the stacks of corpses piled up around the hospitals and carved off arms and legs. Euphemistically the starving Leningrad police called this a "new kind of crime." In the old Haymarket people appeared to sell and buy—to sell any valuable they had to buy bread or other food. In this market of the starving and the dying ventured a new kind of salesman or saleswoman, well fed, tough, hard, calculating. They had meat for sale. Or sometimes stew or sausages. But they gave no answer as to where it had come from. Others sold "Badayev earth," glasses filled with earth from the burned Badayev warehouse, impregnated with burned or melted sugar. There were no longer rats or mice in the city. They, too, had starved or been caught and eaten.

"In the worst period of the siege," a survivor recalled, "Leningrad was in the power of the cannibals. God alone knows what terrible scenes went on behind the walls of the apartments."

In Leningrad's City Museum there is preserved the torn pages of a child's notebook. On them are scrawled these notations:

"Z—Zhenya died 28 December, 12:30 in the morning, 1941.

"B—Babushka died 25 January, 3 o'clock, 1942.

"L—Leka died 17 March, 5 o'clock in the morning, 1942.

"D—Dedya Vasya died 13 April, 2 o'clock at night, 1942.

"D—Dedya Lesha, 10 May, 4 o'clock in the afternoon, 1942.

"M—Mama, 13 May, 7:30 A.M., 1942.

"S—Savichevs died. All died. Only Tanya remains."

Tanya Savicheva was an 11-year-old schoolgirl. The notebook records the fate of her family, which lived at No. 13, Second Line, Vasilevsky Island. Tanya was evacuated in the spring of 1942 to a children's home near Gorky on the Volga. She suffered from chronic dysentery and she, too, died, in the summer of 1942.

Battles to deblockade Leningrad went on listlessly through the winter in the deep forests and bogs around Mga and Tikhvin. But the troops had scant success. Death walked the Leningrad streets. In January by the most conservative estimate deaths were 3,500 to 4,000 a day or possibly 108,000 to 124,000 for the month. The combined January-February total is estimated at about 200,000, probably a low estimate. There is no parallel for these figures in modern history. On January 1, 1942, Leningrad still had 2,282,000 residents.

Gradually in January the ice road began to work better. It brought in 10,300 tons of food in the first 10 days, 21,000 in the second 10 days, and the total continued to rise. Energetic efforts were made to send people out of Leningrad, 500,000 by the end of winter. The ration was raised on January 24 and again on February 11 to 500 grams of bread a day for workers, 400 for office workers, 300 for dependents and children.

By April 15 the ice road had evacuated 554,000 persons including 25,000 wounded.

In late February Vera Inber made the trip across Ladoga. It took only an hour and a half across a plain of ice as desolate as the north pole—white, snow-covered, strewn with antiaircraft installations, carcasses of burned-out trucks and defense posts. The sacrifices of the city had been incalculable, but on the other side of the lake she drank a toast with General Fedyuninsky whose forces had helped to keep the road of life open. The toast was: "To live or not—that is not the question. Our life belongs to Leningrad." By the time the spring thaw forced the closing of the road of life it had delivered, from November to April 24, 271,000 tons of food, 32,000 tons of military supplies and 38,000 tons of fuel.

In April there remained 1,100,000 persons in the city, 800,000 fewer than in January. More people had died in the blockade than in any modern city, more than 10 times the number who died in Hiroshima. The exact total will never be known. The official Soviet figure issued in 1946 was 632,000 for Leningrad and for the whole area including suburbs 671,635. Present-day estimates by Leningrad officials put the total in the neighborhood of 1,000,000. Many Leningraders think this is too low. If deaths in the surrounding area and those which occurred during evacuation are added the number probably comes to 1,300,000 or more.

The exact total is not important. What is important is that it was a sacrifice without parallel in our times, a sacrifice almost entirely of civilians who died in their city and for their city. Nothing like it has occurred in any war of which we have knowledge. Leningrad survived. Hitler did not achieve his ambition of leveling it to the ground. Nor did the city open its gates in the spring and let the starving survivors out to meet the uncertain mercy of their Nazi enemies. Instead, as the thin sun of March melted the ice and snow and exposed the rubble and corpses which filled the streets of Leningrad, the survivors began to put their wonderful northern capital once more in order, each survivor proud of the endurance and bravery which had made this miracle possible.

Many years later on the walls of the memorial at Piskarev Cemetery, where hundreds of thousands of Leningraders are buried, this inscription was carved:

"Let no one forget; let nothing be forgotten."

Tanks coming out of the Kirov steel factory went directly to the Leningrad Front.

A convoy of supply trucks on Lake Ladoga's ice road at night.

THE RED ARMY ATTACKS

This photograph of a soldier by Max Alpert was made into a popular poster of the war.

As cold and hunger grasped Leningrad tightly in its grip, as Soviet forces tumbled pell-mell out of the Ukraine, past Rostov and into the Caucasus, as the Moscow Front shuddered under Hitler's November offensive, Stalin and his top commanders, Marshals Zhukov, Shaposhnikov and Sokolovsky, secretly began to plan a move that would change the course of the war.

Stalin had hesitated for weeks about bringing west substantial forces from his Far Eastern armies. But in October and early November he began his move, certain now that Japan had committed itself to the Pacific rather than Siberia. Stalin's eastern troops would be on hand to halt the Germans if they broke through. If the lines held—perhaps they could be used to turn the tables.

Stalin was greatly encouraged by Zhukov's success in bringing the Nazi drive to a halt at the end of October (but greatly alarmed in the first phase of the November German offensive). His staff began making plans for a counterblow.

Planning went forward for the attempt to break the Leningrad blockade, and on December 8, Tikhvin was recaptured. The staggering troops of the Southern Front finally turned on the overextended Germans, counterattacked and regained Rostov, gateway to the Caucasus and a possible jump-off point for recapturing the Ukraine.

By now Zhukov was convinced that classic conditions were approaching for a sudden reversal of the front. All he must do was to hang on to the Moscow Front until the Germans reached the extreme limit of offensive strength, husband his reserves, position the new armies Stalin had brought west from Siberia—then throw them at Hitler.

He could hardly wait. The plans were complete. Stalin had moved the First Shock Army, the Tenth Army and the new Twentieth Army up to positions behind the Russian Front. The First Shock Army and the new Twentieth were positioned north of Moscow, just east of the Moscow-Volga canal on the Kalinin Front commanded by General Konev. The Tenth Army was placed near Ryazan, south of Moscow and opposite Guderian's tank force. Guderian quickly detected the new Siberian divisions and began to voice concern but this aroused no apprehension in the German High Command, convinced the Russians were in their death agony.

On November 29 Zhukov, itching to launch his attack, telephoned Stalin and asked that the new forces be put under his command so the offensive could start. This was the day Rostov-on-Don fell to the revived Soviet forces in the south. Stalin said he would consult Shaposhnikov.

"Are you sure that the enemy has reached a critical point and is in no position to bring some new large force into action?" Stalin asked.

"The enemy has been bled white," Zhukov assured him.

That evening Stalin turned over the new armies to Zhukov and the Soviet commander gave GHQ an outline of his planned counter-offensive. He proposed to strike out with two strong flanking arms, north and south of Moscow, envelop and smash the main Nazi forces investing Moscow. Hopefully, Zhukov would at least be able to drive the Germans away from Moscow's doorstep.

Stalin approved Zhukov's plans December 2. Late on the night of December 4 Stalin telephoned Zhukov and asked:

"What else can we do to help the front?"

Zhukov asked for more tanks and more air support. Stalin had no tanks available but promised air support. He wanted the Soviet troops to jump off the next morning but because of heavy snow the general attack did not get going until the morning of December 6.

The great German theorist of war, Karl von Clausewitz, called the "culminating point" of battle that moment when, as a result of his losses in the depth of enemy territory, an opponent must go over to the defense.

"For the other side," Clausewitz declared, "this point is the crisis, the moment to strike."

Hitler's military leaders were well aware of Clausewitz's maxim but they did not believe the Russians possessed the strength to strike. In fact, as late as December 3 Field Marshal von Bock was still talking hopefully about the possibility—slight he had to admit—that Moscow still might be taken. The German generals ignored such evidence as they had of a Soviet buildup and when the Russian attack began they misjudged the operations, calling them local attacks. Not until December 7 did the German staff begin to realize that something more serious was underway.

Serious it was. On December 6 the whole Moscow Front burst into flame as reinforced Soviet forces, still holding no real numerical superiority over the Germans, pressed forward.

The first days of fighting were bitter. Gains by the Russians were small, particularly on the Kalinin front. But gradually the Red Army began to move.

For a few days Stalin held back the good news until he could be certain of the results. Then on December 11 an official Sovinformburo announcement was issued. The Nazi attack on Moscow had been halted. Soviet forces had gone over to the counteroffensive. They had surrounded Klin, occupied Solnechnigorsk, recaptured Istra, beaten back Guderian southeast of Tula, and liberated more than four hundred towns and villages.

The battle went on. The Germans fell back. Hitler ordered his forces onto the defense, contending that winter had halted them. But it was the Red Army that was hurling the Germans back. The drive

Far left, Soviet infantry attack. Above, the powerful katyusha rockets fire. Below, a mortar being aimed.

German troops and tanks slogging through the Russian winter of 1941–42.

went on and on. *Pravda* published the portraits of the new hero generals. Zhukov, Lelyushenko, Rokossovsky, Govorov, Boldin, Golikov, Belov and Vlasov, Commander of the Twentieth Army, the man who ultimately would go over to the Germans and give his name to an anti-Soviet force fighting under German command.

It was something to raise Russian spirits—the recapture of Klin, Kalinin, Yelets, Kaluga and Volokolamsk. Guderian had to pull back a hundred miles in ten days, the first time he had ever had to retreat. At some points the Germans were shoved back nearly two hundred miles but in the center of the Moscow Front the Germans hung on stubbornly. They dug in on the Rzhev-Gzhatsk-Vyazma triangle a little more than one hundred miles west of Moscow, there to stay for a long time to come.

The counteroffensive gradually tapered off about December 18, having gained all of its initial objectives. Zhukov was in favor of

continuing the drive but for this he needed more men and more matériel—at least four reinforcement armies. These were not forthcoming, and twenty years after World War II he was still bitter about this.

The first phase of the great war in the East was now ending. It had produced colossal losses for the Russians. The Germans stood at the gates of starving Leningrad, the city still under blockade. The Germans had occupied all of the Baltic states, all of Byelorussia and had only now been pushed back one hundred miles or so west of Moscow. They still held the western sections of Russia proper. They had occupied the great cities of Kiev, Kharkov and Odessa and the Ukraine. The Russians clung to positions in the Crimea and had just shoved the Germans back out of the Caucasus.

But the outcome was by no means certain. Hitler had beaten Stalin in the opening phases of war but now Stalin and the Russian people had risen. For the first time since Hitler had begun his march across Europe in 1933 the Nazi armies had not only been halted, they had been driven back, defeated in open fighting by an enemy whom Hitler had proclaimed a dozen times to be "finally defeated."

Now at the moment of crisis, the moment of the successful Soviet counteroffensive a wholly new—and probably decisive factor— entered the picture. On December 7 the Japanese attacked the United States at Pearl Harbor. Now the U.S.A., too, was at war. The alliance of Great Britain, the Soviet Union and the United States was about to be forged.

Whatever perils and sacrifices lay ahead Stalin and the Russians could now look forward to allied armies fighting a common enemy.

Stalin had won back his self-confidence—not necessarily an entirely desirable development. No longer was he shifty and uncertain as he had seemed to General P. A. Belov when he accompanied Zhukov to see Stalin in the Kremlin November 11. Belov hadn't seen Stalin for eight or nine years and thought he looked twenty years older. Zhukov addressed Stalin sharply in a commanding manner and Belov had the impression that Zhukov, not Stalin, was in charge. Occasionally, a look of something like bewilderment crossed Stalin's face.

Now this was changed. The British Foreign Secretary, Sir Anthony Eden, sailed from Invergordon in the north of Scotland aboard the cruiser *Kent* for Murmansk and meetings with Stalin in Moscow on December 8. He got the news of Pearl Harbor from Churchill just before sailing. Eden arrived in Moscow December 15.

He was greeted with newsreel cameramen, a guard of honor, Foreign Secretary Molotov and a full barrage of newspaper publicity. Stalin was riding high. Already he was looking forward to a victorious end of the war. The next day Eden met Stalin with the Soviet Ambassador to England, Ivan M. Maisky, acting as interpreter. Stalin presented Eden with the text of two treaties—one, an Anglo-Soviet alliance against Germany and a pledge against separate peace, the other covering postwar cooperation. Both were what Eden had expected. However, there was a "most secret protocol" which called for British recognition of Soviet annexation of Latvia, Lithuania and Estonia in 1940, of the incorporation of eastern Poland which Stalin had gotten in his deal with Hitler, Bessarabia and northern Bukovina which Stalin had taken from Romania, plus the port of Petsamo from

Finland. Poland would be compensated with East Prussia, except for Tilsit and German territory north of the Nieman which would go to Russia. Poland's western frontier would be on the River Oder. Both Finland and Romania must permit construction of Soviet bases on their territories. Germany would be partially dismembered, losing not only her eastern territories but the Rhineland and possibly Bavaria. Austria would return to her 1938 frontiers.

Eden had no particular objection to the parts about the Baltic states and eastern Poland, but the Americans were already on record against any "secret accords."

Stalin offered to support British bases in Denmark, Norway and France in return for British support of his proposals. Eden and Stalin did not reach agreement on the territorial questions but the meeting ended on a friendly note after Eden had been given a trip to Klin, the home of the composer Tchaikovsky, which had just been recaptured by the Red Army.

Stalin's demands cast a passing shadow over the emerging grand alliance, a shadow to be remembered as the war went on because his position on Russia's postwar frontiers was to change very little.

Stalin's self-confidence flowed over into the military field. He came to believe that the spectacular Moscow offensive could be duplicated along the whole front. Quite possibly he dreamed of repeating the triumph of the great Russian marshals, Kutuzov and Suvorov, whose portraits now dominated his Kremlin office, relegating those of Marx and Engels to secondary position. They were the Russian military leaders who harassed Napoleon on his retreat from Moscow through the winter snows, turning it into an agony of defeat.

Stalin summoned a meeting of his top political and military leaders to the Kremlin in the late evening of January 5. He had made up his mind. He would launch a general offensive and drive the Germans out of the Soviet Union. The plan of attack was presented by Marshal Shaposhnikov. The main blow was to be struck at the center of the front, west of Moscow. The troops northwest of Moscow, uniting with the left flank of those south of Leningrad, would press to the southwest and produce a double envelopment of the Rzhev-Vyazma-Smolensk triangle. Forces of the Baltic Fleet and the Leningrad Front would rout Army Group Nord which had invested Leningrad. The south and southwest groups would sweep the Donets basin clear of Germans, and the Caucasus forces would cross over the Kerch peninsula and drive the Germans from the Crimea.

By this time Hitler would be in rout.

Stalin observed that the Germans had been stunned by their defeat at Moscow. They were badly prepared for winter and the moment was just right to hit them.

He asked Zhukov his opinion. Zhukov strongly favored continuing the Western Front offensive but insisted it would require heavy reinforcement of men, equipment and, particularly, of tanks. He warned against overextension. The Leningrad and southwest operations would come up against very heavy German defenses and would need strong artillery preparation. Casualties were likely to be substantial. Zhukov was supported by N. A. Voznesensky, Chairman of the State Planning Commission. He didn't think Russia had the means to support widespread simultaneous offensives.

Stalin snapped: "I've talked with Timoshenko and he favors the attack. We must quickly smash the Germans so that they cannot

Above, Germans killed as they tried to flee with loot, including a samovar. Below, one German dressed for the cold and snow carrying a wounded companion. Right, a Red Army cavalryman passes a stricken German tank.

attack us when spring comes."

Police Chief Beria and Party Secretary Malenkov sprang to Stalin's side. They claimed Voznesensky was always looking for unforeseen difficulties. These could be overcome. Stalin asked if anyone else wanted to speak. No one did. "So," said Stalin, "this, it seems, ends the discussion."

Zhukov decided that Stalin didn't really want to discuss his plans but simply hoped to ginger the military a bit. Marshal Shaposhnikov confirmed this as they left the office. "It was foolish to argue," he said. "The Boss had already decided. The directives have gone out to almost all the fronts and they will launch the offensive very shortly."

"Then, why," asked Zhukov, "did Stalin ask for my opinion?"

"I just don't know, old fellow, I just don't know," Shaposhnikov said with a heavy sigh.

The orders for the general offensive reached Zhukov's headquarters the next day. It was kicked off January 10. On January 13 an offensive was opened on the Leningrad front and a drive on Kerch about the same time.

All failed. True, minor gains were made, but nothing decisive. Soviet troops had been weakened by six months or more of continual fighting. Stalin did not have reinforcements. The weather was severe. Snow was deep. The Germans organized skillful hedgehog defenses. There were rows over troop dispositions. Stalin took the First Shock Army away from Zhukov and put it into the GHQ Reserve just at the

German infantry during the
hardest fighting of the winter.
Below, Russian troops moving up.

moment when Zhukov badly needed it for his attack on Vyazma.
When he protested Stalin said: "Don't protest. Send it along. You
have plenty of troops—just count them." When Zhukov tried to argue,
Stalin hung up. Two important fighting groups, General P. A. Belov's
Cavalry Corps and three divisions of the Thirty-third Army,
commanded by Lieutenant General M. G. Yefremov, became encircled
near Vyazma. Belov fought his way out when spring came. Yefremov
didn't make it and finally shot himself rather than be captured.
Ammunition was scarce. Deliveries fell short by two-thirds in
January, and in the first ten days of February Zhukov did not get one
of the 316 carloads of munitions he had been promised. He ran out of
rockets for his katyushas and his guns were rationed to one or two
shells a day.

A series of inconclusive attacks were carried out over the Kerch
peninsula in an effort to relieve the pressure on besieged Sevastopol in
the Crimea. The Sevastopol garrison sallied forth, and Soviet military
specialists believe the operations would have been successful had not
the notorious political-police General Mekhlis been sent to the scene.
His interference impeded the Soviet attacks and not a few Soviet
commanders considered him guilty of treason.

Mekhlis even managed to incur Stalin's wrath. Stalin finally sent
him a telegram saying: "You maintain the strange position of a mere
onlooker who bears no responsibility for the affairs of the Crimean
Front. This position may be very comfortable but it is rotten to the
core. . . . If you had used assault aircraft not for auxiliary purposes
but against the enemy's tanks and infantry, the enemy would not have
broken through the Front and the tanks would not have gotten
through. One does not have to be a Hindenburg to understand this
simple fact."

Mekhlis was fired as Deputy Defense Commissar, reduced in
rank and never again sent as a GHQ representative to a fighting front.
He did, however, survive, as an official of the Interior Ministry, dying
a natural death in early 1952.

Still, Stalin did not give up. On March 20 he renewed his orders
to attack the Germans on the Western Front and in late March and

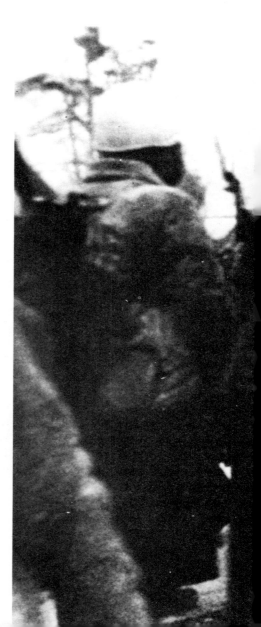

early April the Crimean Front continued to attack. But its strength was spent. On the Leningrad Front, the Second Shock Army, now commanded by the rapidly rising military hero Lieutenant General Andrei A. Vlasov, had fallen into encirclement in the boggy area north of Lake Ilmen, south of Leningrad. Despite every effort Vlasov would find it impossible to fight his way out, eventually surrendering to the Germans.

The score for the winter offensive was not a positive one. The worn-down Red Army had further been weakened. As Zhukov commented dryly: "Stalin was very attentive to advice but, regrettably, sometimes took decisions not in accordance with the situation."

Overleaf:
Dmitri Baltermants's famous photograph of Crimeans searching for kin after the German slaughter of civilians at Kerch, 1942.

Two misconceptions possessed Stalin's mind in the spring of 1942. The first was that Hitler was certain to renew the battle for Moscow. The second was that the Red Army possessed the strength to thwart Hitler's intentions with a spoiling attack.

In line with his first misconception Stalin mobilized his main strength in the area just west and south of Moscow, ready to counter any blow which Hitler might aim.

In line with the second misconception he prepared to carry out an offensive blow which would catch Hitler unaware, possibly even as successful as the Moscow winter attack.

Stalin brought his top military commanders into the Kremlin in late March to discuss the possibilities. Among those who participated were Shaposhnikov, Zhukov, Vasilevsky, Voroshilov, Timoshenko and Bagramyan.

Stalin announced there was no immediate hope for a Second Front by Western Allies and turned the meeting over to Shaposhnikov.

TRIES FOR STALINGRAD

He proposed keeping the Red Army on active defense, concentrating the main reserves around Voronezh in the Central Front where the General Staff expected the principal German efforts.

Zhukov urged that an offensive be launched to the west of Moscow while the rest of the Front stayed on the defensive.

Stalin interrupted angrily: "We cannot remain on the defensive and sit on our hands until the Germans strike first! We must launch preventive strikes on a broad front and probe the enemy intentions." He called Zhukov's proposals "half-measures."

Timoshenko spoke in favor of a strike by the Southwest and South Fronts, a preventive strike. Otherwise, he said, they could expect a repetition of what had happened at the war's beginning, that is, the Germans would seize the initiative. Timoshenko also supported Zhukov's idea for a Western Front attack. Voroshilov agreed with Timoshenko. Zhukov spoke again, advising against dispersing the Red Army's strength in separate operations. Shaposhnikov sat silent,

Nazi armor masses for attack on the Russian position in the Don River region, September 1942.

although he actually favored Zhukov's proposal.

Stalin then cast the decisive vote: Limited operations would be carried out in the Crimea to recapture Kharkov and against the Sixteenth German Army opposite the Northwest Front at Demyansk.

The Crimean operation was a failure and on July 4 the Russians had to surrender the Sevastopol fortress after a nine months siege.

Timoshenko drew up plans for a Southwest Front offensive, aimed at the recapture of Kharkov. His plan was sent to the General Staff April 10, was revised somewhat and approved April 28. Stalin again consulted Zhukov and again Zhukov expressed his doubts.

The attack on Kharkov opened May 12 with Timoshenko as commander and Nikita Khrushchev as political officer. It got off to a fine start—so excellent, in fact, that Stalin reprimanded the General Staff for having opposed the move. But trouble soon began. The first sign, in Nikita Khrushchev's recollection, was the absence of German opposition. The front seemed empty. There had to be something wrong and there was. In fact, the Germans were about to launch a powerful attack of their own in almost the same area. They waited until the Russians committed their troops, then pounced.

The usual controversy broke out as to who was responsible for the catastrophe.

Zhukov had opposed the Kharkov plan from the beginning. Now he remembered being present in "mid-May" when Stalin spoke first with Timoshenko and then with Khrushchev. Both, Zhukov insisted, assured Stalin that everything was going well. But by the evening of May 18 the situation had turned so critical that Marshal Vasilevsky, Chief of Staff in place of an ailing Marshal Shaposhnikov, urged that the offensive be halted. Stalin said no.

Khrushchev was frantic. He realized that the Soviet forces had stumbled into a trap. He begged for permission to pull back. Vasilevsky tried again, but Stalin refused. Khrushchev called Vasilevsky a second time. Vasilevsky said in his characteristic droning voice that he could do nothing. Stalin had gone to his villa at Kuntsevo.

Khrushchev knew that he had arrived at a dangerous point in his career. Stalin, he realized, had considered himself a great military strategist since the Moscow victory. When he called Stalin's dacha, Party Secretary Malenkov answered the telephone and Khrushchev asked to speak with Stalin. He heard Malenkov tell Stalin Khrushchev was on the phone, then Malenkov was back, saying Stalin wanted him to take the message.

That was a certain sign of trouble, but Khrushchev had no alternative. He submitted his plea to Malenkov who talked briefly with Stalin, then told Khrushchev nothing doing. The attack was to proceed. Disaster followed. The Germans surrounded the Fifty-seventh and Sixth armies and part of the Ninth. There were heavy casualties including several important generals. Khrushchev was called back to Moscow. He was ready for anything, including arrest. He knew that he, not Stalin, would be blamed for the failure.

Stalin met Khrushchev with a bland face.

"The Germans have announced they captured more than 200,000 of our soldiers," he said. "Are they lying?"

"No, Comrade Stalin," Khrushchev recalled replying. "They're not lying. The figure sounds about right. We had approximately that number of troops, perhaps a few more. We must suppose that some were killed and the rest taken prisoner."

Stalin dropped the subject, but a few days later he reminded Khrushchev that in World War I a Czarist general who had led his

German infantry firing from behind rocks on Jaila Mountain near Sevastopol in the Crimea.

troops into encirclement had been courtmartialed and hung.

The only thing, Khrushchev thought, which made it difficult for
Stalin to order him shot was that there were many witnesses to the
fact that he had tried to persuade him to withdraw the troops before
it was too late. Finally, Stalin told Khrushchev he could go back to his
post. Still he didn't feel safe. Sometimes Stalin dismissed men but had
them arrested once they were out of his sight.

That was not to be the case. Khrushchev got back safely to his
post and found that Timoshenko's forces had been routed. The troops
had fled all over the countryside. The only way they got some back
was by setting up field kitchens. Gradually the hungry men began to
straggle back.

As the stage was set for the great struggle of 1942, the
advantage in south Russia still turned to the Germans. They had
massed a force of about 900,000 men, 1,200 tanks, 17,000 guns and
1,640 planes against a Soviet force of 655,000 men, 740 tanks, 14,200
guns and 1,000 planes.

The German attack by Army Group B under Field Marshal von
Bock got under way in the Bryansk area June 28, and by July 2 the
Germans had penetrated fifty miles and were nearing the key center
of Voronezh. If they seized Voronezh they could turn north on Moscow
or proceed east and envelop the city from behind. To the south,
German Army Group A under Field Marshal von List was picking up
speed in a push across the Donets basin which soon unhinged the
remaining Soviet defense forces in the eastern Ukraine, opening the

flat grain country of the Don Cossack region to fast-moving German tanks.

Stalin rushed reinforcements into Voronezh and managed to stave off loss of the city but in almost no time the German panzers were deep into the great bend of the Don, whirling forward in enormous clouds of dust. With the Soviet forces broken and morale falling, Stalin issued Order No. 227, a harsh decree enforcing iron discipline against desertion, cowardice, and panicmongers. Violaters were shot out of hand. The injunction to officers and men was "not a step back."

Leading the German spearhead toward Stalingrad was General Friedrich von Paulus, commander of the German Sixth Army which at the beginning of July comprised five corps with eighteen divisions, including two armored divisions and one of motorized infantry. The Fourth German Panzer Army under Hoth was advancing toward Stalingrad, parallel to von Paulus but to the south.

Von Paulus headed into the great bend of the Don, and by the last weeks in July was closing on the Soviet bridgehead west of the Don that protected the approaches to Stalingrad.

Stalingrad, a long, narrow city located on the west bank of the Volga, sprawled for twenty-five miles north to south along the river. The approach was over an open plain but the city itself lay on flat or rising ground with a range of bluffs compressing it close to the river itself. It was a manufacturing center with a population of about

500,000 and possessed several important agricultural machinery
works, particularly a large tractor plant. Another big factory was
called the Red October Plant. Stalingrad was a center of the Volga
caviar fisheries. Before the Revolution it had been called Tsaritsyn
and was the scene of heavy fighting during the Civil War between the
Communist and White Russian forces. Stalin played a major role in
these battles, a somewhat equivocal role it would now appear. But in
his day these exploits were praised to the skies and the city was
renamed Stalingrad in his honor. When he was denounced after his
death by Nikita Khrushchev the name of the city was changed to
Volgograd.

If the Germans captured Stalingrad they would cut Russia in
two, severing the great north-south waterway of the Volga and secure
themselves a position from which they could ransack the Caucasus at
leisure, seize its oil reserves, and push into Persia with its oil and even
to India and its riches. Stalingrad would open a vista of conquest such
as had not been seen since the days of Alexander.

The seriousness of the threat could clearly be seen in the swift
advance of German forces into the Caucasus. As von Paulus and Hoth
drove toward Stalingrad, von Kleist raced for Grozny, Maikop,
Voroshilovsk, Krasnodar and Novorossisk. Budenny and Malinovsky,
with tattered remnants of divisions, retired slowly before the
Germans, taking advantage of mountain heights and narrow passes to
block or delay the Nazi advance.

Men at war. Left, Major General
A. I. Rodimtsev, center, with his
soldiers, Stalingrad, September
1942. Right, German soldiers
during a lull in the Stalingrad
street fighting.

Stalin set up a special Stalingrad Front July 12 and put it under Timoshenko and Khrushchev. They had at their disposal the Sixty-second Army, and the Sixty-third Army, the Sixty-fourth Army and the Twenty-first Army, all of them well below strength. They were given the First and Fourth Tank armies, the Volga river naval flotilla and remnants of the Twenty-eighth, Thirty-eighth and Fifty-seventh armies. The force sounded more impressive than it was. At the end of July it possessed 38 divisions, totaling about 187,000 men, 360 tanks, 337 planes and 7,900 guns. They had to cover a 330-mile front. Against them the Germans massed 250,000 men, 740 tanks, 1,200 planes and 7,500 guns.

Under Directive No. 45 of the Nazi High Command dated July 23 the German objective was to seize Stalingrad and Astrakhan on the Caspian Sea, gain a stronghold on the middle Volga and cut off the Caucasus from the rest of Russia.

If the Caspian approaches to Russia were cut, it would end the rapidly growing Allied effort to set up a major supply route into the Soviet Union via Iran.

A tough, lean, dark-haired Russian with a high forehead named Vasily Ivanovich Chuikov was serving in Chungking as Soviet military attaché when World War II broke out. There he remained until early 1942 when a diplomatic row arose over an interview he was alleged to have given, telling about the great military aid Chiang Kai-shek was receiving from the Russians. Chuikov was recalled to Moscow and in March 1942 went back into active service. He spent a little time as deputy commander of a reserve army and, after suffering minor injuries in an auto accident, was sent with his command to bolster the Stalingrad Front. He arrived with his Army, now designated the Sixty-fourth, in Stalingrad on July 16, appalled at the disorder and lack of morale. Traveling west toward the Don across the blazing steppe he encountered people, eating their last food, overcome by heat. When he asked them where they were going "they gave senseless answers; they all seemed to be looking for somebody on the other side of the Volga." He asked officers where were the German positions and where their units were located. They didn't seem to know. He was not impressed with General Gordov, commander of the Sixty-fourth Army. To Chuikov Gordov's cold eyes seemed to say, "Don't tell me about the situation. I know all about it. There's nothing I can do about it, since such is my fate."

Chuikov's name was to become synonymous with that of Stalingrad. Soon he was to take command of the Sixty-second Army and fight with it through every day and every night of the Stalingrad battle, its unbelievable perils, its unimaginable triumphs.

Chuikov's men went into action July 25 in the southeast corner of the Don bend. After two days of fierce fighting the Russians had lost all their tanks, but Chuikov's lines still held. Suddenly a panic swept through his rear elements—a rumor that Nazi tanks had broken through. There was a rush for the Don river crossing. Nazi dive-bombers spotted the crowd and wiped it out, including headquarters officers trying to restore order.

A few days later Chuikov came upon the colonel of a fresh Siberian division which had been attacked by German tanks and planes while unloading at Kotelnikovo station with losses so frightful the commander was in a state of nervous collapse.

"I am a Soviet officer," the Colonel said, "and I cannot survive the death of a large part of my division."

Tough, aggressive General Chuikov checked the German assault on Stalingrad.

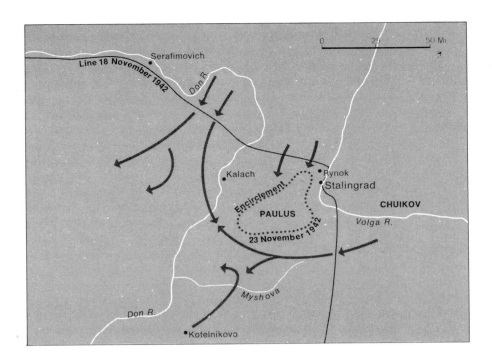

Stalin kept juggling his Stalingrad arrangements. On August 5 he split Stalingrad into two fronts, one for Stalingrad city headed by General Gordov to whom Chuikov had taken such a dislike, and a Southeast Front entrusted to the brash and bold General Yeremenko who still had Stalin's confidence despite his sorry failure to destroy Guderian on the Bryansk Front near Moscow. Nikita Khrushchev doubled as political officer for both commands and soon took as strong a distaste for Gordov as had Chuikov.

Stalin sent Vasilevsky to Stalingrad to coordinate movements for the General Staff. Zhukov also flew in and out, assessing the situation. He was chief of the Western Command, protecting Moscow, a front which turned out to be the quietest in Russia.

Despite every effort the Russians could not halt von Paulus and on August 23 the Nazi 14th Armored Corps slashed through the Soviet Don River defenses at Vertachi, cut the Stalingrad sector in two, and reached the Volga River on a five-mile front between Latoshinka and Rynok, just north of Stalingrad. The Sixty-second Army—the army which Chuikov soon was to command—was cut off and had to be transferred to the jurisdiction of the Southeast Front.

As the Nazi troops reached the Volga the full force of the Nazi 4th Air Fleet was thrown at the city, August 23 and 24. Some 600 planes participated in the attack, flying 4,000 sorties. The whole 25 miles of the long city on the Volga seemed to be in flames. Chuikov had never seen anything like it. Everything was burning. "Sorrow and death entered into thousands of Stalingrad homes," Chuikov observed. General Vasilevsky recollected that at night it reminded him of a giant's bonfire. Nazi propaganda announced that "the fortress of the Bolsheviks is at the knees of the Fuehrer."

At this moment—as always in times of disaster—Stalin sent a special commission into Stalingrad. It was there on the night of August 23—Party Secretary Malenkov, Air Force Commander A. A. Novikov, and V. A. Malyshev, later to be a Politburo member, then deputy for tank production.

Khrushchev got a telephone call from Stalin: "What's this about you starting to evacuate the city?" Khrushchev protested there wasn't a word of truth in it. They would fight to the end. After he hung up he began to wonder who had planted this lie in Stalin's mind. When he found that Stalin had called two other members of the military committee he realized it was just Stalin's way of putting fear into his subordinates.

On the night of August 23–24 telephone communications between Moscow and Stalingrad were destroyed by German bombing. Word of the Nazi breakthrough to the Volga had to be sent to Stalin by wireless. Early on the morning of the 24th, communications were restored and the first message from Stalin said Stalingrad had plenty of strength to throw the Germans back, to do so immediately and not succumb to panic.

A task force managed to drive the Germans back from the Volga shore August 24, but the Russians could not hold and the German breakthrough was more and more firmly established.

Reinforcements were steadily brought up, but the Germans increased their strength as well. Stalingrad turned into a rubble heap. Water mains were destroyed, telephone communications severed, streetcars and railroad services smashed. The city was put in a state of siege and the factories Barricade and Red October were organized to defend themselves shop-by-shop. On the 24th a German attempt on the tractor factory was turned back.

On the evening of August 25 Stalin ordered Vasilevsky to go to the north of Stalingrad where he was accumulating reserves and take charge of the forces for an intended counterblow. Vasilevsky arrived at the concentration point the morning of August 26 where he found the Twenty-fourth Army, the first arriving troops of the Sixty-sixth Army and some divisions of the not-yet completely organized First Guards Army.

Zhukov was cleaning up a small operation on the Western Front on August 27 when he got a call from Stalin's *chef de cabinet* A. N. Poskrebyshev. Poskrebyshev told Zhukov that Stalin on the previous day had named him Deputy Supreme Commander in Chief, that is, No. 2 to Stalin himself. He told Zhukov to stand by for a call from Stalin at 2:00 P.M. Zhukov gathered that Stalin was very concerned about Stalingrad.

Stalin called promptly at 2:00 P.M. He told Zhukov to come to Moscow, leaving his deputy in charge, and to think about who should take over the command. Then he hung up. Zhukov got to the Kremlin in late evening. Stalin had several members of the Politburo with him. He said that the situation in the south was bad and that the Germans might take Stalingrad. The situation in the North Caucasus was equally gloomy. He said it had been decided to name Zhukov Deputy Commander in Chief and send him to Stalingrad. Vasilevsky, Malenkov, and Malyshev were already on the scene. Malenkov would remain but Vasilevsky would return to Moscow.

They drank some tea and Stalin briefed Zhukov on the situation. Stalin had moved all available reserves except for strategic reserves held back for future operations into the Stalingrad area.

Zhukov spent a day thoroughly studying the situation, then took off from Moscow's Central Airport early in the morning of August 29. He was met by Vasilevsky at an airstrip near Kamyshin and drove immediately to Stalingrad Front Headquarters at the village of Malaya Ivanovka about fifty miles north of Stalingrad.

The most urgent task was to try to eliminate the German breakthrough to the Volga and to slow the pace of the Nazi offensive which

Two views of the same Stalingrad square showing destruction from German bombing and the battle which had taken place here.

threatened to swallow up Stalingrad. Zhukov mounted a small attack
September 3. It gained little ground. Later in the day Zhukov got a
message from Stalin that the situation in Stalingrad was worsening,
the Germans were only three miles from the city and might take it
that day or the next. He ordered an immediate all-out attack.

"No delay permissible," Stalin telegraphed. "Delay would be
criminal. Rush all aircraft to help of Stalingrad."

Zhukov telephoned Stalin and said it would be useless to attack on
the third. His troops had no ammunition.

"Do you think the enemy will wait for you to warm up?" Stalin
asked, adding that Yeremenko thought the Germans might take the
city from the north. Zhukov said he didn't agree and asked permission
to delay his attack until September 5. With some reluctance Stalin
agreed.

Zhukov's forces fought for five days attempting to liquidate the
German breakthrough but had no luck. Finally, September 10 Zhukov
reported to Stalin that he did not think the effort could succeed. The
German positions were too strong.

Stalin ordered Zhukov to come back to Moscow for a full-scale
review of the Stalingrad situation and on the evening of September 12
Zhukov joined Stalin and Vasilevsky in Stalin's Kremlin office.

Zhukov described the difficult fighting conditions, the deep
ravines, and high bluffs held by the Germans, their use of long-range
artillery fire, the lack of room for maneuver. Zhukov said that it would
require at least a full-strength army, a tank corps, three tank brigades,
an air army, and four hundred howitzers to blast the Germans out of
their foothold on the Volga.

Stalin studied the estimates while Zhukov and Vasilevsky retired
to a corner to talk. Zhukov whispered to Vasilevsky that apparently
they would have to seek another way out.

"What other way out?" Stalin suddenly asked. Zhukov had not
realized Stalin's hearing was so keen.

Stalin told them to go back to General Staff and spend a day figuring out everything that would be needed for Stalingrad and for the Caucasus as well.

The more they studied the situation the more Zhukov and Vasilevsky concluded that a "Moscow solution" would be best. That is, hold Stalingrad with minimum forces, wear the Germans down. Meanwhile collect new forces from strategic reserves which would be ready in October (including more units from Siberia) and strike a single counterblow into which all the Russian resources would be poured, rather than feeding them in bit by bit.

They could not prepare the estimates in one day but they did sketch the tentative outlines—main blows at the weak German wings, particularly the flank covered by Romanian troops, an effort to encircle the main German forces.

The Russians would not be ready before mid-November. Could the Germans beat them at Stalingrad or the Caucasus in the meantime? This was the key calculation. Zhukov and Vasilevsky decided the Germans could not. They were already bleeding badly at Stalingrad. The armored corps was being worn down. The city of Stalingrad would halt them. The fighting in the streets. The struggle over each block of rubble. The savage combat in the factory buildings, floor by floor and even room by room. By November the Russians would have large motorized formations available. Quantities of T-34 tanks. The Germans were at a disadvantage. They had a few operational reserves.

On the evening of September 13 Stalin saw the commanders at 10:00 P.M. He was not in good temper. "Tens and hundreds of thousands of Soviet people are giving their lives in the fight against fascism and Churchill is haggling over twenty Hurricanes. And the Hurricanes aren't that good anyway," he snapped.

Three scenes illustrating the savage house-to-house combat in Stalingrad.

The generals laid out their plans. Stalin was cautious. He questioned Zhukov closely as to whether the forces would be sufficient. Zhukov assured him they would. As they talked a call came in from General Yeremenko. The Germans were massing armor closer to Stalingrad. Stalin ordered Zhukov immediately to fly back to Stalingrad. In the meantime they would think about the plan. Vasilevsky would fly down to the Southeast Front in a day or two.

That was the way the autumn went—planning in Moscow and the bitterest, most savage, most heroic fighting of the war in the buildings and streets of Stalingrad. General Chuikov took over the Sixty-second Army at 10:00 a.m. September 12. From that time on his life was constricted to a sliver of rubbled land along the Volga River, comprising the northern areas of Stalingrad, a sliver that shrank with each passing week but which never fell out of Chuikov's hands. Again and again and again he appealed for reserves, for replacements for his troops. For the most part he had to hang on with what he had. And he did, making the name of Chuikov, the Sixty-second Army and Stalingrad a legend in the world's record of heroism.

Week by week Zhukov and Vasilevsky commuted between the Stalingrad Front and Moscow. Zhukov flew in any kind of weather. Once he made a forced landing in a small field when his plane iced over completely. Another time as his pilot nosed the plane down through total fog toward what he thought was Moscow's Central Airport, a smoking chimney appeared off the plane's left wing. The pilot flipped up his plane and a moment later came down safely at the airfield. "We almost went up in smoke," Zhukov told the pilot.

The Germans tore into Stalingrad. Chuikov had his command post atop Mamaya Heights, but the German shelling was so fierce he moved it down into a well-furnished dugout that may have been used by Stalin in the Civil War in 1918. But this headquarters suffered a direct hit. Chuikov moved again to a heavily reinforced dugout near the Volga, between the two railroad stations. The fighting for Mamaya Hill went on and on. The Central Railroad Station changed hands three times. Supplies had to come in from the east bank of the Volga, a mile wide at Stalingrad. The crossing was shelled by Nazi artillery twenty-four hours a day. Stalingrad had one strong support —artillery on the east bank of the Volga, heavy guns, katyushas. These weapons kept the Germans under constant fire.

By late September the Germans had most of central Stalingrad and began to penetrate the industrial areas. Oil tanks were set afire and the heavy smoke almost choked Chuikov and his staff in their command post. In October Chuikov had moved his command post to a site near the Barricade Plant when German bombs touched off another oil storage tank. Flaming oil poured around the dugout. Somehow Chuikov and his men managed to survive. But losses were frightful and soon Chuikov had to move his command post again because German artillery had zeroed in on it and he lost a score of men.

Chuikov became more and more grim, especially toward rear element commanders. In mid-October the Germans launched a "final offensive" to break Chuikov's lines. Not more than two miles separated his trenches from the Volga. Chuikov's front lines were surrounded. The Stalingrad Tractor Plant was encircled. The bodies of 3,000 Germans were heaped up around the walls of the Tractor Plant and that night Chuikov evacuated 3,000 wounded across the Volga. Finally,

the Germans captured the Tractor Plant and cut Chuikov's sector in two. They got within 300 yards of his headquarters. In two days two units lost 75 percent of their men. Now the Germans began to close in on the Barricade and Red October factories, driving to within 400 yards of the Volga. A final German offensive was mounted on November 11. The Germans advanced over a three-mile front but made little headway.

It was beginning to become apparent that victory at Stalingrad might well be beyond the grasp of the German command.

On November 7 *Pravda* published an "Oath of the Defenders of Stalingrad" in which Chuikov's troops and all the others pledged to "dear Josif Vissarionovich" Stalin:

"We swear we shall not disgrace the glory of Russian arms and shall fight to the end. Under your leadership our fathers won the Battle of Tsaritsyn. Under your leadership we shall win the great Battle of Stalingrad."

The hour of the turn, the crisis of which Clausewitz had spoken, was again approaching. This time at Stalingrad.

Combat in the Tractor Plant in Stalingrad in January 1943.

STALIN AND CHURCHILL

Stalin had no love for Winston Churchill. In general he was suspicious of the British. He regarded Churchill, correctly, as one of the chief authors of the implacably anti-Soviet policy of the British Government at the time of the Bolshevik Revolution. He had never forgotten the British military intervention in 1918–1920 which had almost beaten the fledgling Soviet state to its knees, nor the anti-Soviet policy of later British governments. He had not trusted Neville Chamberlain in diplomatic dealings on the eve of World War II and regarded Chamberlain's policy of appeasement as chiefly responsible for Hitler's consolidation of power. (He never assumed responsibility for his own policies toward Germany which played a major role in Hitler's rise to power.) His justification of the Nazi-Soviet pact of August 1939 which freed Hitler to start World War II was that the British with French help were trying to turn Hitler against Russia.

After World War II started he rejected with intense suspicion every British effort to establish a closer relationship. His hostility was heightened when the British came close to sending volunteers to help Finland in the winter war with Russia.

This hostility had played a major role in Stalin's refusal to accept evidence that Hitler was preparing to attack in the spring of 1941, particularly evidence that emanated from London. Now in 1942 he was still suspicious of the British and of Churchill in particular.

It was true that Churchill had pledged all aid to Russia, but it was never as much as Stalin needed and he had a feeling what Churchill really wanted was to see Russia bled white so that even if Germany was defeated the Soviet Union could not play a major role in postwar Europe. Stalin was quicker than Roosevelt to see that many of Churchill's strategies were designed to advance British national policy as much as to aid in winning the war.

What Stalin wanted more than anything by the spring of 1942 was an Allied Second Front in Europe. He felt that if the West could draw away from the Eastern Front forty or fifty German divisions, the Red Army would be able to smash Hitler and win the war by the end of the year.

Stalin's estimate was overoptimistic. It did not take into account the terrible damage inflicted on the United States and Britain by the Japanese, the loss of American naval strength at Pearl Harbor, the loss of the Philippines, Hong Kong, Singapore, the sinking of the great British battleships, the *Repulse* and the *Prince of Wales*, the dangerous plunge of the Japanese into Indochina and Southeast Asia and, most frightening to the British, the toll being taken by Nazi U-boats of vital food and war matériel in the Battle of the Atlantic.

Roosevelt was eager to meet with Stalin and plan common strategy, but Stalin's preoccupation with day-to-day conduct of the war made this difficult. Finally Stalin sent Molotov to London and Washington for talks with Churchill and Roosevelt. Already major differences had appeared between Washington and London. Roosevelt wanted a Second Front in Europe in 1942. Churchill concealed his opposition under a curtain of eloquence but did not want a Second Front before 1943. He knew that a Second Front in 1942 meant British troops. He did not think England could stand the physical losses and he knew he could not survive the political losses.

Winston Churchill meets with Josef Stalin in the Kremlin.

Molotov's trip had its lighter side. He brought a pistol along and slept with it under his pillow in the White House where he was F.D.R.'s guest. Two Secret Service men were assigned to see that Molotov, the most conventional, starched-collar kind of man, had an appropriate "night out on the town." On the business side Molotov returned to Moscow with what Stalin thought was a commitment for a 1942 Second Front. But even before Molotov got back to the Kremlin, Churchill was hard at work overturning the decision, and getting Roosevelt to agree to a North African invasion instead.

From the moment of the Nazi attack on the Soviet Union the British had been diverting guns, ammunition, planes, and tanks from shipments from the United States, sending them to Arctic Murmansk over a perilous, cold and stormy northern route from Scapa Flow off Scotland, or east of Iceland around the northern tip of Norway and into Murmansk. At first the ships had gotten through without great difficulty, but with spring and the rapidly lengthening Arctic daylight (by June the sun never set on the convoy route) the Germans were inflicting serious losses on shipments to Russia.

The British Admiralty wanted to halt convoys until fall when short days and foggy weather would give better protection. But the Russian need was too great and Roosevelt would not hear of it.

In June 1942 preparations were underway to send a major convoy, code-named PQ 17, to Murmansk. The Germans knew of the convoy and had their battleship *Tirpitz* stationed at Trondheim. They had the pocket battleships *Scheer, Lutzow* and *Hipper*, plus eleven destroyers and three large torpedo boats in northern Norway, a number of them based in Narvik, just off the convoy route. The Germans had concentrated a large group of bombers and reconnaissance planes in northern Norway, as well as a wolfpack of U-boats. When the convoy reached the vicinity of Jan Mayen island north of Norway, the Germans planned to attack with bombers. The naval force would close in and drive for the kill once the convoy had reached a position east of Jan Mayen. Submarines would complete the cleanup off Bear Island.

The British had obtained the German battle plan from interception and decoding of the German naval traffic by their Ultra technique.

PQ 17, comprising 34 British, American and Russian freighters, three rescue ships, carrying 157,000 tons of tanks, planes and war supplies sailed from an assembly point east of Iceland June 27, 1942. It had a close escort of six destroyers, four corvettes, three minesweepers, four trawlers, two antiaircraft ships and two submarines. Four cruisers, two of them American, provided closeby cover. The battleships *Duke of York, Washington* (American), and *Victorious* provided distant cover. Thirteen submarines, including four Russian, were positioned off North Cape.

Simultaneous with the sailing of PQ 17, the empty returning convoy QP 13 sailed from Murmansk. Both trips were uneventful until July 2 when the two convoys were passing each other midway between Jan Mayen and Bear Island. Here the Germans sighted them and *Tirpitz, Hipper* and the German destroyers left Trondheim. *Lutzow* and *Scheer* left Narvik. Three of the four German destroyers accompanying *Tirpitz* hit an uncharted rock and were out of action. *Lutzow* also ran aground.

PQ 17 plowed ahead. It suffered no losses July 3. On July 4 it lost

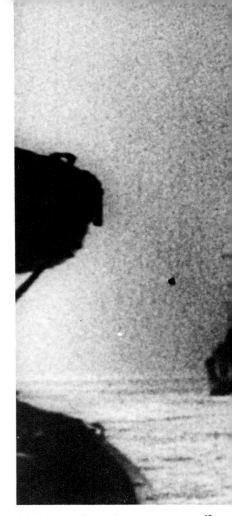

A British-American convoy sailing north of Norway to arctic Murmansk with military supplies for the Russians. Below, a ship sunk by Germans.

three ships sunk by air attack. A fourth was damaged.

That evening at 9:00 P.M. the convoy's cruiser escort was suddenly ordered to withdraw to the west at high speed. Half an hour later the convoy was ordered to disperse and proceed singly to Murmansk.

The orders, caused by a misinterpretation of decoded information at the Admiralty, doomed the convoy. The instruction was based on the belief that *Tirpitz* was about to attack the convoy. In fact, *Tirpitz* did not reach the open sea until 3:00 P.M. the afternoon of the 5th. In the meantime the dispersed merchant ships, deprived of protecting escort, were sunk at random by Nazi planes and submarines. Twenty-three freighters and one rescue ship were sunk; eleven freighters and two rescue ships struggled into Murmansk.

There was endless controversy over PQ 17. Arguments pro and con still go on among British naval specialists. Many blame Admiral Sir Dudley Pound, who authorized the order to disperse the convoy. They contend he was opposed to the convoys in principle and specifically to the sailing of PQ 17, and that his mind had been made up before the convoy was dispatched.

The consequences were catastrophic. The sending of convoys was immediately halted by Churchill. On July 18 he announced his action in a long cable to Stalin in which he said that the western Allies were "building up for a really strong Second Front in 1943." This was a double-barreled blow to Stalin at the moment when the peril of the Nazi drive on Stalingrad was becoming clear. Not only was Churchill calling off the convoys and the shipments Stalin badly

A British Hurricane coming in to join a camouflaged mate on snow in Russia.

needed; he was, in Stalin's opinion, also welching on the pledge to
open the Second Front in 1942.

Stalin replied that he could "not tolerate the Second Front in
Europe being postponed until 1943."

As for discontinuance of the convoys he said: "The Soviet Union
is suffering far greater losses and I never imagined that the British
Government would deny us delivery of war matériel precisely now
when the Soviet Union is badly in need of them."

Winston Churchill flew into Moscow August 12, 1942, for his
first "visit to this sullen, sinister Bolshevik State I had once tried so
hard to strangle at its birth." He was prepared to talk man-to-man
with Stalin but he compared his task to "carrying a large lump of ice
to the North Pole."

The two men had it out. Stalin told Churchill "you can't win wars
if you aren't willing to take risks" and "you must not be so afraid of
the Germans." Stalin, Churchill recalled, said "a great many
disagreeable things," including a charge that the British had broken
their word. On one occasion Churchill replied: "I pardon that remark
only on account of the bravery of the Russian troops."

Averell Harriman who accompanied Churchill concluded that
the Russians were really desperate: "Stalin's roughness was an
expression of their need for help. It was his way of trying to put all
the heat he possibly could on Churchill."

Stalin told Churchill of a conversation he once had with Lady
Astor in which she blamed Churchill for the intervention against the
Bolsheviks in 1918. Churchill admitted there was truth in Lady
Astor's statement.

"I was not friendly to you after the last war," Churchill told
Stalin. "Have you forgiven me?" Stalin responded: "All that is in the
past. It is not for me to forgive. It is for God to forgive."

Before Churchill left Moscow he had a seven-hour evening with
Stalin, just the two of them, in a conversation that rambled over the
horizon. They talked of stationing British air squadrons in the
Caucasus to protect the Baku oilfields, of a great counteroffensive the
Russians would soon launch against the Germans to cut them off in
both Stalingrad and the Caucasus, of the possibility of Roosevelt,
Churchill and Stalin meeting in Iceland in November 1942, of a
British-Russian operation to occupy the Finnish port of Petsamo, of
the British being "sea animals" and the Russians "land animals."
Before they broke up early in the morning after many toasts in vodka,
Stalin told Churchill that great as was the strain of war on Russia it
was not as bad as the crisis over collectivizing Soviet agriculture. "It
was fearful," said Stalin. "Four years it lasted."

Churchill and Stalin were never to be friends; each was too
strong in the defense of the special interests of his own country. But
the long, frank, open and acrimonious discussions laid a basis for
mutual respect which would carry the two old opponents through the
remainder of the war.

Harriman's trip with Churchill had another practical consequence.
Harriman was a railroad man. His father had been the
builder of the Union Pacific Railroad. Harriman stopped off in Iran
going in and out of Russia. The supply route manned by Russians and
British was trying—but not always succeeding—to deliver about
3,500 tons daily of matériel to the Russians via the Persian railroad.
Harriman concluded the total could easily be upped to 6,000 tons a

day. By May 1943 the total topped 10,000 tons a day and it continued to rise until the war's end. Long since the dangerous, difficult Arctic route had been abandoned, the Persian Gulf rail-and-truck route provided the Russians with tens of thousands of trucks, jeeps, tanks, railroad material, steel and food supplies.

Allied aid to Russia in 1942 totaled about 1,700,000 tons of which 1.2 million tons was American. In 1943 the Americans shipped 4.1 million tons, including 2,000,000 tons of food. Between June 22, 1941, and April 30, 1944, the United States provided the Soviet Union with 6,430 planes, 3,734 tanks, 112 naval vessels, 200,000 trucks and motor vehicles, 3,000 antiaircraft guns, 476,000 tons of high octane aviation gasoline, 100,000 tons of aluminum, 184,000 tons of copper, 42,000 tons of zinc, 1,200,000 tons of steel, 20,000 machine tools, 245,000 field telephones, 5,500,000 pairs of army boots. The British shipped 5,800 planes, 33,000 tons of copper, 4,292 tanks, 103,100 tons of rubber and 6,000 machine tools. By the end of the war the United States had shipped more than 15,000,000 tons of matériel including 427,000 trucks, 13,000 combat vehicles, 2,670,000 tons of gasoline and oil, 4,478,000 tons of food and an enormous amount of railroad equipment.

Soviet figures indicate the Russians produced about 100,000 tanks, 120,000 planes, 360,000 guns, 1,200,000 machine guns and 9,000,000 rifles during the war.

If the Soviet figures are not exaggerated the United States and Britain provided Russian with about 15 percent of its heavy equipment; that is, tanks and planes.

At left, Russians building road near Murmansk. Below, Murmansk after German destruction.

VICTORY AT STALINGRAD

Russian artillery at Stalingrad firing in front of remains of factory.

In the simple code being employed by the Kremlin Vasilyev was
Stalin; Konstantinov was Marshal Zhukov; Fedorov was General
Vatutin; Ivanov was General Yeremenko. The telegram from Stalin to
Zhukov authorized him to fix the date of the start of the Stalingrad
counteroffensive, now nearing jumpoff point.

Zhukov and Marshal Vasilevsky had fine-tuned the plans. They
had assembled the greatest force the Russians had yet gathered for a
single operation—more than 1,000,000 men, possibly a quarter of the
total roster of the Red Army; a quarter of its air strength; 60 percent
of its armored and mechanized divisions. No longer was the Red
Army fighting against desperate odds. It was not alone. On November
8 the Western Allies landed in North Africa. It was not the full-scale
Second Front Stalin wanted. But it was better than nothing.

As of November 1 the Germans had a total of probably 6,100,000
troops on the Eastern Front, 266 divisions, 70,000 guns, 6,600 tanks
and 3,500 planes. The Russians had 6.1 million men, 72.5 thousand
guns, 6,000 tanks and 3,000 planes. The Soviet Supreme Command
now possessed a strategic reserve of 25 divisions, 13 armored corps
and seven independent brigades.

In preparation for the Stalingrad attack the Russians moved into
place 11 armies, a number of independent armored, cavalry and
mechanized corps, 13,500 tons, 900 tanks and nearly 1,500 combat
planes.

The Germans did not detect this movement.

The Russians employed 27,000 trucks in moving up their forces.
The railroads behind Stalingrad on the east side of the river brought
up 1,300 carloads of matériel a day. From November 1 to November
19 Volga ferries carried 160,000 troops, 10,000 horses, 430 tanks, 600
guns, 14,000 trucks and 7,000 tons of ammunition across to the west
bank.

The Germans did not detect this movement.

From the last weeks of October through the first two weeks of
November Zhukov and Vasilevsky were in constant movement from
Moscow to Stalingrad and back. They inspected personally every site
of the proposed attack; they consulted with each of the commanders;
they examined every major unit; they solicited every possible
suggestion from the Red Army Commanders. But they kept the
tightest security. Not a single operational paper changed hands
between Moscow and the Front. No papers were carried on planes.

Only at the very final moment were the commanders briefed on what was about to happen. There was not one breach of security.

Zhukov and Vasilevsky (Comrade Donskov in the primitive GHQ code) fixed zero hour at November 19 for their forces north and northwest of Stalingrad. The rest would join November 20. They did not wish to precipitate a quick withdrawal by von Paulus. First the armies from the northwest would hammer down, closing one jaw of the pincers. Then the troops south of Stalingrad would dash forward and seal the ring.

It was, in a sense, a reprise of the successful Moscow operation. The long wait until the enemy wore out his strength and bogged down. The painful, dangerous fighting to hold off the Nazi advance while enormous strike forces were collected. The sudden blow just as the enemy's last offensive vigor was spent and it was too late for him to withdraw from his dangerous overextension. A classic from Clausewitz' textbook.

All was ready. A scant forty-eight hours to jumpoff remained when Zhukov and Vasilevsky were urgently summoned back to Moscow. They were escorted into a meeting of the State Defense Council presided over by Stalin and confronted with a letter sent to Stalin by General V. T. Volsky, Commander of the 4th Mechanized Corps. Volsky's corps was to be the southern arm of the pincers designed to trap the Germans at Stalingrad. Volsky's letter warned Stalin, "as an honest Communist," that the Stalingrad operation was doomed to disaster for lack of manpower and matériel. Zhukov and Vasilevsky were compelled to go over their arguments again and justify their plans and dispositions. Stalin then telephoned Volsky in the presence of the two generals and the Defense Council. Volsky withdrew his objections and agreed to carry out his orders.

The rationale for this strange confrontation never was to become clear, although some suspected Stalin wanted to put on record a charge which could be leveled against Zhukov and Vasilevsky if the Stalingrad operation failed.

Vasilevsky immediately flew back to the front. Zhukov stayed on in Moscow to coordinate the operation and to engage on planning further operations which depended on success at Stalingrad.

In the German trenches and dugouts before Stalingrad there was apprehension. For days and weeks the troops had been going with little sleep. They were living on alcohol and drugs. Neither side took prisoners any more. It had been that way for a long time. All they had to look forward to was frostbite, wounds or death. The day of November 18 was cold and overcast and worrisome. There was too *little* gunfire. Nothing but occasional spitting machine guns, the intermittent crash of a shell. The night was quiet, cold and foggy.

At 7:32 A.M. the guns of the Southwest Front, facing the Third Romanian Army, opened up on enemy positions near Serafimovich on the Don, northwest of Stalingrad. Soon the infantry and tanks of the Soviet Fifth Armored and Twenty-first armies swung into action, looming out of the frost and mist. They drove through the 3rd and 4th Corps of the Romanians. The guns hammered steadily. The crescendo rose as more and more weapons took part. The katyushas screamed overhead without let. Before daylight on the 20th the Russians had pushed more than twenty miles south of the Don and everything in front of them was in pell-mell retreat.

German soldiers carry mail and provisions through a trench at night. At right, Germans at a Stalingrad barricade in autumn 1942.

Dead German soldiers and disabled tank after an engagement. Bottom, mounted guards of the 1st Corps commanded by General Belov on attack.

The Germans brought up heavy reinforcements of armor but before they could go into action the principal Soviet tank force had wheeled south for Kalach, directly behind and west of von Paulus. It was here that the ring was to be closed.

Now the southern Soviet front erupted, smashed through the Sixth Romanian Army, despite losses suffered from their own artillery, and wheeled madly for Kalach, racing the German Fourth Panzer Army to the junction.

On November 23, just four days after the attack was launched, scouts of General Kravchenko's Soviet 4th Tank Corps saw white-clad tankmen coming toward them across the steppe. It was 4:00 P.M. The men were a patrol from General Volsky's 4th Mechanized Corps. The linkup had been made. Twenty German divisions, an antiaircraft division, two mortar regiments, two Romanian divisions and a Croat regiment were encircled.

Stalin was in no hurry to bring the good news to the country. The communiqués of November 19, 20, 21, made no mention of Stalingrad. But late in the evening of November 22 the first bulletin was made public. The Russians had captured Kalach, cut Paulus' supply lines and inflicted 30,000 casualties on the Germans.

The battle, of course, was far from over. As soon as the scope of the Russian offensive became clear to the Germans, von Paulus was ordered by Army Group B to break off his engagement in Stalingrad and wheel his panzers around to face the Russians at his rear. Actually Army Group B was getting von Paulus prepared to withdraw before it was too late. However, Hitler telephoned from Berchtesgaden to keep the Sixth Army in place.

When the Russians captured Kalach and completed their first ring of encirclement November 23, von Paulus sent Hitler a message asking permission to act on his judgment, noting that only by concentrating his forces and withdrawing to the southwest could the Sixth Army survive. At this point his force was in excellent shape and only one corps had been attacked by the Russians.

The chances that Hitler would have responded positively to von Paulus were slight. His tendency (like that of Stalin) was to hold on

German infantrymen trudge through snow at Stalingrad.

until it was too late to withdraw. This bias was strongly confirmed when Air Marshal Hermann Goering on the morning of November 24 promised he could keep von Paulus supplied by air. Hitler acted on this advice, declared Stalingrad a "fortress" and ordered von Paulus to stand fast.

At the moment of this order von Paulus had within the circle about 284,000 men, 1,800 guns, 10,000 trucks, 8,000 horses. At minimum levels he needed 750 tons of supplies a day. The Luftwaffe had a total of 750 Junker-52 transports, but they were scattered all over Europe and Africa. Von Paulus had seven airfields, six of them airstrips and only one usable at night. As it turned out Goering delivered an average of 90 tons a day. The best single day was December 19 when 290 tons were delivered.

Stalin was eager to liquidate the encircled Nazi forces as rapidly as possible. The task was entrusted to General Rokossovsky. While he closed in on von Paulus, Soviet forces on the outer edge were to strike southwest toward Rostov-on-Don with the aim of trapping the German armies still lodged deep in the Caucasus.

This operation did not work out according to plan. The Germans realized that extraordinary measures would have to be taken to save von Paulus and his Sixth Army. The task of driving a liberating wedge through the Soviet encirclement was entrusted to General Fritz von Manstein who put together a strong armored column headed by General Hoth and part of his Fourth Panzer Army. The column drove out December 12 from the area of Kotelnikovo, 110 miles southwest of Stalingrad. It made excellent progress and by December 18 von Paulus could hear the artillery exchanges between von Manstein and the Russians. Hoth broadcast a message to the Sixth Army: "Hold on. We are coming." But it was not to be. Rokossovsky's Second Guards Army rushed to the River Myshkova and Soviet reinforcements poured in. The Nazi rescue column was halted.

Manstein still saw a possibility of saving von Paulus if von Paulus massed his Sixth Army and broke out in the direction of Hoth's armor. But von Paulus had endless objections. He needed time to prepare. He didn't have enough fuel. His chief of staff, General Schmidt, a Nazi, insisted: "It is quite impossible to break out just now. This would be an acknowledgement of disaster. The Sixth Army will still be in position at Easter."

On Christmas eve 1942 General Hoth ordered his forces to withdraw from the Myshkova River. They pulled back under hot pursuit by Soviet forces. Hoth was needed to repel a new Soviet attack which had broken through from Voronezh into the eastern Ukraine. Other Soviet units pressed south to Rostov to join forces with Soviet troops from the Caucasus. Rostov was ultimately retaken and the Germans ordered a complete pullout from the Caucasus. The dreams of Baku oil, the Persian Gulf and India disappeared rapidly.

All that remained was the disposal of von Paulus. There was no hope for him now. Rokossovsky finally turned to the task. He had 280,000 men, 39 divisions, to carry out the job. There were not quite 200,000 Germans remaining in the doomed "fortress." The Russians called on von Paulus to surrender January 8. He refused. The final attack began on January 10. It was opened by a barrage laid down by 7,000 guns. German resistance was most bitter against General Chuikov and his embattled Sixty-second Army, now blasting its way out of the jungle of dugouts, fractured buildings and rubble in which

it had lived and fought and died for six endless months.

On January 17 the Russians again broadcast an offer to von Paulus to surrender. He had no authority to do this. By January 22 the Germans had retired into Stalingrad city and by the 24th the Russians were closing for the kill. Hitler named von Paulus a Field Marshal to dramatize his role. The last small Nazi planes flew off von Paulus' last airstrip. On January 26 the Russians broke through across Mamaya Hill to Chuikov's still-isolated Sixty-second Army. On January 31 von Paulus had moved his GHQ to the basement of the Univermag Department Store, a concrete-reinforced building largely shattered by gunfire, in the heart of Stalingrad.

Lieutenant Fyodor Yelchenko, a young artillery officer, was bombarding the Univermag that day with mortar fire from the opposite side of the broad square. An officer popped out the side door of the Univermag and waved at Yelchenko, yelling: "Our big chief wants to talk to your big chief."

Yelchenko said his "big chief" was too busy fighting and the officer would have to deal with him. He took two armed men from his unit and went into the basement of the department store. It was jammed with hundreds of men, dirty and hungry. The stench was overpowering. They were escorted to Major General Raske and Lieutenant General Schmidt, Paulus' chief of staff, who said they wanted to negotiate a surrender. There was talk back and forth and finally the young Red Army man was taken in to see von Paulus. He lay on an iron bed wearing his uniform, unshaven.

"Well," said Yelchenko, "that finishes it."

The Germans asked permission to have von Paulus taken away by car so that he would not be killed. Yelchenko agreed. A car was found and von Paulus was driven over to General Rokossovsky.

Rokossovsky was with Artillery Marshal N. N. Voronov when von Paulus was brought in with an interpreter. The HQ building was lighted by electricity and the two general officers were sitting at a small table. Von Paulus was ushered in. Rokossovsky described him as

German Field Marshal von Paulus being taken by the Soviets. Below, Paulus being interrogated by General Rokossovsky and Marshal Voronov. Left, German prisoners being herded through Stalingrad.

Mounds of German dead after the Battle of Stalingrad. Below, two German prisoners.

tall, thin, well knit, wearing an officer's field uniform. He was under great tension and very upset. Rokossovsky invited the German commander to sit down, offered him a cigarette and a glass of hot tea. Von Paulus was running a high temperature. His face kept twitching and his hands shook. The Stalingrad epoch was over.

Something like 300,000 Germans were taken prisoner at Stalingrad. Zhukov estimated total German losses in the Volga-Don-Stalingrad area at 1,500,000 men, 3,500 tanks, 12,000 guns and 3,000 aircraft. Actual losses were probably about half this number but never had Hitler and his Wehrmacht suffered like this. Nikita Khrushchev walked over the battlefield. Thousands of corpses lay on the open steppe, thousands more in the city streets and buildings. Khrushchev gathered army forces and prisoners to gather up the frozen corpses. They were stacked like cordwood on alternate layers of railroad ties, then set afire.

"I went once to watch," Khrushchev recalled, "but I didn't go a

second time. Napoleon or someone once said that burning enemy
corpses smell good. Well, speaking for myself I don't agree. It was a
very unpleasant smell and altogether a very unpleasant scene."

Khrushchev saw German corpses that had been stripped half
naked, their boots and trousers missing. It was not, he added, the
wolves who had gotten to them. At other points he found great heaps
of German soldiers, all of them shot. He asked General Volsky about
these neat heaps of bodies: "Were these men executed?" Volsky
insisted they were killed in battle. Khrushchev did not accept that. He
thought the Germans had been shot down by advancing Russians who
ignored their effort to surrender.

Stalingrad shook the world. All of Russia knew after Stalingrad
that Germany would lose the war. So did the Western Allies, gradually
mustering strength to cope with war on a dozen fronts, the Atlantic,
the Pacific, Asia, the continent of Europe. And so from now on
did more and more Germans. Now Stalin had the advantage of Hitler.
He would never let him go.

Stalingrad, the Hero City of Russia, February 2, 1943.

THE GREATEST

Shell exploding in front of German tank at Kursk, the largest tank battle ever fought.

BATTLE OF THE WAR

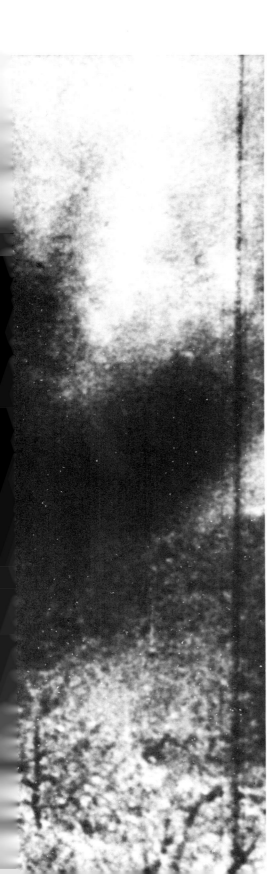

In the grim early months of the war and even after the Russian success in the December snows at Moscow, General Staff officers had noticed that Stalin never put his name to military orders and directives. Either they were signed by the Chief of Staff Marshal Shaposhnikov, or they were issued in the name of the "State Defense Committee."

With the Moscow victory generals like Zhukov and Konev got page one publicity, but Stalin still kept a low profile. Stalingrad changed that. Now the decrees were signed with Stalin's name. Now *Pravda* began to speak for the first time of the military genius of the Soviet leader. New titles and new ranks appeared. General Vasilevsky stepped out of his plane one day, on returning to Moscow, and found himself surrounded by men wearing broad new shoulderboards sparkling with golden emblems of rank. It took him a moment to realize he was in the company of his old associates, now wearing new uniforms which remarkably resembled those of the Czar's old armies. A table of ranks had long since replaced the simple Red Army designations of Commander and Commissar. Already Stalin was fitting himself for the supreme title of Generalissimus. He appeared in military uniform instead of the revolutionary blouse he had affected since 1917. The chests of the generals were beginning to bulge under the weight of new orders and medals. After Stalingrad Zhukov was awarded the first medal of the new Order of Suvorov, First Class. Vasilevsky, Voronov, Vatutin, Yeremenko and Rokossovsky got theirs soon thereafter.

It was a heady time and Stalin was eager to do everything at once. An operation was mounted in January 1943 to deblockade Leningrad. On January 18 the Leningrad and Volkhov fronts linked hands, but the Leningrad blockade was yet not completely broken. The Germans stood firm on the iron ring of the suburbs west and northwest of the city but a narrow corridor was blasted out which enabled limited rail service to be restored. By now Leningrad's population had fallen below 500,000. The rest had died or been evacuated. With trains running again the city could begin the long preparation for finally breaking the clamp of the Nazi armies and restoring normal life to Russia's second city.

Offensives were mounted on the Western Front where the Germans still held the Vyazma triangle. They had no notable success. But a Soviet attack westward from Voronezh began to unhinge the Nazi position in the Ukraine. The Russians recaptured Kharkov and pushed toward Dnepropetrovsk and Zaporozhe on the Dnieper. Hitler, conferring with his frantic commanders at Zaporozhe, came under Russian fire a few hundred yards at Zaporozhe airport.

But Nazi panzer units, notably Hoth's 48th and 57th Armored Corps, saved the day for the Germans. The units had been equipped with the heavy new German Tiger tank, a rival of the 60-ton Voroshilov. With remarkable rapidity the Germans turned the tables.

A street in Kharkov, destroyed by Germans in retreat.

They recaptured Kharkov March 13 and the immediate Russian threat melted away.

Once again Stalin had paid the price of overconfidence. It was only too apparent that the Germans remained a dangerous and deadly foe who might still muster strength for a devasting summer offensive.

The long Russian front sank into comparative quiet after the Nazi recapture of Kharkov. The Russian defense lines held and the German pressure eased off. It was a moment when commanders on both sides could step back, look at the situation and plan for the future.

The first thing about the Eastern Front in the spring of 1943 which caught the eye was the Kursk salient. This was a prominent bulge in the Russian lines just north of Kharkov and Belgorod. Here the Front swung sharply to the west, protruding 150 miles into German-held territory. The bulge was 175 miles wide, curving sharply back to the east near a small town called Dmitrovsk-Orlovsky, southwest of Orel, which was still in Nazi hands. There the Front turned sharply east again for a distance of nearly 150 miles before resuming a gentle curve to the north.

The big manufacturing city of Kursk stood squarely in the center of this bulge, which stuck out like a fat thumb into Hitler-occupied Russia.

For military men a salient of this proportion represents an irresistible temptation. For Hitler the temptation was to try to hack it off from both sides, north and south. For Stalin the temptation was to thrust outward at both ends of the salient and try to square off the Front.

By this time Zhukov was acting as Stalin's deputy for military affairs and as he and Stalin and the other top commanders looked at the map they saw Kursk precisely in the terms stated above. Zhukov did not believe Hitler had the strength to mount a major offensive directed at the deep Volga or the Caucasus. But he was sure Hitler would attempt to regain his prestige with a major attack. The obvious spot was Kursk.

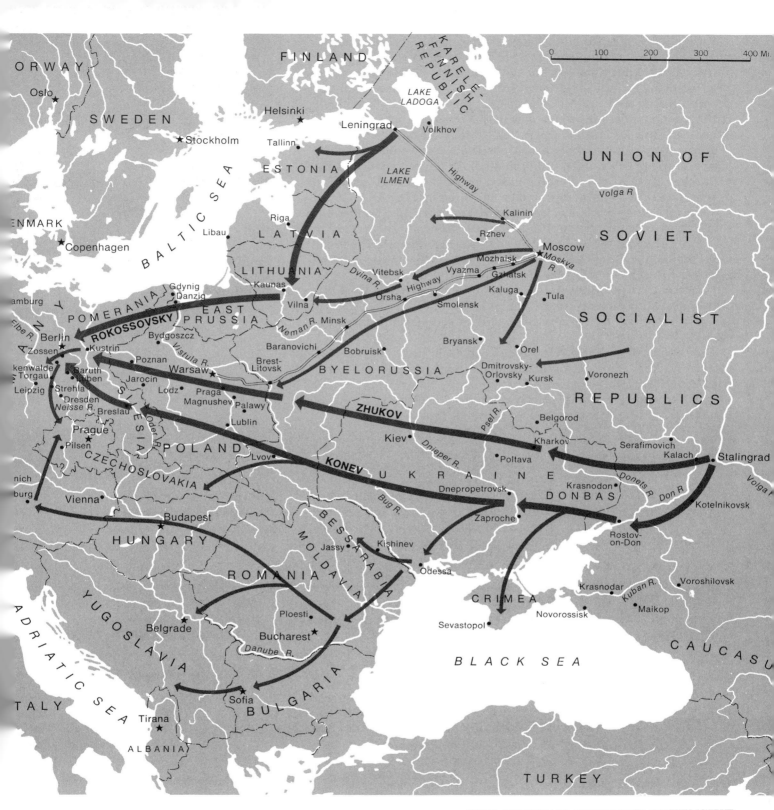

THE RUSSIAN COUNTER-OFFENSIVE

On Hitler's side the situation was envisaged just as Zhukov imagined. Von Manstein had hoped to attack the Kursk salient in March after taking Kharkov, but the combination of Soviet defenses and the spring thaw was too much for him. By April, discussions of a move on Kursk were underway at Hitler's headquarters. Not all of Hitler's commanders favored a new major offensive but in early May opinion solidified. Plans for Operation Citadel to blast the Russians out of Kursk were painstakingly prepared. The Nazis would have new, powerful weapons available—60-ton Mark VI Tiger and 45-ton Mark V Panther tanks and the Ferdinand self-propelled gun. Albert Speer promised that 324 Panthers would be delivered by May 31.

Operations Order No. 6, issued by Hitler April 15, specified that Kursk must be "a victory to shine out like a beacon to the world."

Even so doubts remained. At a conference on May 10 the great tank commander Guderian said: "My Fuehrer, why do you want to attack the East at all this year?"

To which Hitler replied: "You are quite right. Whenever I think of this attack my stomach turns over."

Field Marshal Keitel interposed: "We must attack for political reasons."

Guderian responded: "How many people do you think even know where Kursk is? It's a matter of profound indifference to the world whether we hold Kursk or not."

Hitler said he was not entirely committed to Operation Citadel. But in fact he was. The plans moved forward.

On the Russian side plans for Kursk had been in gestation since mid-March. On March 13 or 14 Zhukov flew into Moscow to confer with Stalin about the Kharkov situation. The Germans were about to recapture the city. Stalin was tied up in a long conference about energy matters that lasted until nearly 3:00 A.M. Then he telephoned and asked Zhukov if he had had dinner. He had not. Zhukov and Stalin talked until 5:00 A.M. about the situation on the Kharkov front and at 7:00 A.M., falling asleep the moment he boarded the plane, Zhukov went off for a first-hand inspection. The Germans took Kharkov March 16 but were halted immediately thereafter. In the interim Zhukov inspected the entire area with care. When he got back to Moscow preliminary plans for Kursk began to be drawn up.

On April 8 Zhukov formally reported to Stalin his conviction that the major German thrust for 1943 would be in the Kursk area with the objective of smashing the Russians there and then tackling Moscow. He proposed mobilizing Soviet forces in the Kursk area but warned against a preventive strike.

Two days later Stalin got a report from General Malinin, Chief of Staff of the Central Front, which concurred in Zhukov's judgment that the Kursk front was where the Germans would concentrate their efforts. Two days later a report from General Vatutin and Khrushchev from the Voronezh Front gave a similar evaluation.

Formal planning for Kursk began in the Kremlin April 12. Zhukov had returned to Moscow April 11 and Vasilevsky had already begun drafting plans. Zhukov, Vasilevsky and General Antonov worked all day April 12 preparing for the meeting with Stalin. Vasilevsky and Zhukov made a detailed outline of the campaign. Antonov put together operational charts of the Kursk salient.

The materials were presented to Stalin that evening. He accepted the recommendations although still expressing concern about Moscow.

A Soviet tank factory producing Russian tanks, shown below, on the attack.

Zhukov and Vasilevsky had proposed a remarkable defense in depth of the Kursk salient. Nothing like it had been attempted. None of the rapidly building up strategic reserves of the High Command were to be committed to action. Instead they would be held in the newly created Steppe Front for use in the summer offensive.

With the intensive care and attention to detail that were becoming the hallmark of the staff work of Vasilevsky and Zhukov, preparations began. There were command reorganizations, refitting of armies, equipping units with new weapons, particularly tanks and armored vehicles, providing infantry divisions with truck transport instead of horses, mechanizing divisions with the flood of American trucks, jeeps and command vehicles pouring in via the Persian Gulf Command, outfitting the air force with improved LA-5s and Yak-9s, and establishing eight new corps of long-range bombers. The Soviet Air Force had now outstripped the German Air Force in numbers. Each Soviet front command had its own air army of 700 to 800 planes. Artillery was given motorized traction. Signal companies with mobile wireless equipment were set up. Hundreds of thousands of new recruits were carefully trained. Five new armored armies, each incorporating one mechanized and two tank corps were established.

By the summer of 1943 the Soviet Union had 6.4 million men under arms with 99,000 guns, 2,200 units of rocket artillery, nearly 10,000 tanks and 8,500 combat planes. German strength was estimated at 232 German and allied divisions, 5,300,000 men, 56,000 guns, 5,850 tanks and self-propelled guns and 3,000 planes.

For the first time the Red Army had a decided superiority in strength over the Germans.

For the intended Kursk offensive the Nazis concentrated about 50 divisions, including 17 panzers and motorized divisions, 10,000 guns, 2,700 tanks and 2,000 planes. Manpower totalled more than 900,000.

On the Soviet side the Red Army mustered 1,330,000 men, more than 3,600 tanks, 20,000 guns and 3,130 planes.

Soviet intelligence was first class. By the beginning of June Zhukov knew virtually all the details of the German strike plan. He was fully informed about the new Nazi armor, the Panthers, the Tigers and the Ferdinands. Stalin was receiving extremely accurate intelligence from a spy code-named Lucy, in reality Rudolf Rossler, a Soviet agent in Switzerland. Front intelligence was good and Moscow had finally begun to work in close liaison with underground groups in the German rear which provided detailed reports on German troop concentrations and movements.

The Soviet forces were echeloned in extraordinary depth. In some areas where the main Nazi attack was expected, the Russians installed as many as 148 guns and mortars per mile of front. In slightly less dangerous sectors there was a density of 25 guns per mile in the first line and another 23 per mile in the second line. Concrete bunkers and firepoints studded the region as far back as 100 miles. Back of that was what Zhukov called the "national defense line" on the River Don, 150 to 175 miles to the rear.

The Soviet plan called for a box defense. If the Germans penetrated the initial shield they would find themselves enclosed in a square of fire from the second line, the sides and the reversed first line. If they broke the second line they would enter another square of fire. Antiaircraft batteries and antitank batteries studded the region so that the fronts could cover any objective with double, triple, quadruple or even quintuple fire.

What it was like. Frames from film footage taken before and during tank battle.

In the weeks just before July 1 there were several flutters. Stalin verged on the point of launching several local spoiling attacks, urged on by local commanders. But Zhukov and Vasilevsky stood firm. Hold back everything until the Germans attack, they warned. Once they are engaged, pin them down under murderous fire. Once they have committed themselves and suffered heavy losses, swiftly go over to the offensive, hurl in the strategic reserves of the Steppe Front, now carefully positioned behind the north and south flanks of the Kursk bulge, strike with all possible speed, crush the Germans and bag them if possible in a new "Stalingrad kettle."

The Zhukov-Vasilevsky tactic was remarkably like that which the Germans had unfolded a year earlier when they let the overconfident Red Army launch its Kharkov offensive, then swiftly turned tables, smashed the Kharkov attackers and sped on to the Volga and Stalingrad.

There was an air of enormous professionalism and self-confidence about the Soviet preparations. The commanders and men knew their roles. For the first time they had not only a plan but the time and the matériel with which to put it into execution.

A Soviet tank captain commented: "At the beginning of the war everything was done in a hurry and time was always lacking. Now we go calmly into action."

For the first time the Soviet High Command possessed complete confidence in its ability to impose *its* will and *its* pattern on the battlefield.

The German attack started at 4:00 P.M. the afternoon of July 4 in the southern sector of the Front. As the great German armored monsters lumbered out of the depressed roadways where they had lain hidden close to the Front, the Russian guns laid down a hurricane of fire. The Russians had sown the terrain with an unbelievable density

of mines—as many as 2,400 antitank and 2,700 antipersonnel mines per mile. The mines were laid in a pattern in which open lanes intersected the explosive terrain. The Soviet guns were registered for fire into the lanes. If a Nazi tank became disabled in a minefield Soviet antitank weapons from four sides opened up on it. If the tank tried to navigate the mine-free lanes it ran into progressively registered Soviet artillery fire. Tank after tank bogged down. Tank after tank burst into flame. Tank after tank blew up, sending fragmented armor plate over the fields. The German tank crews had orders not to halt to help disabled comrades. If disabled they were to stay in their places and continue to fire. This made them sitting ducks for the registered fire of the Soviet guns. The Russians had set up tank-destruction commandos, squads that darted into the battlefield under the noses of the immobilized German monsters, blasting off turrets and nozzeling the occupants to death with liquid fire.

Zhukov was at the Orel sector command post with Rokossovsky when the German attack began. It was no surprise. A captured prisoner had told Vasilevsky at the Voronezh command post that the attack was beginning and would spread to the northern sector at dawn July 5. About 2:00 A.M. July 5 Rokossovsky's men captured a German sapper of the 6th German Infantry who confirmed the northern attack would start at 3:00 A.M.

Zhukov ordered Soviet guns to open up immediately on the German positions. He then called Stalin and told him what he had done. Stalin was nervous, keyed-up and could not sleep.

The Soviet guns started at 2:30 A.M., beginning what Zhukov came to call "the grand symphony of the great battle at the Kursk bulge." There was a continuous thunder of the heavy guns, and the eerie whish of the katyusha rockets.

Stalin called ten minutes later at 2:30.

"Well, have you begun?"

"Yes, we have."

"What's the enemy doing?"

Zhukov said the Germans were trying counterbattery fire but it was not effective.

"All right," Stalin said. "I'll call you again."

The German Air Force took off about 5:30 A.M. and began to bombard Soviet positions as the German armor and infantry moved out of their holding positions.

The Germans plowed forward under terrific fire but sheer weight enabled them to penetrate six miles in two days into the Russian hedgehog.

This time Stalin did not withhold the news of the battle from the people. The communiqué of July 6 on the first day's fighting gave the extraordinary figure of 586 German tanks crippled or destroyed. The

Corpse of a German soldier beside his destroyed tank.

next day it was 433. The day after 520 and the next day 304. Russians did not necessarily accept those figures as literally accurate, but they gave them some measure of the magnitude of the engagement and a clear indication that the Russians were winning.

The climax of the battle came on the morning of July 12, when Zhukov and Vasilevsky threw General P. A. Rodmistrov's 5th Guards tank army, with two armored and one mechanized corps, a fresh force of 850 tanks and self-propelled guns, into battle to meet a final lunge by Hausser's SS Panzer Corps along the River Psel. The Nazis were moving forward in attack with about 600 tanks, all that remained of their original force. The Russians plunged full speed into the Nazi armor, firing at them with new 85-mm guns, specially designed to knock out the German Tigers and Panthers. There was an incredible tangle of armor, the Soviet T-34s driving in to use their guns at point-blank range against the larger Nazi panzers. Nazi Stukas and Soviet dive-bombers plunged into the smoke of the burning vehicles.

By nightfall more than 300 German tanks, including 70 of the huge Tigers, lay smashed and smoldering on the battlefield along with 88 self-propelled guns and more than 300 trucks. Half of Rodmistrov's army had been destroyed. No one, Russian or German, had seen anything like what the surviving Nazis called the *Blutmuhle von Belgorod*, the Bloodbath at Belgorod. The battlefield was a gigantic heap of broken steel, broken human bodies, burned-out carcasses, human and metal.

On July 13 Hitler called off his offensive. He had lost strength which he was never to regain. The Russians put the totals at 70,000 Nazis killed, 2,900 tanks, 195 self-propelled guns, 844 cannon, 1,392 planes. The Germans never announced their losses but they were probably not far below the Russian estimate. The Russians, of course, lost large numbers of tanks. They entered the engagement with about 3,800 and by July 13 had only 1,500 operational. But they won the battlefield. This meant they were able to reclaim not only all their own damaged tanks but all the German damaged tanks. In a little more than two weeks the number of Russian tanks operational rebounded to 2,750.

The wild ride of the SS Death's Head panzers into Rodmistrov's 5th Guards Armored Force proved to be the high tide of Hitler in Russia. Never again would the Germans muster an offensive operation in the East. Never again would the Third Reich seriously threaten its great Soviet opponent. No one after Kursk could doubt the final outcome.

The Russians made good their losses and took up the long, painful pursuit and pressure that was not to halt before Berlin. For the Germans it was the beginning of a nightmare without end, the long, stubborn bloody retreat over the land they had devastated until once again they were back in what was to become the rubbleheap of Hitler's Thousand-Year Reich.

Hitler turned back to try to cope with the Allied invasion of Sicily which had occurred on July 10. Stalin a bit later ordered the salute guns of Moscow to fire what was the first in an unbroken series of victory salutes—12 salvoes from 120 guns celebrating the recapture of Orel and Belgorod by the victors of Kursk.

Kursk had changed history. To this day the titanic armored struggle, hardly known in the West, is studied in the world's military academies as the classic pattern of contemporary armored warfare.

BABI YAR

Westward the wheels of the Red Army rolled through the bright sunshine of late summer 1943 and the crisp autumn days that followed. It was no parade. The Germans fought every inch but the Red Army was irresistible as the tide. The Germans stood and fought, then retreated. They stood again and fought, then retreated.

Kharkov fell on August 22 and this time it fell firmly in the hands of the Russians. The Donbas was cleared in early September and Poltava, site of an ancient battle between Peter the Great and Charles of Sweden, went to the Russians September 23.

The Red Army slugged forward across the black lands of the Ukraine, driving for the historic capital of Kiev, lost in the terrifying disaster of the summer of 1941.

On the morning of November 6 the Russians marched in. Nikita Khrushchev, Party boss of the Ukraine before the war and still its boss, rode into the city with some Ukrainian leaders. To him it was the most familiar of scenes, the highway he had driven on a thousand times to and from his dacha outside the city.

He drove through the suburbs and into the center of the city, the Kreshchatik, the curving chestnut-lined boulevard beloved by Kievlyans. The chestnuts were gone. So were many big buildings, some blown up by the Russians by remote control when they abandoned the city in September 1941, some blown up by the Germans a few hours before. The Communist Party's Central Committee building where Khrushchev had his offices still stood. So did the Academy of Science building and the theaters. But the Bolshevik and Kreshchatik factories had been destroyed. The Bolshevik Factory went up as Khrushchev drove into Kiev.

Khrushchev and his comrades walked down the Kreshchatik and turned into Lenin Street. It was a curious experience. Kiev, so noisy, so gay, so full of life, was an empty shell. A handful of people began to emerge from the cellars. As Khrushchev neared the Opera House a young man came running to him, screaming hysterically: "I'm the only Jew left! I'm the last Jew in Kiev who is alive."

He told Khrushchev he had a Ukrainian wife who had hidden him in the attic or he would have perished with the other Jews.

How many Jews died in Kiev will never be known. The prewar population of the city was about 850,000, of which Jews numbered about 170,000. About three-fifths of Kiev's population was evacuated before the Germans entered. Probably 50,000 Jews remained.

On September 28, 1941, two thousand posters were pasted up on the walls of Kiev. They said:

All Jews of the city of Kiev and its environs must appear at the corner of Melnikov and Dokhturov Streets (beside the cemetery) at 8:00 A.M. on September 29, 1941. They must bring their documents, money, valuables, warm clothing, etc. Jews who fail to obey this order

Bodies of Jews slaughtered by the Nazis at Babi Yar, Kiev.

*and are found elsewhere will be shot. All who enter the apartments
left by Jews and take their property will be shot*

Rumors promptly spread that the Jews were to be evacuated
from Kiev.

The posters had been put up by Einsatsgruppe C. Sondercommando 4A, a 150-man unit assigned to deal with Jewish "problems." This particular unit was attached to German Army Group
South and was charged with carrying out a secret order issued by
Hitler in May 1941, calling for the extermination of all Jews, gypsies,
insane, "Asiatic inferiors," racially and mentally "inferior elements"
and Communist functionaries.

The Sondercommando had not expected more than 6,000 Jews to
answer the summons. To their surprise more than 30,000 gathered at
the street corner by the cemetery. The Sondercommando had to call
in two police regiments to help with their task.

The long procession marched slowly along the Lvovskaya
Prospekt, mothers with babies at their breasts, children in baby
carriages, elderly men and women, even paralytics, pulled in hand
carts.

They reached the entrance to the cemetery in late morning or
early afternoon. There a barbed-wire barricade had been set up. The
victims were made to remove their clothing, pile it and their belongings
neatly on the sidewalk. Then they were marched in close-rank
columns to Babi Yar, a ravine just beyond the cemetery. Here they
were run through a gauntlet, beaten with sticks and truncheons by
polizei from the Western Ukraine. In batches they were compelled to
lie face down at the bottom of the ravine and shot with automatic
rifles. A little earth was shoveled over the bodies and another row was
made to lie down. Some were simply machine-gunned. Small children
were thrown in alive. The ravine rapidly filled with what one of the
participants was to call "a glutinous mass."

It was arduous work for the Sondercommando. A squad would
shoot for an hour, then take a rest, being replaced by another squad.
At nightfall the task was far from finished. The remaining victims were
herded into empty garages, kept overnight, and shooting resumed in
the morning. By the time the exercise had been completed the
Sondercommando was able to report that exactly 33,771 Jews had
been killed in 36 hours. The ravine was dynamited to put a cover of
earth over the bodies.

As the German occupation went on other victims were shot and
buried at Babi Yar, possibly 100,000 in all—more Jews, Soviet POWs,
partisans, Communists. According to a postwar estimate made by a
special commission under Khrushchev's chairmanship, about 195,000
persons were executed by the Nazis in the Kiev area.

Before the German pullout the Sondercommando had another
task—to try to conceal the extent of their crime. Slave labor excavated
the site and burned the remains of the bodies in a pyre over a period
of six weeks.

Babi Yar in the post-Stalin years became a symbol of German
atrocities in Russia, particularly against the Jews—a symbol in spite
of itself, for Soviet authorities were not eager to perpetuate the
memory of a crime directed so specifically against the Jews. At one
time there were plans to bulldoze Babi Yar and put up a housing
development or an athletic center. After much bitterness a memorial
monument was finally erected to "all" the victims, Russian and Jewish,
at Babi Yar.

**Russians leaving a concentration
camp after being liberated by
the Red Army. Below, two
civilians being executed by Nazis
in Minsk during the early days
of the war.**

Babi Yar was only one of thousands of sites of atrocity uncovered as the Red Army moved west. It had been known from the beginning that the Nazi attack had been accompanied by cruelties of an unspeakable kind directed against any class of people Hitler or his politicians and generals chanced to decide upon.

Hitler had incorporated into his Nazi ideology an old Neitszchian concept of the "superman." The superman in his definition was a German "aryan," blond, clean-cut, healthy, obedient. Hitler was waging war, he insisted, to provide *lebensraum*, living space, for this new breed of super-German. He proposed to clear the eastern spaces of *untermenschen*, that is, all subhuman species such as Russians, Ukranians, Poles, Jews, "Asiatics," etc., etc.

The German armies moved eastward with special orders, such as the "commissar" order under which every Communist official who was captured would automatically be shot. There was also the "kugel" order, a bullet in the head for any prisoner who attempted to escape or was believed to be thinking of escaping.

Under this philosophy millions of Russians, Jews and Poles died. There were six million Jewish victims in Europe including possibly two million in Russia. The Germans did not always bother with bullets or concentration camp furnaces. They simply starved their victims to death. The Germans captured about 5,754,000 Russian soldiers

in the war. The number who survived as prisoners of war was a little more than 1,000,000. That is, only one in five or six of the men and women who fell into German hands survived to the end of the war. (And, shameful to say, most survivors were sent straight from German prisoner camps to Soviet labor camps by Stalin.) Several million Russians were driven into Germany as forced labor. Probably half this total died of starvation and disease.

No one knows how many persons in Russia were killed by the Germans out of hand, as in the case at Babi Yar. But there was no doubt that the number ran to millions.

Many of those killed by the Germans were partisans, underground fighters, Soviet men and women, particularly young men and women, who remained in the occupied zones and carried on the fight for their motherland.

In the early phase of the war the partisans fought almost entirely on their own. In the 1930s at the time of the Spanish Civil War, an elaborate organization had been set up in Byelorussia along the route of any German invasion of organized Communist bands which would stay behind the lines in case the Nazis rolled over the frontier.

Bases were established, ammunition, arms, foodstuffs and radio equipment was placed in caches ready for use in the deep forests and marshlands in case of emergency. But just before the war the system was liquidated. The depots were cleaned out and the organizations dispersed by Police Chief Beria. No reason has ever been given for the action, but many Russians believe that Beria convinced Stalin the bases might just as easily be used against Stalin as against Hitler; better take no chances.

Zoya Kosmodemyanskaya, a fabled Soviet partisan who set fire to German stables, was captured and hung by the Nazis. Below, a photo taken after her execution.

When war broke out a central partisan administration was set up under P. K. Ponomarenko, a long-time Byelorussian official. It was created in July 1941, but not until July 1942 was Ponomarenko given permission to start operations.

But partisans did operate from the start of the war. A young schoolteacher named Zoya Kosmodemyanskaya headed a partisan band in a little village named Petrishchevo not far from Moscow near Kalinin. She was captured by the Germans in December 1941 and hung in the village street where her lifeless body was found by Red Army troops when they recaptured the town. She was made into a national hero. Newspapers carried her photograph and endless stories about her exploits. There were supposed to be 10,000 partisans operating in the winterclad forests around Moscow at the time of the Battle of Moscow, and they were credited with killing 18,000 Germans. A group of young people in the town of Krasnodon in the Donbas set up an underground organization which took a deadly toll of the Germans until they were captured and executed. Their story became the subject of a best-selling novel by the writer Alexander Fadeyev, called *The Young Guard*. After the war he had to rewrite the book because he had written the story as it actually happened, that is, that the youngsters fought entirely on their own. In the rewrite he was compelled to claim that the Young Guard carried out their operations at the instructions of the higher Communist Party leadership.

Nowhere were partisans more active than in the forests of Byelorussia and nowhere were German reprisals more fierce. In one antipartisan operation carried out June 5, 1943 called Cottbus the Germans killed 5,000 persons with a loss of 59. In Kaluga province the Germans killed 20,000 civilians. Near Bryansk they killed 2,000 and deported 5,000 as slave labor.

At the time of the Orel offensive in July 1943 the partisans of the Bryansk and Orel districts carried out 17,000 individual attacks on the German rail network.

But it was not the statistics that counted. It was the deadliness of the conflict. Mercy was a word erased from the vocabulary of German official orders. Keitel ordered his troops December 16, 1942: "If the repression of bandits in the east . . . is not pursued by the most brutal means the forces at our disposal will before long be insufficient to exterminate this plague. The troops, therefore, have the right and the duty to use any means, even against women and children. . . . Scruples of any sort are a crime against the German people and against the German soldiers."

Yevgeny Yevtushenko, the Russian poet who skyrocketed to fame in the Khrushchev days, wrote a poem to Babi Yar in 1961. Bestial as had been the Nazi atrocity against the Jews, it still was against Communist Party policy to mention Babi Yar publicly in the Soviet Union. Yevtushenko spoke out regardless of the official outburst he knew would greet his words:

> The wild grasses rustle over Babi Yar
> The trees look ominous as judges,
> Here all things scream in silence. . . .
> And I myself am one massive, soundless scream
> Above the thousand thousand buried here
> I am each old man here shot dead
> I am every child here shot dead
> Nothing in me shall ever forget.

An extraordinary photograph of a
guerrilla detachment assisting
the Red Army in the Carpathian Mountains.
The man in the civilian hat,
as well as some of his companions, seem
to have just been hit by German fire.

WARSAW

Two horses wander through the ruins of a Hungarian city.

AND OTHER BATTLES

Stalin, Churchill and Roosevelt met for the first time at Tehran on November 28, 1943. The three leaders flew to the Persian capital—Roosevelt and Churchill from Cairo where they had a preliminary meeting with Chiang Kai-shek—and Stalin from Moscow, absenting himself for the first time since the start of the war.

The meeting had moments of unexpected drama. About midnight on the evening of Roosevelt's arrival on the 27th Molotov summoned Harry Hopkins to report the discovery of a "German plot" to assassinate the Big Three. Stalin offered Roosevelt shelter in the big Soviet embassy just across the road from the British embassy so that security could be improved. Roosevelt accepted the offer and moved in on the 28th. His effort at Tehran was to do everything he could to win Stalin's confidence.

Churchill was not amused. Nor was he pleased by the quick emergence of a firm American agreement with the Russians that the Second Front must be started as soon as possible in Europe by a cross-Channel invasion. He tried with all his eloquence to persuade Roosevelt and Stalin to shift to the Balkans, the "soft underbelly of the Axis," as he liked to call it. But he lost the argument.

The Tehran meeting broke up December 2 with a firm commitment for a Second Front in June. Stalin agreed to consider letting the Americans set up shuttle bombing bases in the Soviet so that the American 8th Air Force from England and the 15th Air Force from Italy could bomb Germany, land in Russia and repeat the mission on the way back. He agreed to consider joining the war in the Far East at an appropriate moment.

As for Europe, Stalin made clear that he considered the Baltic States part of the Soviet Union and intended to be the dominant factor in postwar Poland. He continued his fierce antagonism to the Polish emigré government in London although the London Poles had Army and Air forces fighting beside the Western Allies and a powerful underground organization in Warsaw.

Roosevelt left Tehran riding the heights. He thought he had attained all his major objectives. The threat of trouble over Poland was hardly perceived. Churchill was downcast. A few days later in Cairo as he sat lunching with General Brooke he kept swatting flies and building up a small hill of dead ones beside his plate. Again and again he said: "It is all quite simple; there are just three areas." Then he would swat another fly.

This was the beginning of a collapse that put Churchill out of action for some weeks, resting in desert seclusion to regain his nervous control.

Stalin did not leave Tehran swatting flies. Like Roosevelt he left with confidence. Back in Moscow he vigorously directed his armies forward. Shortly after the turn of the year the Red Army went into action again. By the end of the month the ring around Leningrad was broken, the Germans blasted out of the three-story concrete-and-steel redoubts in which their siege guns had been sunk. By January 29 the siege was finally and formally lifted and Red Army troops drove the battered Nazis westward.

The Russians kept the pressure on. Smolensk was recaptured and the German defense nucleus that had so long resisted in the center of the Front was liquidated. The drive across the Ukraine went ahead in the black spring mud. Odessa fell by Easter and the ramshackle Romanian regime in "Transdniestria" scrambled for home. A month later the Crimea was liberated, the Germans gunned down in the Sevastopol fortress with the same desolation that had befallen the Russians two years before. In vain 20,000 Nazis making a last stand on a tiny peninsula waited for rescue craft that never came. Most died in bursts of Russian gunfire. Only those Germans fortunate enough to be clustered in knots of 1,000 or 2,000 men managed to succeed in surrendering as prisoners of war.

In June came two dramatic events.

On June 5 the first American shuttle bombers flew into three U.S. airbases carved out of the rich Ukrainian lands around Poltava. In two years a squadron of French fighter pilots, the Normandie squadron, had fought on the Eastern front. But Poltava was the first—and only—major U.S.-Russian operation of the war. It involved thousands of Russian workers, thousands of American Air Force

American B-17s flying over the railroad marshalling yards at Ploesti, Romania. At left, Stalin, Roosevelt, and Churchill at 1943 conference in Tehran.

ground technicians, enormous quantities of supplies and high octane gasoline brought in over the Persia supply route, and intimate collaboration between U.S. and Russian staffs.

The first American flight came in from the Italian bases, having bombed Ploesti en route. The 70 B-17 Flying Fortresses touched down on the Ukrainain soil to the cheers of a crowd of GIs, Ukrainian peasant girls, American and Russian reporters.

Next day there was bigger news. The Allies had landed in Normandy. D-Day at last. There were celebrations on the streets of Moscow, toasts in the newly opened "commercial" restaurants where almost any kind of food could be bought at high prices off-ration. A week later Stalin declared the Normandy invasion:

"Unquestionably a brilliant success for our Allies. One must admit that the history of wars does not know of an undertaking comparable to it for breath of conception, grandeur of scale and mastery of execution. . . . History will record this action as an achievement of the highest order."

Now the Red Army went into high gear. Stalin had told Roosevelt at Tehran that he had a superiority over the Germans of 70 divisions. He concentrated 166 divisions along the Byelorussian front, 31,000 guns and mortars, 5,200 tanks and self-propelled guns and 6,000 planes. The Russians had a superiority of two to one over the Germans in manpower, 4.3 to 1 in tanks. To back this up they had a fleet of 12,000 trucks, most of them American, capable of transporting 25,000 tons a load.

The Russians kicked off between June 23 and 28 on four fronts, breaking through and surrounding large German forces in Vitebsk and Bobruisk. They took 20,000 prisoners in the two encirclements and recaptured Minsk, capital of Byelorussia, July 3, capturing another 100,000 Germans and killing and wounding 40,000.

On July 17 Moscow was treated to a spectacle. Through silent crowds, mostly grim women and some children, the Russians marched 57,000 German prisoners through the streets of the capital. The Germans were led by 40 or more officers. For the most part the streets were so quiet you could hear the slurp of the German boots as they beat on the pavement. Occasionally a child would shy a pebble at the prisoners, quickly to be stopped by a scowling mother.

The Germans fell back, trying to turn Byelorussia into a desert zone as they retreated. More than a million peasant huts were burned or blasted to the ground. The little remaining livestock was slaughtered. There were mass graves of civilian victims, sometimes 2,500 bodies in a single trench.

The Russians took Baranovichi July 8, Vilna July 13 and on July 18 Rokossovsky, himself born a Pole, led his forces across the border into Poland. Lublin, the first big Polish city, was captured July 27 and Brest-Litovsk July 28. The Germans had lost between 25 and 28 divisions, at least 35,000 men, in Byelorussia.

Soviet troops crossed the Vistula River near Magnushev and Palawy on July 25. The same day they took Lvov and Belostok and the next day captured another Vistula bridgehead at Sandomir. All of Byelorussia and the Ukraine had been cleared. So had most of Lithuania and on July 31 the right flank of the First Byelorussian Army, commanded by Rokossovsky, reached the outskirts of Praga, the Warsaw suburb just across the Vistula from the Polish capital.

The next day the "Home Army," the Warsaw underground military force allied to the London Polish Government and led by General Bor-Komarowski, rose against the Germans. A furious fight ensued. The Poles seized most of the city. Gradually the Germans closed in on the Polish force which numbered about 35,000 men. The Poles cried for help—from the Russians, from the West, from their countrymen in London. They got little from anyone.

Their action touched off a political quarrel of such magnitude that its aftereffects can be felt today. There seems no doubt that the Soviet's original expectation was that Rokossovsky would roll forward and take Warsaw. He had secured a number of Vistula crossings not too close to Warsaw, but the task of undercutting the German position was not great in the scale of operations the Russians had been carrying on. In *Pravda* August 2, the day after the uprising, a Soviet correspondent named Makarenko, dating his dispatch "Outside Warsaw," wrote: "On to Warsaw! In an offensive there is a moment when the military operation reaches its culminating point and having acquired its necessary pressure and impetus goes ahead without any doubt as to what will happen next." The next day the Soviet press published a map showing the front line close to the Vistula just east of Praga. The expectation in Moscow was that Warsaw would fall in less than a week.

But it did not. Rokossovsky did not advance. The Russians remained deaf to the pleas for aid from the Home Army. They rebuffed requests from Churchill and the Americans. The Germans closed in, snuffing out the Home Army.

For years the Russians have contended that their pause (which continued until January) was not deliberate but that Rokossovsky's

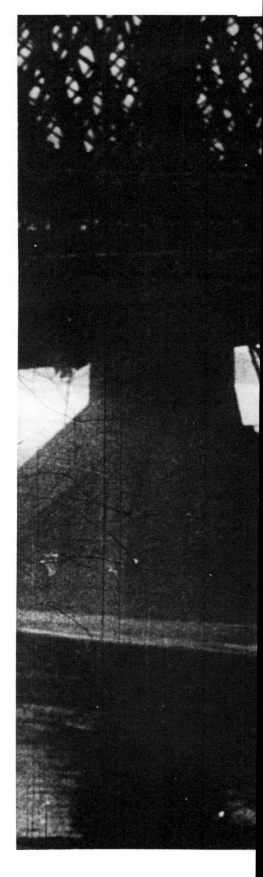

Russians surveying the damage to a bridge over the Vistula River in Poland.

troops were exhausted, the Germans so strong the Red Army could not get across the Vistula. Because of the intense political involvement —Stalin was adamantly opposed to the London Poles, was just then setting up his "own" provisional Government in Lublin, was engaged in difficult and obscure negotiations with Stanislav Mikolajczyk, head of the London Polish government who was then in Moscow (and who was not on good terms with his colleagues)—the suspicion has persisted that Rokossovsky was halted to let the Poles exhaust themselves. If the Home Army was wiped out by the Germans, Stalin's political task of setting up a pro-Soviet Polish government would be eased. As for the Home Army there was no question but that it wanted to set up its own regime ahead of a Russian-sponsored one.

The truth may never be known. All sides make contradictory charges. But one curious bit of evidence has surfaced. General Guderian, in his memoirs, noting the bridgeheads which the Russians pushed across the Vistula, gave his opinion that the Russians were actually trying to reach Warsaw (at least as of August 12) but had been halted by fierce Nazi resistance.

Whatever the facts the tragedy for Warsaw was total. When Soviet forces finally entered the Polish capital in January 1945 some 300,000 Poles had died. More than nine-tenths of the city lay waste. No city in Europe had been so savagely handled by Hitler as Warsaw. He had destroyed the Warsaw ghetto in 1943. Now the Old City of Warsaw, the classic medieval town, was gone. Walking across it was like walking across a desert, nothing but stones, dust and sand. Later the Poles neatly piled up the stones and made little alleys through which pedestrians could walk, like an old-fashioned English garden with twisting paths through high hedges. But the hedges were made of the bones of a city and the paths led to nowhere.

The Soviet forces pushed westward in their "liberation" mission. They entered Romania and drove to the gates of Bucharest. There, too, they paused before going on in. The Russians had approached the Romanian frontier as early as April 1944 when they offered the Romanians an armistice which was declined. Heavy fighting followed before they finally broke the back of the German defenders in the Jassy-Kishinev offensive. Behind the scenes there was complex diplomatic negotiating. A group around young King Michael was trying to take Romania out of the war behind the backs of the Germans and their puppet Antonescu. The group had the support of the Romanian army. Finally a coup was carried out with Communist Party backing August 23. Although the Russians had been carefully informed of the preparations by Romania to switch sides, the Soviet commanders could not bring themselves to trust these movements. They pushed forward with armored units, seizing the Ploesti oilfields which they feared the Germans might sabotage and sent armored columns racing to Bucharest. They did not relax—even when they were greeted by the city's inhabitants with flowers and songs when they entered August 31.

The story was much the same in Bulgaria. Here the Russian position was more delicate. Russia and Bulgaria were not at war. Bulgaria was at war with the Western Allies, but because of traditional Slav closeness to Russia had never gone to war with the Soviet Union.

As the Red Army approached the border the Russians proposed

Trolley car in liberated Warsaw. Sign at right in German and Polish says, "Only for Germans." Below, Romanians welcome liberation by the Red Army.

EIN U. AUSSTIEG
NUR FÜR DEUTSCHE
WEJSCIE i WYJSCIE
TYLKO DLA NIEMCÓW

to smash ahead or, as Marshal Shtemenko put it in his memoirs: "We had to cope with the fact that formally Bulgaria was not at war with the U.S.S.R."

The General Staff coped with this problem by making comprehensive plans to invade Bulgaria by land and sea. Marshal Zhukov was put in charge of the planning. Once Soviet troops were at the Bulgarian frontiers the Sofia government was given an ultimatum on August 30 to halt all movement of German troops through Bulgarian territory.

The Bulgarian government resigned. For two days there was no government. Zhukov signed off the plans for the invasion. It was to be launched by land and sea September 10. Ultimatum followed ultimatum as the Bulgarians tried to find a formula which would suit Moscow's pleasure. Bulgaria broke off relations with Germany and asked for an armistice. It even declared war on Germany. This did not halt the Soviet invasion, which began at 11:00 A.M. September 8. The military action was broken off after twenty-four hours, at least in theory, because by this time an uprising had been organized by the Communists to take power into their hands.

Unorthodox Soviet actions in Bulgaria continued. The German embassy staff fled Sofia. On September 13 or 14 Stalin in Moscow thought to ask what had become of them. No one knew. Marshal Shtemenko in charge of the Bulgarian operation had no idea. Marshal Tolbukhin, chief of the Front, was ordered to try to find the missing Germans. Tolbukhin deputized Colonel General S. S. Biryuzev to locate them. He found no sign of them in Sofia. After much investigation he discovered that they had left a week earlier by special train for the Turkish frontier. An army police force was sent to the border crossing. They found that the diplomats, after exhausting their food supplies while waiting for Turkish visas (Turkey no longer had diplomatic relations with Germany), had set out for the Greek frontier. Finally the Russians overtook the diplomatic party and put it in custody, under what provisions of international law the Soviet military did not bother to concern themselves. An order from Stalin was an order they obeyed.

Each time the Red Army approached a foreign capital, military action took second place to political action.

The case of Budapest resembled that of Warsaw. The Hungarians began to try to get out of the war September 21, 1944, when Admiral Horthy secretly sent a mission to contact the Western Allies in Italy. Soviet troops had already entered Hungary and were moving briskly in the direction of Budapest. The British and Americans told Horthy's emissary that he would have to deal with the Russians. In late September a Hungarian mission secretly slipped through Russian lines and reached Moscow October 1 where they began negotiations for surrender.

The negotiations dragged on and on. Postwar Soviet commentators blame the Hungarians, but the fact that Stalin put his most disreputable political police general, L. Z. Mekhlis, in charge of the talks probably had much more to do with it. Agreement after agreement was reached, then overturned by the Russians on one pretext or another. The Germans got wind of the Hungarian effort and put more troops into Hungary. In the end Soviet forces did not enter Budapest until February 13, 1945, after violent fighting and artillery and air bombardment which so devasted the ancient city that for two

A Russian machine gunner in clean-up. Below, German soldiers surrender to Russians as they walk out of building.

To the front and back. Muddy roads put great strain on people and vehicles in the chaos of the German retreat. Right, the soldiers of the Third Ukrainian Front cross the Danube in 1945.

decades the ruins of its architectural gems stabbed the sky like broken swords.

Every effort by anti-Nazi elements in Hungary to cooperate or collaborate with the Russians failed. In the end a puppet Communist regime, manned by carpetbaggers from Moscow, was installed. Hungary had been "liberated" at the cost of hundreds of thousands of Russian and Hungarian lives, terrible destruction to Budapest and other Hungarian cities, after a delay of many months.

On a minor scale the events at Vienna followed the same pattern. There were early contacts between anti-Nazi Austrians and the Russians, plans for an uprising to take over the city, quibbling by the Russians over details and in the end an armed assault by the Red Army which suffered heavy casualties and did major damage to the Austrian capital.

The Red Army entered Vienna April 13, after 10 days of desperate fighting. Blame for the breakdown of efforts to surrender the city without damage and without casualties was placed by Soviet propagandists on the Austrians and, as an added touch, on Allen Dulles, then chief of American intelligence in Switzerland who was said to have plotted against the Russians with non-Communist Austrian elements.

Prague was the last Eastern European capital to fall from Nazi clutches. Its liberation came May 5—but not at the hands of the Red Army. The Czechs themselves rose against the dying Hitler regime. In their patriotic hour they had strange allies—the Russian

Typical victims of the war seen everywhere in Europe in 1945.

troops of General Andrei A. Vlasov, Stalin's most promising protégé in the days of the Battle of Moscow but since capture by the Germans in 1942 the leader of an "independent" Russian Army formed out of Russian POWs. Vlasov and his men, dedicated fighters against Stalin and his regime, saw little actual combat on the Eastern Front. Although his movement was supported by the Germans and encouraged by some of the factions around Hitler, it was not really trusted. It went contrary to Hitler's theory of the Russians as being *untermenschen*, subhumans.

Now in the death agonies of the Third Reich Vlasov and his men found themselves in Czechoslovakia. They knew that if they fell into Russian hands it would be short shrift—the firing wall or a quick bullet in the head beside the road.

Vlasov made a desperate effort to surrender his men to the British or Americans. The Americans under the thrust of General Patton's Third Army were already deep into Czechoslovakia and within forty miles of Prague. Had they not been held back by a zone line previously agreed upon by the Americans and Russians they could quickly have entered Prague.

Vlasov sent an emissary through the lines to headquarters of the American Seventh Army, commanded by Lieutenant General Alexander Patch. Patch had never heard of Vlasov and his Russian Army. The only Russians he had encountered were fighting side by side with the Germans in France, helping the repell the Allied invasion. Vlasov's officers explained that *their* Russian army had never fought the western allies. Patch shook his head. These Russians were a puzzle he couldn't understand. He put it up to Eisenhower who said the question could be decided only in Washington. The emissaries ultimately were sent to an American prison camp.

On the morning of May 5 the Czechs rose against the Germans, led by a group of nationalists and communists. The Germans were slow to react but by the next day had begun to attack the Czechs with SS troops and police formations. At this point Vlasov's men were already marching on Prague to lend a hand to their fellow Slavs. On May 7 they captured the Prague airport and forty-six planes. They fought their way through SS detachments to the center of Prague and at 5:00 P.M. the afternoon of May 7 the Vlasov blue-and-white banner was raised beside that of Czechoslovakia on the Prague City Hall. Three hundred of Vlasov's men had been killed in the fighting. The Czechs cheered their Russian protectors.

The next day it was announced that the American advance on Prague had been halted in the vicinity of Pilsen, the agreed checkline. Pictures of Vlasov and his national banner began to disappear in Prague and were replaced with red flags and pictures of Stalin.

On the evening of March 9 the Vlasov forces silently marched out of the liberated city and on the 10th most of them and Vlasov, himself, crossed the demarkation line and surrendered to the Americans. The next day Vlasov was turned over to the Russians by the Americans. A few thousand of Vlasov's men managed to escape. The rest were shot by the Russians out of hand or sent back to perish in prison camps. Vlasov was returned to Russia, formally tried, and shot.

The Russians entered Prague May 11. They reported that casualties in the Prague uprising had been 3,000 killed, 10,000 wounded. Soviet troops had been standing to, ready for an attack on Prague for a week. Once again they had been held back by Stalin while politics took center stage.

ON TO BERLIN

November 7 is the great holiday in Moscow—the anniversary of the Bolshevik Revolution. November 7, 1944, was a real holiday, the first since the start of the war. The weather was fine, a great parade through Red Square was organized. Generalissimo Stalin and his marshals in their long-skirted gray-wool uniform coats with gold buttons, gold embroidery and gold epaulets on their heavy shoulder-boards, tall karakul *papka*, the high Cossack fur hats, stood atop Lenin's Mausoleum and took the salute. It was not yet victory, but victory was in the air.

All the great marshals had come back to Moscow for the occasion, leaving deputies in charge of the front—the greatest of them, Marshal Zhukov, Stalin's deputy; Marshal Rokossovsky, the brilliant Pole, Commander of the First Byelorussian Front; Marshal Konev, Commander of the First Ukrainian Front; General Zakharov, Commander of the Second Byelorussian Front; Marshal Feodor I. Tolbukhin, Commander of the Second Ukrainian Front; General Ivan D. Chernyakhovsky, Commander of the Third Byelorussian Front; General Vasilevsky, Chief of Staff; and his deputy, General Antonov. Every top military man of the Red Army was there. So were the leaders of the Politburo—Foreign Minister Molotov, Party Secretary Georgi Malenkov, Police Chief Lavrenti P. Beria, Lazar Kagaonovich, Anastas Mikoyan—the elite of the Soviet ruling circle.

They stood atop the Mausoleum as the battle-hardened troops, the great Voroshilov tanks, the katyusha rocket formations paraded past and the fleets of new YAK fighters and bombers roared overhead.

This was a Russia triumphant. How much longer the Third Reich might last no one could say for sure. But it would not be for long. The Western Allies were driving into Germany from the west. The Red Army was cleaning up the Balkans and stood ready at the German frontiers, poised for the final attack.

The planning for the final offensive was well underway. It had begun in October under the direction of General Antonov and the supervision of Marshal Zhukov. The final plans were worked up in the last days of October. They were submitted to Stalin November 1 or 2 and were ready for the big meeting which Stalin had arranged with his marshals at the November reception.

Operational halts had been imposed on the five great Soviet armies while the November 7 consultations went forward.

The final push into Germany was envisioned in dramatic terms. There would be a continuous advance on Berlin with no halts. It would be carried through in forty-five days. The first strike from the Bydgoszcz-Poznan-Breslau line was to take not more than fifteen days. Thirty more days—no more—was alloted to the extinction of the Nazi forces and the capture of Berlin. Colonel General S. M. Shtemenko, chief of operations, thought this a conservative timetable.

After November 7 Zhukov stayed on in Moscow, working on the plan. The draft plan provided that Berlin would be taken by the First Byelorussian Front, that is, Rokossovsky's command. Zhukov had discussed the operation in detail several times with Rokossovsky and

Russian antitank team advancing across Eastern Europe toward Berlin.

his chief of staff General M. S. Malinin.

Zhukov left Moscow for Lublin, Poland, then site of Stalin's pro-Soviet Provisional Polish Government, on November 15. The next day he received orders to take over the First Byelorussian Front from Rokossovsky with General K. F. Telegin as his deputy.

Stalin had changed the order and the rank of the players. Zhukov had been given the plum—he was to be the hero of Berlin.

Rokossovsky was desolate.

"I had just been at Supreme Headquarters discussing plans for the operations of the First Byelorussian Front toward Berlin. Our proposals had been accepted without comment and now I was getting a new assignment. I could not help asking the Supreme Commander in Chief: 'Why am I being penalized?' Stalin answered that his deputy, Marshal Zhukov, was being named Commander of the First Byelorussian Front and I would learn the other necessary information at Supreme Headquarters."

It was a nasty letdown for Rokossovsky, even though he was compensated, in part, by being given General Zakharov's Second Byelorussian Front.

Stalin announced that he would personally coordinate the Army groups which would participate in Berlin's capture, something he had never before done. Always in the past he had placed a senior commander in that post, probably in order to have a scapegoat at hand if something went wrong. Clearly, *nothing* was going to go wrong with the Berlin operation.

Vasilesvky was left without a function since Stalin would be acting as his own chief of staff. Then, providentially, General Chernyakhovsky, Commander of the Third Byelorussian Front, was killed in action and Vasilevsky was given his command.

There was clearly no operational reason for displacing Rokossovsky. But Zhukov was Russia's top commander and Stalin was letting him have the payoff—for the moment, at least.

Nor was there any question about Stalin's intentions. He laid down lines of front demarkation which prevented any of the other generals, and specifically Konev who commanded the powerful First Ukrainian Front just south of Zhukov, from operating in the Berlin direction. Zhukov and Zhukov alone was to capture Berlin. That was that.

But Konev was a powerful and ambitious rival. He was not to be shouldered easily out of the great prize of World War II.

Zhukov and his staff busied themselves working out every detail of the complicated operation.

The Soviet Union by now had built up an extraordinary superiority over the German armed forces. At the end of 1944 the Red Army had at its disposal in the field 6,000,000 men, 91,400 guns, 14,000 tanks and self-propelled guns and 14,500 planes. The total German strength in the field was estimated (overestimated is a more appropriate term) at 5,300,000 of which it was said to have 3,100,000 on the Eastern Front with 28,500 guns, 4,000 tanks and 2,000 aircraft.

The commands of Zhukov and Konev, the principal forces in the final drive on Berlin, would have at their disposal 2,200,000 men, 32,000 guns, 6,500 tanks and 4,700 planes. This constituted nearly a third of the Soviet armed strength and more than 40 percent of its armored forces.

Opposing Zhukov and Konev was Colonel General Harpe's Army Group A. The Soviet held a superiority of 5.5 to 1 in manpower, nearly 8 to 1 in guns, 6 to 1 in tanks and more than 17 to 1 in

Russian soldiers have turned upside down a sign announcing, "Attention—Border of the Reich." At right, a wounded Russian artillery commander at his post despite head wound.

planes.

Zhukov won approval of his battle plans by late November and Stalin tentatively fixed D-Day for January 15–20.

The first task of Zhukov's forces would be to cross the Vistula on a large scale and the final barrier before Berlin would be the River Oder forty to fifty miles east of the German capital. Zhukov worked out detailed plans for the offensive. The first objective of Zhukov's front was to be Poznan, 125 miles east of Berlin. It was to be achieved by February 1. In spite of Stalin's guidelines Zhukov knew he would be in a race with Konev who would drive in a southwesterly direction to the Oder.

Zhukov went to Moscow in late December and discussed last-minute problems with Stalin and the High Command, particularly coordination of operations between himself and Konev. Konev's plans were also confirmed and GHQ authorized the launching of the final attack. After January 1 only minor alterations were made in the grandiose operation.

Difficult as the situation was in which the German command found itself, it still possessed an intelligence capability. General Harpe's information was that the Soviet attack would be launched January 12.

In December the Western Allies advancing toward Germany had suddenly been struck by the German Ardennes offensive, a remarkably successful tactical operation which had caught them by surprise and sent their forces reeling back. There was danger the Germans might capture the Allied supply port of Antwerp. While energetic measures by General Eisenhower gradually brought the situation under control, there was a dramatic moment of suspense. In this situation Churchill, acting with Eisenhower's approval, cabled Stalin directly on January 6. He expressed the hope that Stalin might activate the Eastern Front which, except for Balkan operations, had been in a state of repose since September. "The battle in the West is very heavy," Churchill said. Stalin instantly responded that the Soviet offensive then in preparation would go forward at a "forced pace," disregarding weather conditions, "not later than the second half of January."

Stalin was as good as his word. He had General Antonov telephone Konev January 9 and order the offensive launched January 12 instead of January 20. Konev asked no questions. He said he would meet the new deadline. He kicked off his First Ukrainian Front as ordered on January 12 from his Vistula bridgehead at Sandomir. His objective was Breslau.

The Second Byelorussian Front under Rokossovsky went into action on the second day, January 13. His objective, as was that of the Third Byelorussian Front, was to knock out the German forces in East Prussia, cutting them off from East Pomerania, Danzig and Gdynia.

Zhukov's First Byelorussian Front went into action January 14, driving straight west from the Vistula toward their initial objectives, Lodz and Poznan.

The attack roared ahead. By the 17th the First Byelorussian and the First Ukrainian fronts were neck-and-neck. Encircled and broken German units lay everywhere behind the fast-moving Soviet panzers. Warsaw, Lodz and Bydgoszcz fell. By January 30 Konev was due to approach the Oder south of Zesno. On January 25 Zhukov trapped a large German force at Poznan and, operating closely with Konev, reached Jarocin.

Both Soviet commanders were far ahead of their objectives as

Soviet troops crossing Bug River, which flows from the Ukraine to Poland.

planned in November and there were clear signs that a race for Berlin was in the making between the two. The Germans, preoccupied with the new Allied offensive in the west, were falling back in increasing disorder.

Stalin telephoned Zhukov about noon January 25 and asked what he planned next. Zhukov reported that the Germans were demoralized and seemed unable to put up serious resistance. He proposed to drive on to the Oder and try to seize a bridgehead at Kustrin, forty miles from the capital. His right wing would advance north against the Germans in eastern Pomerania. He did not believe these formations posed a threat.

Stalin pointed out that Zhukov would be almost one hundred miles from Rokossovsky's Second Byelorussian Front when he got to the Oder and that this was too great a gap. He would have to pause ten to fifteen days to let Rokossovsky catch up. However, Zhukov got permission from Stalin to continue his offensive, pointing out that it would be more difficult later on when the Germans had a chance to stiffen their defenses. He also asked for another Army to protect his right flank—that is, his connection with Rokossovsky. Stalin said he would think it over.

Zhukov broke into the German fortified zone at Meseritz the next day, found it only partially manned and ordered his main force to speed ahead to the Oder and secure bridgeheads. The main force constituted the First and Second Guards armored armies, the Fifth Shock Army, most of the Eighth Guards Army commanded by General Chuikov, and several other units. Zhukov faced another group of armies north to maintain liaison with Rokossovsky and detached one army to mop up at Poznan.

That same day, January 26, Zhukov concluded the Germans would not be able to hold on the Oder line. He advised Stalin that by January 30 he would be just short of the Oder and proposed to resume the offensive in force February 1, cross the Oder without a halt and drive on to Berlin (only thirty-six miles distant), bypassing the city, if possible to the north, northwest and northeast.

His recommendation was approved by Stalin January 27.

As General Shtemenko at General Staff put it, Zhukov advised the General Staff that he was pausing on January 26 to move up supplies and that he would resume his offensive February 1–2 with the Second Guards Tank Army and the First Polish Army in the vanguard, force the Oder on the march, and follow with a lightning blow at Berlin. The Second Guards Army would strike from the northwest, the First Guards Tank Army from the northeast.

On the next day, January 27, Konev advised Stalin that he was moving ahead without any measurable pause, opening an attack February 5–6 that would reach the Elbe (the agreed dividing line for Soviet-American forces) while his right wing in cooperation with Zhukov captured Berlin.

"Both fronts aimed to take Berlin without any kind of pause," Shtemenko recalled.

There was one detail about the plans of Zhukov and Konev which bothered the General Staff. Stalin had alloted Berlin to Zhukov. Konev was not to poach in that preserve. Stalin's plan called for Konev to pass south of Berlin. There was no way on the basis of Stalin's directives that Konev could get a crack at Berlin.

All of this was well known to the General Staff. Nonetheless, on the theory that "we would be able to correct this stupidity in some way in the course of the operation," the General Staff approved both Zhukov's and Konev's plans (each calling for a strike at Berlin) as well as the demarkation line which separated them.

Zhukov consulted repeatedly with Stalin. On January 31 he asked that Stalin instruct Rokossovsky to launch an immediate advance by his Seventieth Army to close the gap on Zhukov's right flank. He also asked that Konev be instructed to move up to the Oder line as rapidly as possible.

Zhukov advised his commanders that the Germans had no forces capable of carrying out any substantial counterattacks, nor had they any continued defense line. He instructed his forces that in the next six days (apparently from February 4) they were to bring up all possible supplies with double ammunition and double fuel requirements, preparing for an assault to capture Berlin February 15 or 16. Between February 4 and 8 they were to obtain a series of bridgeheads on the Oder and be ready for what Zhukov called the "decisive phase" of the operation by February 9 or 10.

Stalin, in Zhukov's words, finally agreed with Zhukov's estimate of the situation but insisted that Zhukov secure his right flank without additional forces.

There was every indication that the race for Berlin had already

A Red Army tank unit passes through a town near Berlin that is cleared of the enemy.

started. Zhukov's forces seized a bridgehead on the Oder at Kuestrin February 3.

World attention focused on the Soviet drive. *The New York Times* reported on January 30 that Berlin seemed to be doomed. The next day it reported the Red Army was twenty miles closer to Berlin. By February 2 the threat had so enlarged that Berlin was placed in a state of siege. The Red Army was said to be less than sixty miles from the German capital.

On February 3 the second great Allied meeting of the war opened at Yalta. Once again Churchill, Roosevelt and Stalin met to determine the course of the war and, quite possibly, the design and fate of the world. Each of the three knew that the war was won. Each had his eye on the shape of the postwar world. For Churchill this meant, primarily, the shape of Europe and the viability of the Empire. He had not, as he said, become the Queen's First Minister to preside over the dissolution of the British Empire. But he already knew that Britain in the postwar era would be vastly weakened. Much of the Empire probably would go. And he was steadily losing his battle to keep as much influence and strength as possible for Britain in Europe while holding Russian gains to a minimum.

Roosevelt was concerned first with the task of defeating Japan after the war in Europe came to its victorious conclusion. He and his military advisers shuddered to think of the hundreds of thousands of American lives which still might be expended in defeating an intransigent Japan. He wanted Stalin's help against Japan. So did all of his generals and he knew he would have to pay a price for that.

Both Churchill and Roosevelt were concerned at Stalin's growing independence as far as Eastern Europe was concerned. Both realized Stalin was determined to have his way in Poland. Churchill more or less acquiesced in that, hoping to keep a foothold on other parts of Eastern Europe. Roosevelt still thought there was room for diplomatic maneuver. Churchill was, as usual, more conscious and more aware of the manner in which Stalin had used the Red Army in recent weeks to mop up the Balkans politically. Roosevelt was prepared to draw lines (and did) which would enable the Red Army to take Berlin. Churchill was reluctant. He understood, as Stalin did, the symbolic and political consequence of this act.

The three men were playing poker for very high stakes. Stalin was growing more suspicious of his Western Allies. He understood Churchill's game. He knew there were strong forces in the West that would like to deny Russia's fair share of the spoils. He was determined that Russia would play as strong a hand as possible.

The conference opened February 3. Stalin's armies stood on the threshold of Berlin. The plans had been drawn. The orders issued. The commanders were lashing the troops forward. They believed— and with substantial realism—that Berlin might fall within ten days; that, in fact, the Yalta meeting might hardly conclude before the Red flag was run up over Berlin.

It was a tricky moment for Stalin—to maximize his advantages, minimize his weaknesses, to get what he could from the West while he was strong and while their aims had not been fulfilled. Stalin had a strong strain of paranoia. He was surrounded by a vicious court of favorites and rivals who played for advantage by feeding his suspicions, never a difficult task.

The Yalta meeting opened with great fanfare. Roosevelt and

190

Stalin and Churchill share a light moment in the Crimea in February 1945.

Churchill, in separate planes, flew in from Malta to the Crimean airport of Saki. Molotov met them and was host at a picnic lunch in a tent with champagne, caviar, sturgeon, fresh bread and butter, cheese and hard-boiled eggs. There was a six-hour ninety-mile drive to Yalta on hairpin mountain roads which had been blasted to bits by the retreating Germans and hastily repaired for the meeting.

President Roosevelt stayed at Livadia, the fifty-room palace built for Nicholas II only six years before his fall, a two-million ruble chateau of marble and limestone. It was furnished with carpets and furniture hastily flown from Moscow's Metropole Hotel and installed under the eye of Ambassador Harriman's daughter, Kathleen. Churchill was put up in the Vorontsev palace, Aliupka. Bedbugs were a problem. The waiters and kitchen help came from Moscow's National Hotel. Stalin stayed at the lovely Koreis villa which had belonged to the Yusupov family.

The conference opened February 4 and in the first day or two Stalin and his military aides carefully cross-examined Roosevelt, Churchill and General George C. Marshal on the military situation in the West, the prospects for Allied offensive action, the numbers of German divisions engaged, the likelihood of transfer of German divisions from Italy and Norway to the east and estimates of when the war might end (the most frequent guess was in the autumn of 1945).

On February 6 Zhukov called a meeting of his leading commanders—generals Berzarin, Kolpakchi, Katyukov, Bogdanov and Chuikov, the scrappy commander of the Eighth Guards Army. The meeting was at the headquarters of the Sixty-ninth Army and the discussion concerned the developing attack on Berlin.

In the midst of the meeting the telephone rang. Chuikov was sitting next to Zhukov and heard every word of the conversation.

Stalin was calling. He said:

"Where are you? What are you doing?"

"I'm at Kolpakchi's headquarters. All commanders of the Group's armies have gathered here. We are planning the operation against Berlin."

"You're wasting your time. After first consolidating on the Oder, you must turn as many forces as possible to the north to Pomerania and together with Rokossovsky crush the enemy's Army Group Vistula."

Zhukov was instructed to present his plans for this operation as soon as possible. Chuikov said that Stalin's instructions came as an obvious surprise to Zhukov. As soon as his talk with Stalin was completed Zhukov broke off the conference with his commanders without dining with them and left for his own Front headquarters.

The drive to capture Berlin was off.

What had happened? Stalin's armies had gained between three hundred and four hundred miles in ten days. Opposition had been almost nil. They were fewer than forty miles from Berlin at the closest point. They had gained footholds across the Oder. The armies were ready to start the final dash. Some had already begun. Konev's troops were pushing ahead with equal élan. There was no organized opposition ahead of Zhukov and Konev and hardly a chance that the stricken Germans could establish any. Every sign indicated that chaos was growing and could not be halted. The Third Reich was in extremis and the estimate of careful and competent military men both Russian and non-Russian was that Hitler could hardly survive beyond mid-

February.

Suddenly the mighty Soviet machine ground to a halt. Stalin turned his armies to the north and south, to the north to clean up the Pomeranian and East Prussian groupings, to the south to continue to clear Silesia, Austria and Czechoslovakia.

What was going on?

This is precisely the question which was raised by the peppery Chuikov twenty years after the event.

"In February 1945 there was not even a trace of those defenses on the approaches to Berlin that we encountered in April," Chuikov said. "Furthermore the enemy was greatly demoralized. The statement of many of Hitler's military men, including Chief of the General Staff Guderian, give convincing evidence of how catastrophic the situation was for the Hitlerites in the Berlin sector in early February."

The question of the failure to advance on Berlin was first raised semipublicly at a military conference in Berlin of Soviet commanders, shortly after the end of the war. It was not pursued at that time because it obviously implied criticism of the Supreme Commander, Stalin, and this was unthinkable. But the very raising of the issue showed clearly that it was a real one in the minds of the Soviet military.

When Chuikov raised the issue in 1964 Khrushchev was still the Soviet chief and criticism of Stalin's wartime military leadership was not only permitted but encouraged. Criticism of Zhukov, then out of favor, also was permitted. Within a few weeks of the appearance of Chuikov's article in which he criticized Stalin and asked why Zhukov accepted Stalin's decision, Khrushchev was overthrown and in the new Brezhnev government Zhukov came back into favor.

Zhukov quickly made public a polemical article disputing Chuikov but actually conceding many of his points. Konev's views on the specific issue were never published. The official line was laid down that Chuikov was simply mistaken, that he did not understand the military situation, the great strength of the Germans, the relative weakness of the Soviet forces, their need for new supplies, etc.

The arguments failed to convince.

As Chuikov insisted:

"To this very day I do not understand why Marshal Zhukov, as first Deputy Supreme Commander in Chief and as someone who knew the situation perfectly well, did not attempt to convince Stalin of the necessity of waging the offensive against Berlin instead of Pomerania. All the more so since Zhukov was not alone in his view; he was well aware of the mood of the officers and the troops. Why then did he agree with Stalin without a murmur?"

The answer is difficult to find. Some have suggested that Zhukov went along because Stalin had promised him that he would capture Berlin and he did not want to jeopardize that honor. As for why Stalin made the strange decision there is no clear answer. It lies buried somewhere in the politics of the Kremlin and quite possibly in the politics of Yalta. Some statement by Roosevelt or Churchill may have convinced Stalin, who was obviously already wavering in his determination to push on immediately to Berlin, that it was to his advantage to wait a bit and clear up other business first.

One thing, however, was clear. Berlin and its capture was to follow the same curious course of each of the other European capitals —Warsaw, Bucharest, Sofia, Budapest, Vienna, Prague (Belgrade and Tirana are somewhat different cases because Yugoslav and Albanian partisan movements played the major roles in their recapture). This is, a Red Army advance to the outskirts of the capital and then a pause for sometimes a very extended time while political considerations were worked out. These pauses invariably led to extremely high Soviet casualties and usually to the destruction of the capital in question. Berlin was to be no exception.

Top left, General Chuikov and staff inside Germany. Below them, General Zhukov plans the final drive on Berlin. Below right, General Konev, center, outside of Berlin.

Ruins of Hitler's seat of government, the Reichstag, May 1945.

BERLIN

There was a meeting in Stalin's Kremlin office April 1, 1945, to which the Soviet dictator summoned his top military commanders, Marshals Ivan S. Konev and Georgi K. Zhukov. They sat at the long table under the portraits of the great heroes of Russia's war against Napoleon, Marshals Suvorov and Kutuzov.

In addition to Stalin, Zhukov and Konev, the members of the State Defense Committee, including Foreign Minister Molotov, Party Secretary Malenkov, Anastas Mikoyan, the Chief of the General Staff A. I. Antonov, and Chief of Operations General Semyon M. Shtemenko were present.

Stalin opened the meeting by having Shtemenko read a telegram which reported that a field group of Anglo-American forces under command of Field Marshal Montgomery was being formed with the intention of striking north of the Ruhr and capturing Berlin. The source of this "telegram" has never been given by any Soviet publication. Zhukov said it came from "a foreign well-wisher."

The operation, it was said, was to be carried out as speedily as possible. While the Elbe had been agreed upon at Yalta as the demarkation line in the west between the American-British and the Soviet sectors it was technically possible for the Western Allies, should they wish, to try to capture Berlin. There had been some agitation for this move by Prime Minister Churchill but no plans were ever made. Whether Stalin believed in the report cannot now be ascertained. All that is known is that he acted as though he did and many of his military commanders were convinced of the reality of an effort by the Western Allies to seize this main prize of the war.

After Shtemenko had read the telegram, Stalin turned to Zhukov and Konev and said:

"Well, who is going to take Berlin, we or the Allies?"

Konev spoke immediately. He said the Russians would take Berlin and they would take it before the Allies.

"So that's what you're like," Stalin said with a grin. "And how will you be able to build up a grouping for it? Your main force is on your southern flank and apparently you will have to carry out a large-scale regrouping."

Both Konev and Zhukov assured Stalin they were ready to go for Berlin—an easy assurance to make since both had been straining at the leash for precisely two months, ever since Stalin had put the Berlin operation into the deep freeze.

It was plain to everyone that Stalin was deliberately setting up an intense competition between his leading military commanders. Each went to the drawing board and in twenty-four hours turned in to Stalin independent plans for capturing Berlin. The operation was to start April 16. Stalin had let stand the old demarkation line which still kept Konev from attacking Berlin directly. That honor was still reserved for Zhukov.

But Stalin gave a clue to a revision in his thinking. He penciled on the map the demarkation line between Konev's troops and Zhukov's. But he stopped his pencil when he got as far as Lüben, forty miles southeast of Berlin. If the line had been continued beyond Lüben, Konev would have been diverted south and west of Berlin. But Stalin lifted his pencil from the map at that point. He said nothing. Both Konev and Zhukov thought they understood his meaning. Lüben was the point Konev was supposed to reach on the third day of the operation. "From this point," as Konev observed, "it was tacitly assumed that the Army Group Commanders could show their own initiative."

Konev understood that this meant Berlin was to be a horse race. He was not going to lose it. Neither was Zhukov. Both men rushed back to their headquarters to get ready. Konev took off from Moscow Central Airport two minutes after Zhukov.

The understanding of Konev and Zhukov was correct. A bit later Stalin said to Shtemenko and Antonov at GHQ: "Whoever reaches Berlin first—let him take it."

Zhukov was leaving nothing to chance. He held a meeting of all his top commanders April 5 to 7 at which the final operation was run through, using maps and models. Supply services checked every demand for matériel and rechecked to be certain there would be no last-minute shortage of fuel or ammunition. From April 8 to 14 war games were run through at lower levels. Zhukov decided to launch his attack two hours before dawn, using 140 searchlights to illuminate the battlefield.

For two days before the attack on April 14 and 15 Zhukov carried

Broken armor left after battle for bridge over the River Spree, Berlin.

out forced reconnaissance of the Front. His reconnaissance detachments probed every sector to pinpoint enemy fire positions, defenses and strength. The Germans understood this was preliminary to a general attack.

Zhukov put Chuikov's Eighth Guards Army at the head of the ram which he aimed at Berlin, backing Chuikov with the First Guards Armored Army under General M. Ye. Katukov. On a narrow front the Russians had concentrated 68 infantry divisions, 3,155 tanks and 42,000 guns for the breakthrough. They had 23 pontoon bridges and 25 ferry crossings for the take-off over the Oder.

About 3:00 A.M. on the morning of April 16 Zhukov went to Chuikov's observation post. His deputy, General K. F. Telegin, was with him. About 4:45 A.M. very strong hot tea in glasses was served by a young girl named Margo. Three minutes before the opening of the artillery barrage at 5:00 A.M. the generals left Chuikov's dugout and took their places in a sandbagged observation post.

At 5:00 A.M. the thousands of guns opened up. The katyusha rockets filled the air for thirty minutes like the thunder of the gods. At 5:30 thousands of flares burst in the sky and 140 powerful searchlights, stationed 200 yards apart, switched on, illuminating the battlefield with more than 100 billion candlepower and, supposedly, blinding the enemy. Actually the searchlights blinded everyone. They were switched on and off, disorienting observors.

"The searchlight beams ran into a solid curtain of gunpowder, smoke and earth," Chuikov observed. "The most they could penetrate this curtain was 150 to 200 yards, no more. From my command post [the same from which Zhukov viewed the scene], which was situated at an elevation of 270 feet, several hundred yards from the row of searchlights, we could not observe the battlefield."

Chuikov added dryly that "among the actual participants in the fighting it is unlikely that you will find anyone who would attest to the advantages of this 'new weapon.' "

On the other hand Zhukov called it "an immensely fascinating and impressive sight" and said that "never before in my life had I felt anything like what I felt then." Of course, the searchlights were his own idea.

Now the tanks surged forward, followed by infantry. By daybreak the Russians were through the first defense lines. In the two months' halt which Stalin had decreed, the Nazis had enormously strengthened their approaches. What would have been an open road in February was now strewn with tens of thousands of tank and antipersonnel mines, concrete machine gun points, tank traps, hedgehogs, barbed wire and every obstacle human minds could concoct.

Never in World War II had artillery been so lavishly used. It resembled the enormous concentrations of the Somme or Ypres in World War I—1,236,000 shells in the first day, 2,450 railroad cars of ammunition, almost 100,000 tons of metal, 6,550 air sorties.

Despite the depth of Nazi defenses Zhukov advanced four to six miles in the first hours and pushed ahead to the approaches to the Seelow Heights where the Germans were echeloned in depth. The Germans had brought out additional forces from the Berlin city ring to defend the Seelow position. At 1:00 P.M. it was obvious to Zhukov that he would have to add weight to the Seelow attack. He pushed ahead the armored forces of General Katukov and Bogdanov and could see that they were breaking through the outer defense lines. He expected to capture the Seelow Heights by the evening of April 17.

Stalin promptly gave him the needle. Konev had started off at the same hour as Zhukov under a smoke barrage and had gotten across the Neisse by 6:55 A.M. He laid light pontoon bridges in fifty minutes, bridges for his medium tanks in two hours and for the heavy Voroshilov monsters in four or five hours.

He had penetrated about twice as far as Zhukov into the German defenses.

Stalin gave Zhukov this news and told him to bring in his dive bombers to assist the armor in breaching the Seelow Heights and give him another call in the evening.

At the evening call Stalin criticized Zhukov's use of his armor and asked him if "you have any certainty that you will take Seelow Heights tomorrow?"

Stalin's remarks incensed Zhukov but he tried to keep his temper and assured Stalin he would scale the heights the next day. Stalin then told him he was thinking of switching Konev toward Berlin and ordering Rokossovsky and the Second Byelorussian Front into action on Berlin's northeast approaches.

Zhukov recalled telling Stalin that Konev ought to be able to advance from the south but he did not think Rokossovsky could get into action in time to do much good.

As Stalin doubtless anticipated Zhukov redoubled his efforts and in the course of the 17th managed to break through in several points on Seelow Heights. By the next morning the elevation had been taken.

That was the day Zhukov forwarded to Stalin a deposition from a Nazi prisoner, saying that the German troops had been ordered to fight to the last against the Russians, even if this meant letting the Americans advance behind the Russian lines.

After Stalin had received the good news that Zhukov was breaking

Soviet infantry supported by
self-propelled guns attacking
German positions.

through to the Seelow Heights, he sent Zhukov a message to ignore
the German rumor. Hitler, he said, was just trying to "spin a spider
web around Berlin so as to cause dissension among the Russians and
their allies."

"The thing to do," he said, was to cut through the web by taking
Berlin. "We can do it and we must do it," he added.

That day, Konev had set up his command post in an old castle on
the Spree. His advance had continued successfully and he called
Moscow to report to Stalin. He had not completed his report when
Stalin interrupted and said:

"Things are pretty hard with Zhukov. He is still hammering at
the defenses."

After a moment of silence Stalin added:

"Is it possible to transfer Zhukov's mobile forces and send them
on to Berlin through the gap on your Front?"

Naturally, Konev was not going to turn over his Front to Zhukov.
He said he had plenty of men and forces to utilize the gap himself. He
could easily turn his two armored armies in the direction of Berlin.
They could turn, Konev said, at Zossen, about fifteen miles south of
Berlin where, as both he and Stalin knew, the General Staff had its
headquarters.

"Very good," said Stalin, "I agree. Turn your tank armies toward
Berlin."

That was the end of the talk. The direct race to Berlin between
Konev and Zhukov was on.

The Germans were fighting as they had never fought before.
The closer they fell back on Berlin the tougher the opposition became.
Every source of fighting power was mobilized, even though it might
have little capability—teenagers, members of the Hitler Youth, old
men, women, anything to aid the faltering Wehrmacht. The death
agony had begun but the Germans were going to take with them as
high a toll of Russian lives as they could.

Zhukov had two more hard days of fighting before he got up to
Berlin. It took all day of the 18th to clear the Seelow Heights and as
the Germans pulled back into the outer ring of the Berlin city defense
zone the Red Army found the going tougher and tougher.

It was no easier for Konev than for Zhukov. It was not a simple
task to switch the direction of Konev's armor. He gave his orders
within three hours, but the forces worked the entire night to get onto
the new salient. On the morning of April 19 Konev's armor was
beginning to move toward Zossen and Luckenwalde. However, as the
tank army of General P. S. Rybalko approached Zossen, resistance
grew stiffer. Because of the terrain Rybalko's tanks could not advance
in open battle formation.

Konev was infuriated. Zhukov, having started slowly, was picking
up speed. He might yet win the race. The angry commander
messaged Rybalko:

"Comrade Rybalko: You are again moving like a snail. One
brigade is fighting, the entire army standing still. I order: Cross the
Baruth-Luckenwalde line through the swamp along several routes
and in deployed battle order. Report fulfillment."

April 20—both Soviet and German commanders agreed—was
probably the fiercest day of battle. It was also Hitler's birthday.
General Helmuth Weidling, commander of the German 56th Panzer
Corps defending Berlin, recalled:

"April 20 was the harshest day for my corps and probably for all the German troops. They had suffered tremendous losses in previous fighting; they were worn down and exhausted, and were no longer able to resist the tremendous thrust of the superior Russian forces."

This was the day that Zhukov won the race to Berlin. At 1:50 P.M. the long-range artillery of the 79th Rifle Corps of the Third Shock Army, commanded by Colonel General V. I. Kuznetsov, opened fire on Berlin proper. The final battle had opened. On the next day elements of Zhukov's Third Shock Army, Second Guards Tank Army and Forty-Seventh Army broke into the city and engaged the German defense force, now down to an estimated 200,000 troops.

Within Berlin there was panic and hysteria. Hitler sent an advance detachment to Salzburg to get his Alpine Redoubt in shape so that he could transfer there immediately. He had concentrated hoards of weapons, foodstuffs, ammunition and fuel there. He was building fire points, life-support systems, underground caverns where, in his fanciful mind, he might hold out indefinitely even if Berlin fell.

Various diplomatic initiatives were undertaken. Himmler tried to approach the Western Allies through Count Bernadotte of Sweden. Special SS tribunals were set up on the streets to shoot anyone suspected of desertion. As the Russians pounded into the city they found bodies of German soldiers, hung from trees or telegraph poles on charges of cowardice or desertion.

The Allies were slashing toward Berlin from the west. The circle around the city grew smaller and smaller. On April 22 a final opera-

On left, Hitler shakes hands with a twelve-year-old Hitler Youth soldier, after awarding him the Iron Cross in March 1945. Below, Hitler congratulates General Schörner, whom he has appointed Commander in Chief of the non-existent Wehrmacht.

The last moments in Berlin.
A Soviet detachment carries the Soviet
flag toward the Reichstag.

tional conference was held in Hitler's bunker under the Reichschancellory. Chief of Staff Alfred Jodl proposed withdrawing all German forces still opposing the British and Americans and bringing them to Berlin to hold off the Russians. At Goebbels' request Jodl's proposal was submitted to Hitler who ordered Jodl, Field Marshal Keitel and their staff to leave Berlin immediately and take charge of the counteroffensive. Hitler himself would command Berlin and assume responsibility for the relief operation. Jodl and Keitel left immediately and on April 24 General Wenck's Twelfth Army was turned away from the advancing Americans and headed for Berlin where he was to link up with the Ninth Army of Colonel General Schörner.

The situation became more and more unreal. Hitler sent out a succession of wireless messages: "Where is the Twelfth Army?" "Why is Wenck not advancing?" "Where is Schörner?" "Advance immediately." "When will you start advancing?"

By this time he was living in a world of fantasy. The Ninth and Twelfth armies were under attack by the Russians. They could move nowhere. His orders went nowhere. He commanded little more than the bunker. And far to the west of Berlin Soviet and American forces on April 25 joined hands in the region of Strehla and Torgau on the River Elbe.

Wenck's Twelfth Army was furiously engaged by Konev's forces which had been blasting their way into Berlin from the south across the Teltow Canal in some of the heaviest fighting in the city.

By April 27 the Germans had been compressed into a narrow strip one to three miles wide, running from east to west and about nine miles long. It was no walkover for the Russians. They lost eight hundred tanks in the climactic battle. The River Spree with its high concrete embankments proved a formidable obstacle. So did the fortified Silesian Railway Terminal. The Fifth Shock Army of Colonel General N. E. Berzarin forced its way closer to the center of Berlin. Its objectives were Wilhelm's Palace, the Berlin Town Hall, the Reichschancellory and the Reichstag.

Already Berzarin had been named Soviet Commandant and Chief of the Soviet Garrison of Occupation. On April 29 in bitter fighting the 1008th and 1010th regiments of the 266th Infantry captured the Berlin Town Hall, blasting their way in by dynamiting the walls.

Every effort was being made by the Red Army commanders to complete the capture of Berlin by May 1, the traditional Soviet spring holiday.

"The battle in Berlin had reached its culmination," Zhukov recalled. "We were all anxious to write 'finish' to the Berlin group by May 1. But the enemy, though agonized, nevertheless continued to fight, clinging to every house and every cellar, and every floor and roof."

On April 30—with only twenty-four hours to go to the holiday—the 150th Idritsk Infantry Division of the Third Shock Army, commanded by General V. M. Shatilov, opened an attack on the Reichstag building and by 2:25 had captured most of it. At 3:00 P.M. the Army Commander, V. I. Kuznetsov, telephoned Zhukov with the news.

"Our Red Banner is on the Reichstag!" he reported.

Fighting, he said, was still going on in the upper floors and cellars.

That evening when he returned from his observation post in

The Soviet star, hammer, and sickle go up on the Reichstag.

Johannisthal General Chuikov had a call from Marshal Zhukov.

"Is there any hope of mopping up Berlin entirely for the First of May?" Zhukov asked.

Chuikov sadly reported that there seemed little hope of this. The Germans were weakening but there was no sign of capitulation. The Nazis still held the Tiergarten and the government block which included the Chancellory where Hitler's bunker was located in the courtyard. That evening Martin Bormann jotted down in his diary: "Our Reichschancellory is being turned into ruins."

Here in the heart of Berlin Hitler had made his last stand and here, as the clock turned to midnight and the great Soviet May Day holiday began he was, as far as Stalin, Zhukov and the generals knew, still directing the battle of Berlin to the bitter end.

HITLER KAPUT

Hitler inspecting damaged Reichstag with SS adjutant Julius Schaub. Ten days later Hitler was dead in his bunker

arshal Chuikov was having a jolly dinner at his Eighth Shock Army Headquarters in Schulenburgren on the evening of April 30. It was the eve of May Day, traditional evening for Russian parties, the war was in its last days, the mood of everyone was high. It was especially high because in addition to his staff Chuikov had some old friends as guests, writers who had been with the Red Army from the start of the war to its dramatic Berlin days—Vsevolod Vishnevsky, a great bear of a man, a native of Leningrad, writer of sea stories, correspondent with the Baltic fleet in the Tallinn evacuation, survivor of the Leningrad blockade; Konstantin Simonov, the most distinguished of Russian wartime writers, the man who had gone through Stalingrad in the trenches and whose novel, *Days and Nights*, had become a wartime classic; the poet Yevgeny Dolmatovsky, the composer Tikhon Khrennikov and the artist Matvei Blanter.

There was schnapps and vodka on the table, caviar and salmon, German sausage, Polish ham, radishes, onions, chocolate cake. The war was over. Everyone knew this. To be sure, the fighting was not done. Hitler was still holding out like the madman he was. Berlin still shuddered with the roar of mortars, the blast of hand grenades, the rasp of rifle fire. Not all the lives that would be lost had been lost. But these old comrades at arms rested and relaxed for a moment in the glow of victory and their own survival.

The evening had hardly gotten underway—only the first toasts had been drunk and the first tastes of the caviar—when Chuikov was called to the telephone. Lieutenant General V. A. Glazunov of Chuikov's 4th Corps reported that a German emissary under a white flag had approached the lines wanting to talk with a responsible Russian commander. He said he represented the German Government.

Time went by. The group sat drinking and smoking. It was 2:00 A.M. Then 3:00. Then 3:30. It was beginning to get light on the morning of May 1.

Finally the German emissary appeared, an Iron Cross on his chest, a swastika on his gauntlet. He was General Hans Krebs, last Chief of Staff of Hitler's Army. He made a Nazi salute to Chuikov and handed him some papers.

"I want to talk of a secret matter," Krebs said. "You are the first foreigner to whom I have told this. On April 30 Hitler, of his own free will, departed from us, taking his own life."

Chuikov concealed his amazement behind a poker face and calmly replied: "We know that."

Krebs told Chuikov that Hitler had committed suicide about 3:00 P.M. April 30. He then read Chuikov a declaration by Goebbels, attesting that before Hitler's death he had transferred all authority to the triumvirate of Admiral Karl Doenitz, Goebbels and Bormann. Goebbels proposed opening peace talks.

Krebs handed Chuikov the testament dated 4:00 A.M. April 29, 1945. Chuikov telephoned Zhukov who asked what Krebs was

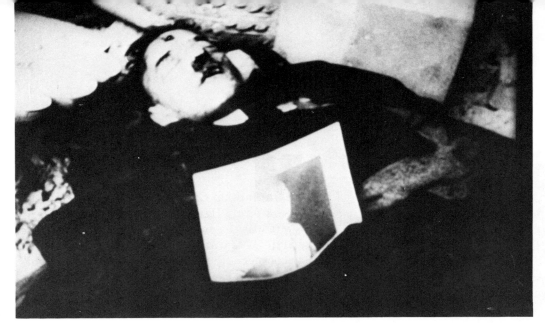

Purported photograph of Hitler dead in his bunker. This photograph was taken from an image projected onto a movie screen.

empowered to do. It developed that Krebs had been asked to try to get an armistice so that the new German Government could assemble in Berlin and deal with the Russians.

The night was spent in discussion with Krebs. Chuikov kept reminding the German that only total surrender was acceptable to Russia and her allies. At 5:00 A.M. tea and sandwiches were brought in. Outside the roar of katyushas could be heard. It had grown light. Zhukov sent General Sokolovsky over to question Krebs. Moscow was getting a sentence-by-sentence report on the conversations.

Krebs said that Hitler's body had been burned in accordance with his instructions. Only Goebbels, Bormann and Krebs were left in Berlin. Admiral Doenitz and Jodl were in Mecklenburg. Essentially what Goebbels wanted was that the Russians give him time to assemble the new "government" in Berlin and then open negotiations for surrender. Both Himmler and Goering had gotten out of Berlin and were attempting to negotiate on their own with the Western Allies. This, Goebbels felt, was "treason" to his dead Fuehrer. He was more bitter at his fellow Nazis than at the Russians.

As soon as the situation was clear to Zhukov he telephoned Stalin. It was after 4:30 A.M. on the morning of May Day. A duty officer answered. Stalin was at his country house outside Moscow and had just gone to bed. Zhukov insisted that Stalin be awakened and told him the news about Krebs and the report of Hitler's death.

"So that's the end of the bastard," Stalin replied. "Too bad it was impossible to take him alive. Where is Hitler's body?"

Zhukov told Stalin it had apparently been burned. Stalin said there could be no negotiations with Krebs or anyone else. It was unconditional surrender—or else. He told Zhukov not to call him again. He wanted some rest before the May Day parade which would be starting in a few hours in Red Square.

Krebs was sent away. Within twenty-four hours he had killed himself, as had Goebbels with his wife and six children. The Third Reich was winding to its end. Zhukov ordered his forces to open up with everything they had. Under a hurricane of fire the Russians smashed through to the Reichschancellory. Chuikov had had no sleep for three days but somehow he kept on functioning.

Chuikov's artistic friends—Simonov, Vishnevsky, Dolmatovsky, Khrennikov and Blanter—wandered off to the Brandenburg Gate.

There from the top of a tank Dolmatovsky read his verses while Roman Karmen, the famous Soviet war photographer, took shots of the scene with his movie camera.

"Where is the Unter den Linden?" Karmen asked Dolmatovsky. The poet pointed to the rubble. Karmen went off and pried down a street sign as a memento.

The end had come. Just before dawn the next morning two German missions entered the Russian lines and made their way to Chuikov. The first represented Dr. Hans Fritsche of the Propaganda Ministry. He offered to go on the air and announce surrender, explaining that since his voice was very well known his name would carry weight with the troops. He was followed by General Weidling, Commander of the 58th German Panzer Corps and Commandant of Berlin.

Weidling told Chuikov of the suicide of Krebs and Goebbels and said he had issued an order to his troops to cease fighting. Chuikov also issued an order halting the fighting in his sector.

"So," said Chuikov, "this is the end of the war?"

"In my view," Weidling replied, "every unnecessary casualty is a crime, madness."

By 11:30 on the morning of May 2 everything was settled. The surrender order had been drafted and signed by General Weidling who cut a record which was broadcast to the city: "I hereby order that all resistance be stopped immediately."

Fighting in the center of town, around the Reichstag, the Chancellory and the Tiergarten had come to an end. At last everything in Berlin was quiet.

There was one more flurry. The general German surrender was signed at Rheims. The Germans, represented by Admiral Karl Doenitz, had contacted Eisenhower May 4 and said they wished to arrange a surrender. Eisenhower informed the Soviets of the approach and said he would accept only the surrender of the Germans facing the Western Front and Norway. A ceremony was hurriedly arranged at Rheims, participated in by the German commanders Jodl, Doenitz and Keitel. Eisenhower advised General Ivan Susloparov, Chief of the Soviet Military Mission, of the arrangements at his headquarters on the evening of May 6. He gave Susloparov a copy of the surrender documents and asked him to advise Moscow immediately and get their approval. The surrender was to take place at 2:30 A.M. May 7 in the operations room of Eisenhower's SHAEF Command.

Susloparov cabled Moscow but by the time of the surrender had received no instructions. At 2:41 A.M. May 7, acting on his own initiative, he signed the document along with the others but appended a protocol saying this did not rule out the signing of another document if any power should so desire.

Another power did so desire. Stalin was furious. He had developed a full-fledged case of paranoia against the Western Allies in the closing period of the war, a paranoia fed by clever Nazi propaganda, hostile maneuvers by Churchill and a brooding row with Roosevelt just before the President's death April 12. Stalin had no idea what kind of man the new American President was, but he had no trust in Harry S Truman.

Stalin's instruction to Susloparov, received a few minutes after the ceremony, was: "Don't sign any document." When he heard Susloparov had signed the surrender he telephoned Marshal Voronov,

One of Hitler's soldiers at the Reichstag ruins, May 1945.

Chief of Soviet Artillery, and demanded to know what manner of men Voronov had in his artillery corps (Susloparov was an artillery officer). He told Voronov that he had ordered Susloparov back to Moscow immediately for "strict punishment," which meant that he would be shot. As for Voronov, there was no assurance that he too would not meet the same fate. In the end Susloparov was not shot, but he had a narrow squeak. To satisfy Stalin a whole new surrender ceremony had to be staged May 8 in Berlin at Karlshorst. Field Marshal Keitel, Admiral Friedeburg and Luftwaffe Colonel General Stumpf were flown in under British guard. Air Chief Marshal Arthur Tedder and Air Force General Carl Spaatz represented the Western Allies. Marshal Zhukov signed for the Russians. Stalin flew in Andrei Vishinsky, the man who had conducted all the purge trials, to be at Zhukov's side during the signature ceremony. Then Vishinsky was appointed to be Zhukov's watchdog in the Marshal's new role as Commander in Chief of Soviet Occupation. Stalin wanted no more unpleasant surprises.

The second surrender was signed at fifty minutes after midnight, May 9. To this day May 9 is Victory Day in the Soviet Union.

On May 24 Stalin invited his generals, his ministers, his political associates, his top police executives, the big factory bosses, his civilian ministers, the Party secretaries, the important scientists, the stars of the ballet, of the stage, of the cinema, the great Soviet writers and musicians of his regime to a victory reception in St. George's Hall of the Kremlin. A splendid ballroom, decorated entirely in white and gold with massive crystal chandeliers, the hall has the names of every man and every regiment which won the Czar's medal for bravery, the St. George's Cross, enscribed on its walls. St. George's Hall had never presented a more glittering aspect than on that night, not even in the days of the Czar's court.

Here Stalin offered a toast which many thought was one of the most revealing statements he ever made. He said:

"Our Government made no few mistakes and there were desperate

moments in 1941–42 when our armies retreated, evacuating our native villages and cities of the Ukraine, Byelorussia, Moldavia, the Leningrad region, the Baltic states and the Karelo-Finnish Republic, evacuated them because there was no other choice.

"Another people might have said to the Government: You have not fulfilled our expectations. Get out and we will form another Government which will conclude peace with Germany and secure our peace.

"But the Russian people did not do that because they believed in the correctness of the policies of their Government and made the sacrifices which made certain the defeat of Germany. And in this confidence of the Russian people for the Soviet Government lay the decisive force which secured the historic victory over the enemies of mankind, over fascism."

A month later. The date is June 24. Red Square. A rainy black-skied day. On the reviewing stand atop Lenin's Mausoleum the chiefs of the Soviet Government. Stalin. His generals, the Politburo, Police Chief Beria, Molotov, Malenkov, the others. Taking the salute on a white horse, Marshal Zhukov, a boyish grin on his face. The katyushas pour through the Square, the heavy artillery, the tanks, the veterans of the Red Army, their commanders.

A great band plays martial music.

The music halts. Total silence in the vast square. Silently the rain pours down. Suddenly hundreds of drums rattle in a tattoo. Silence again. Two hundred Red Army men in dress uniform appear. Heads high. They march in cadenced steps, each carrying a Nazi war banner, the flag and emblem of a Nazi fighting unit.

Each trooper marches to the Mausoleum, makes a right turn, hurls the swastika banner to the wet granite at the foot of Lenin's tomb. The flags, the emblems, the swastikas pile up. One on the other at the feet of Russia's rulers.

The war against Germany is over.

General Zhukov takes salute from General Rokossovsky in Red Square victory parade. Below, Muscovites celebrate victory in Red Square after Red Army parades with captured Nazi insignia. Overleaf, Red Army soldiers dump enemy banners at foot of Lenin's mausoleum in Red Square.

THE LAST ACT

A truckload of Japanese generals on their way to surrender to the Russians.

The war was over, but there was one more act to be played. At Yalta Stalin had finally given his promise. He would join the war against Japan two or three months after conclusion of peace in Europe.

The Yalta agreement had come as no surprise to the Soviet High Command. Marshal Vasilevsky, Soviet Chief of Staff, had known that this was a strong possibility since the conclusion of the Tehran conference. In the summer of 1944, after the successful Byelorussian campaign, Stalin had told Vasilevsky that he would be named commander in chief of the operation against Japan.

On the way to Yalta Stalin asked Vasilevsky and his deputy, A. I. Antonov, how soon after victory in Europe Russia could be ready to fight Japan. They told him they could be ready in two or three months if truck transport was available in the Far East. The United States resolved this question by agreeing to deliver the needed trucks and also locomotives on the spot in Vladivostok.

Actually, beginning in 1944, Stalin had started to stockpile supplies in the Far East, diverting them from the enormous U.S. shipments now pouring in. More than 50 percent of U.S. aid was coming in through the Far Eastern port. So much matériel was piled up that Far Eastern authorities began to complain. They did not realize that the buildup for Japan was already under way.

Throughout the war Stalin had tried to maintain a force of at least forty divisions in the Far East to deal with the Japanese in case they attacked. The reserve had been drawn down only twice, once for the Moscow counteroffensive in December 1941 and again for the Stalingrad counteroffensive in November 1942. Each time, as quickly as possible, the Far Eastern force was rebuilt to the insurance level of forty divisions. As early as the spring of 1943 Stalin named new generals who had combat experience in the west to command the Far Eastern Red Banner Army. They were Colonel General M. A. Purkaev, a very able man, and Major General F. I. Shevchenko, his chief of staff. These men were to organize the Far Eastern forces and make preliminary plans against Japan.

Actual movement of substantial forces began in March 1945 when tank units began to move east. In April and May some 670 T-34 tanks were shipped. The staff of the Second Ukrainian Front and the Karelian Front were sent east, beginning in May, together with a large number of their divisions. The Fifth and Thirty-ninth Armies were among the first to be shipped, followed by the Fifty-third and the Sixth Guards Tank Army.

Stalin massed a force of 1,577,725 men, 26,137 guns, 5,556 tanks and 3,500 planes for his blow against the Japanese. Vasilevsky was commander in chief. His three principal commanders were marshals Malinovsky and Merestskov, two of the best battle-hardened veterans of the war against Germany, and General Purkaev. Vasilevsky had eleven armies and one armored army for the strike.

At Yalta Stalin made clear that his principal objective in going to war against Japan was to redress the defeat of Russian arms by Japan in the war of 1904–05. He was to regain southern Sakhalin, lost to Japan in 1905, as well as the Kurile Islands. He would also maintain the Russian status quo, that is the protectorate, over Outer Mongolia, and regain Russia's special status in Manchuria, including railroad rights and ports.

In preparation for the attack Stalin renounced his neutrality pact with Japan in April 1945. A few days later he told Harry Hopkins (who had come to Moscow to allay Stalin's suspicions about the new President, Harry Truman, and vice versa) that he would be ready to attack Japan August 8.

Actually, the Japanese had been trying since February 1945 to get out of the war. They wanted Russia to act as an intermediary in peace talks with the United States. Foreign Minister Togo tried repeatedly to persuade the Russians to let him come to Moscow to talk about peace. The Russians resolutely ignored these proposals. The Japanese persisted. As late as July 12, on the eve of the Potsdam Big Three meeting, Emperor Hirohito was trying to get the Russians to let Prince Konoye come to Moscow to start peace talks. The Russians cold-shouldered this move as they had the others. Stalin was not going to be denied his revenge for 1905.

The last Big Three conference opened at Potsdam July 17. Already one of the original three, Roosevelt, was gone. Before the meeting ended, a second, Churchill, had left, replaced by Clement Attlee whose Labor Party had defeated Churchill's Conservatives at the British polls.

The atmosphere at Potsdam was less sanguine than at Tehran or Yalta. Although the war in Europe was over, the problems and conflicts among the Allies had mounted. Relations were edgy. On July 17 Secretary of War Henry Stimson got a cable in code at the U.S. headquarters at Babelsberg:

"Operated on this morning. Diagnosis not yet complete but results seem satisfactory and already exceed expectations. Local press release necessary as interest extends great distance. Dr. Groves pleased. He returns tomorrow. Will keep you posted."

The telegram meant that the Los Alamos test of the A-bomb had succeeded. For Truman this raised a question. To tell Stalin? And to tell him his aid was no longer needed in the Far East? Churchill was against revealing anything. The less Stalin knew the better. But Truman would not go that far. He believed he must tell Stalin, but he would tell no more than he had to. On July 24 he approached Stalin during a pause in the talks and mentioned casually that the United States had a new weapon of unusual destructive power. Stalin kept a straight face. He congratulated Truman and expressed hope the United States would "make good use of it" against the Japanese.

Truman and Churchill were pleased. They thought they had fooled Stalin. They had not. Hardly had he gotten back to his quarters than Stalin told Foreign Minister Molotov and Marshal Zhukov what Truman had said. Molotov reacted immediately: "Let them! We will have to talk things over with Kurchatov [head of the Soviet Academy of Science] and get them to speed things up." Zhukov in his memoirs recalls that he knew immediately that the talk concerned the atom bomb.

Stalin could play the same game. He had not advised Truman of

the many Japanese peace feelers, but he did tell him on July 18 about the Emperor's desire to send an emissary to Moscow. Stalin asked Truman whether he thought it worthwhile to answer the message. The two agreed that Stalin would send back a stalling message to "lull the Japanese to sleep."

What Stalin didn't know was that Truman, through the American decrypting of Japan's coded wireless traffic, had already been advised of the Emperor's feeler.

Thus, the two great Chiefs of State, Truman and Stalin, played poker with each other—and with the lives of millions of their countrymen and those of their enemy, neither realizing that the other long since had peeked at his opponent's hole card.

On August 6 the first American A-bomb fell on Hiroshima, devastating the city and taking the lives of approximately 200,000 persons. The course of world history had been changed. On the evening of August 8 Molotov called in the Japanese Ambassador to Moscow, Sato, and told him that as of midnight the Soviet Union considered itself in a state of war with Japan. He gave the same notices to the American and British ambassadors, Averell Harriman and Sir Archibald Clark-Kerr.

At ten minutes after midnight the morning of August 9 Soviet forces poured over the frontiers. They had been positioned in Outer Mongolia and along the Amur and Ussuri rivers. They advanced with lightning speed, sending armored columns on forced marches across the deserts of Mongolia, divebombing Japanese strongholds, dropping parachute assault forces ahead of motorized and armored thrust columns. It was a blitzkrieg in the most professional style of the early days of World War II.

When Ambassador Harriman saw Stalin in the Kremlin the evening of August 9—the day a second A-bomb was dropped on Nagasaki—Stalin told him the Red Army was moving very well, resistance was slight. Harriman and Stalin had a little talk about the atomic bomb. Stalin showed great interest in it. He said they had found evidence in German laboratories of Nazi efforts to produce the weapon. Soviet scientists, he said, were working on the problem but had not solved it. The bomb, Stalin said, could mean the end of the war. But its secret would have to be closely kept.

Within twenty-four hours the Russians had advanced one hundred miles into the territory of north China and Manchuria occupied by Japan's Kwantung Army. But already the war was coming to an end.

A little before midnight August 10, just twenty-four hours after the Nagasaki bomb, the Japanese formally sued for peace. Molotov and Harriman went into immediate consultation. Molotov was in no hurry to end the war and there was some argument about the terms for Japan. Harriman was quite tart. He did not think the Russians had grounds for arguing about how to end a war in which they had been engaged for a little more than a day whereas the United States had been in it since December 7, 1941.

During the inevitable diplomatic exchanges between the United States and Japan the Russian armies in the Far East pounded ahead. By August 12 the Sixth Guards Armored force had crossed the Great Khingan Range and broken into the Manchurian plain, heading for Mukden. Soviet troops pushed across Inner Mongolia and North China, racing against time. On August 14 Japan announced its surrender. The news reached Moscow at 1:00 A.M. at a reception

The Big Three Conference at Potsdam: Churchill, Truman, and Stalin, July 1945.

being given for General Eisenhower, then visiting Moscow as the personal guest of Marshal Zhukov. The toasts went on at the American Embassy residence, Spaso House, until early in the morning.

But the Soviet forces did not halt. General Antonov made an official statement on August 16 that Hirohito's surrender was just a general statement, that there had been no capitulation of the Kwantung Army and that the Soviet offensive would continue. However, an ultimatum was sent to General Uemura, the Kwantung Army commander, on August 17. Meantime, paradrops were organized by Red Army forces. A group of 120 was dropped on the Harbin airport at 5:00 P.M. August 18 and quickly took over the field. At 11:00 P.M. the Kwantung Army surrendered. After another Soviet parachute drop at Changchun the next day the Japanese commander and the prime minister of the Japanese-sponsored state of Manchukuo surrendered. At Mukden August 19 Henry Pu-Yi, the puppet emperor of Manchukuo, was taken into custody. Assault parties entered Korea. Port Arthur and Darien, which had fallen to the Japanese in 1905, were captured. The Soviet Navy seized Sakhalin and the Kuriles.

The Soviet blitzkrieg was a stunning example of military art. If the war had begun on June 22, 1941 with an almost incredible demonstration of Soviet military ineptitude, it ended with the carrying out of one of the most devastating strikes in the history of modern warfare. Granted Japan was on the ropes. Granted the Japanese (as later became perfectly clear) were prepared to surrender before Stalin launched his Far Eastern strike, nonetheless as an exhibition of perfect coordination of all the branches of contemporary technological warfare, the Soviet campaign was classic. It employed masses of tanks and armored troop carriers, armored gun mounts, almost totally motorized infantry, intimate coordination of armor, tactical aircraft and strategic air bombing, parachute landings behind the Japanese lines, concentration on strategic centers, air and naval bases, all the lessons which the Red Army had learned in four years of grueling combat.

Because the Red Army campaign was so swift, because it came at a moment when Japanese resistance in general was coming to an end and when world attention was focused upon political and diplomatic events, few in the West bothered to ponder the significance of the Soviet feat of transferring in a matter of a few weeks so huge a modern striking force nearly four thousand miles from west to east, deploying it with such skill and utilizing it with such competence.

On September 2 the Japanese signed the formal act of capitulation aboard the U.S. battleship *Missouri*. General Douglas MacArthur took the Japanese surrender. He had not wanted a Soviet representative present, resenting what he regarded as a last-minute Russian attempt to "muscle in" on his own brilliant victory. However, General Derevyanko, the Soviet staff representative at MacArthur's headquarters, was present and signed the document for the Soviet Union.

On the day of the signature of the Japanese surrender Stalin spoke in a radio broadcast to his people. Russia, he said, had waited since 1904 (the year of the fateful Russo-Japanese war) for this day. The earlier defeat, he said, had left a bitter memory in Russian minds.

"Our people," he observed, "waited and believed that this blot would some day be erased. We people of the older generation waited for this day for forty years. Now this day has come."

Stalin did not mention the cost in settling accounts with Japan.

German and Japanese dignitaries in a reviewing stand during the war.

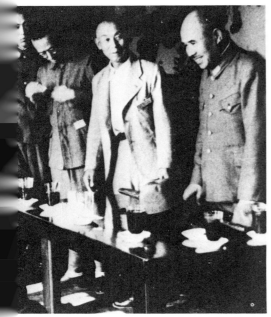

Below, the Japanese surrender to the Russians. At bottom, Americans accept surrender on board U.S. Missouri.

But Soviet official figures put their losses at 8,000 dead, 20,000 wounded. The Japanese dead were estimated at 80,000.

So the last battle had been fought and won on the Eastern Front. Russian strength had been tested as never before in the history of the modern Russian nation and it had proved strong enough despite every obstacle: the paranoia of its leadership which had wiped out the whole commanding corps of the Red Army only three years before World War II; the failure of Stalin to employ effectively the breathing spell against Hitler which he won by the Nazi-Soviet pact of 1939; his incredible failure of judgment in misevaluating the stunningly accurate intelligence which piled up on his desk concerning Hitler's decision to attack, including the scope of his plans and the date for the beginning of war; and Stalin's criminal mishandling of the Red Army's valiant forces in the early months of the war, leading to the stupendous losses at Kiev, Leningrad and Moscow.

All of this the Russian people had managed to survive. They had fought without their best leaders and in spite of blindly stupid leadership. They had died in numbers so vast the Soviet government for years would seek to conceal the totals—probably 20,000,000 of them at the front alone. Some privately said that of every one hundred men who went off to fight in World War II only four came home. Probably that is an exaggeration but more Russians died than the totals for all the other combatants put together. More Russians died than had died in the wars of the past two hundred years put together, including Napoleon's invasion, the Turkish and Balkan wars, and the Crimean War. Russia's losses, including possibly another 20,000,000 civilian casualties, deaths in Hitler's and Stalin's concentration camps, deaths by starvation and disease, were greater than the losses of all nations put together in World War I. Villages were left without a single man or with only one or two 70-year-olds, a child or two and a few cripples.

But Russia had endured. Stalin with his faults and phobias had survived. The Soviet state had not fallen apart. Indeed, it would pull together and tighten all its repressive powers. And Hitler was gone along with his generals, his Nazi chiefs, his dream of a thousand-year Reich, and his plan to wipe Russia from the face of the earth and repopulate its vastness with his own "master race." All of these dreams had been blown to bits by the Russian cannon which blasted their way into the heart of Berlin and seized the bunker in the Wilhelmstrasse which was the pyre of the Third Reich.

Russia was victorious but in the hour of victory the seeds of new conflict already were sprouting. It had been a difficult task for the diverse states and systems of the Soviet Union, Great Britain and the United States to work together, but the common cause of defeating Hitler and Japan had provided the necessary cement. Already before the last gun had stilled, the angry voices of contention about the postwar world were rising, quarrels over Germany and its future, about Poland, about eastern Europe, about Stalin's intentions and whether the United States would lend a helping hand to its Soviet partner in the tasks of peacetime reconstruction.

The Russian armies streamed back from Germany. Some went east to fight Japan but more hurried back to the fields and factories, to the terrible task of rebuilding a nation whose European littoral lay in ruins. There would be no rest for weary Russian bodies. The war had ended but true peace, comfort, contentment and security for Russia's millions still lay far ahead in some unsighted future.

219

INDEX

References to photographs
are set in boldface.

PHOTO CREDITS

ABOUT THE AUTHOR   **Harrison E. Salisbury** has spent much of his lifetime studying and writing about Russia and knows it as well as any American. He first went to Moscow as a war correspondent in 1944 and traveled thousands of miles to the Red Army fronts, to Siberia, the Urals and central Asia. He returned to the Soviet Union in 1949 as correspondent for *The New York Times* during the last years of Stalin and the early years of the Khrushchev regime. Mr. Salisbury has won the Pulitzer Prize and other important awards. He has written extensively about the Soviet Union, most notably in *The 900 Days: The Siege of Leningrad* and *Black Night, White Snow: Russia's Revolutions 1905–1907*. Now, in *The Unknown War*, Mr. Salisbury focuses on an important and little-known story in the annals of war history.

STAFF   **Senior Editor:** Jean Highland
Assistant Managing Editor: Nancy Wiesenfeld
Photo and Map Research: Barbara Whiteman
Layout: Cela Wright, Christian von Rosenvinge, Philip Abrams, Mabelle Chieng, Donna Marxer
Traffic: Alice Romanelli
Maps: Frances & Shaw, Inc.